I0119413

THE HOMO & THE NEGRO

MASCULINIST MEDITATIONS ON POLITICS & POPULAR CULTURE

by

JAMES J. O'MEARA

SECOND, EMBIGGENED EDITION

EDITED BY GREG JOHNSON

Counter-Currents Publishing Ltd.
San Francisco
2017

Cover image:
Anthony van Dyck,
Portrait of Lord John Stuart and his brother Lord Bernard
Stuart (later Earl of Lichfield), circa 1638,
National Gallery, London

Cover design by Kevin I. Slaughter

Published in the United States by
COUNTER-CURRENTS PUBLISHING LTD.
P.O. Box 22638
San Francisco, CA 94122
USA
http://www.counter-currents.com/

Hardcover ISBN: 978-1-940933-13-9
Paperback ISBN: 978-1-940933-14-6
E-book ISBN: 978-1-940933-15-3

The Library of Congress has catalogued the first edition as follows.

O'Meara, James J., 1956-
The homo & the Negro masculinist meditations on politics & popular
culture / by James J. O'Meara.
p. cm.
Includes bibliographical references and index.
ISBN 978-1-935965-47-3 (hardcover : alk. paper) -- ISBN 978-1-935965-
48-0 (pbk. : alk. paper) -- ISBN 978-1-935965-49-7 (ebook : alk. paper)
1. Masculinity. 2. Conservatism. 3. Homosexuality. I. Title. II. Title:
Homo and the Negro masculinist meditations on politics and popular
culture.

BF692.5.O596 2012
306--dc23

2012028370

CONTENTS

Brigit Brat, d. 2011

Sound

Alisdair Clarke, d. 2008

Vision

FOREWORD

My many intellectual debts will be easily seen in the pages that follow. But first I must thank Greg Johnson, White Eminence of the North American New Right, for encouraging me to write for his flagship blog, *Counter-Currents*, and then having the notion that some of those pieces would look very nice between hard covers.

In writing these and others I have benefited from online discussions with Ean Frick as well as many commentators, including about half a dozen loyal, possibly deeply disturbed, Constant Readers of my blog, and real-time discussions with Collin Cleary, Jef Costello, and Derek Hawthorne.

I would also like to avail myself of the wise words of the moral philosopher Richard Taylor, who disclaimed the customary "responsibility for any remaining errors," reasoning that one can only be responsible for what one is aware of, and if he had been aware of any errors, he would have corrected them.

Vive, vale!

James J. O'Meara
Rust Belt, USA
June 13, 2012

"You must choose, brothers, you must choose."

— Brother J. C. Crawford, Zenta New Year Invocation
October 30–31, 1968
The Psychedelic Stooges and The MC5
Russ Gibb's Grande Ballroom, Detroit

FIVE YEARS ON:
PREFACE TO THE EMBIGGENED EDITION

"When you can assume that your audience holds the same beliefs you do, you can relax and use more normal means of talking to it; when you have to assume that it does not, then you have to make your vision apparent by shock—to the hard of hearing you shout, and for the almost-blind you draw large and startling figures."
> —Flannery O'Connor, *Mystery and Manners*

"In normal times, evil should be fought by good, but in times like this, well, it should be fought by another kind of evil"
> —Aereon (Judi Dench) near the beginning of
> *The Chronicles of Riddick* (2004)

"Five years, what a surprise!"
> —David Bowie, "Five Years" from *The Rise and Fall*
> *of Ziggy Stardust and The Spiders From Mars* (1972)

If, as Dr. Johnson said, no man but a blockhead ever wrote for anything but money, the author of this one must be a blockhead of Peanuts proportions.

At the risk of what has come to be called "virtue-signaling," may I say that this was simply an attempt, not to make money, but to bring the Good News and to change the world for the better.

So what was I trying to do?

At the time, I was heavily reading the work of Julius Evola; this itself represented an evolution of sorts, as I had been introduced in my teens, through Alan Watts,[1] to the ideas of René

---

[1] See Greg Johnson's "Remembering Alan Watts: January 6, 1915 to November 16, 1973," https://www.counter-currents.com/

Guénon and Ananda Coomaraswamy, the so-called "Traditionalists," and later induced, under the tutelage of Dr. John N. Deck, to revere the more purely Western Neo-Platonists, especially Plotinus.[2]

Evola, however, while firmly upholding the work of Guénon, took it in a new direction, one which emphasized social concerns and even geopolitics.[3] This seemed much more interesting than just waiting around for the end of the Kali Yuga, however spectacular that promised to be.

Steadily searching the intertubes for more on Evola, one day I came across the writings of Alisdair Clarke, a theorist of what was then called the English New Right. Clarke had given Evola's work another turn of the screw, and developing certain hints in Evola's later books about Orders and Elites in the creation of Aryan culture, had begun to explore the historical role of the *Männerbund*, the bands of warrior youths, through his blog, *Aryan Futurism*.[4]

2017/01/ remembering-alan-watts-2/; and my own "There and Then: Personal and Memorial Reflections on Alan Watts (1915–1973)," https://www.counter-currents.com/2015/01/there-and-then/. Watts, of course, ultimately rejected the Traditionalist view, stating in *Beyond Theology: The Art of Godmanship* (New York: Pantheon, 1964) that "there is not a scrap of evidence that the Christian hierarchy was ever aware of itself as one among several lines of transmission for a universal tradition"; for a Traditionalist reply, see "Anti-Theology and the Riddles of Alcyone" by Whitall N. Perry, *Studies in Comparative Religion*, Vol. 6, No. 3, Summer, 1972, http://www.studiesincomparativereligion.com/public/articles/Anti-Theology_and_the_Riddles_of_Alcyone-by_Alan_Watts.aspx.

[2] See John N. Deck, *Nature, Contemplation, and the One: A Study in the Philosophy of* Plotinus (Toronto: University of Toronto Press, 1967; Reprinted: Burdett. N.Y.: Larson, 1991).

[3] See John Morgan, "What Would Evola Do?" https://www.counter-currents.com/2017/05/what-would-evola-do/, and my own "Two Orders, Same Man: Evola and Hesse," https://www.counter-currents.com/2017/06/two-orders-same-man-1/.

[4] For the historical background, see, herein, "A Band Apart: Wulf Grimsson's *Loki's Way*."

A not entirely irrelevant point was that these bands were, as a friend once usefully put it, "homoerotic though not necessarily homosexual." Jack Donovan, who would give this line of thought its most intensely practical developments, later began calling them "androphilic."[5]

At this point the penny dropped, and I had what might modestly be described as a world-shattering, epoch-making epiphany. As George Carlin said about capitalism, I had nailed together two things that had never been nailed together before.

There was a fatal inconsistency at the heart of the "radical Right," which tirelessly banged on about The White Race, Western man, Aryan Culture, Odinism,[6] etc., yet under the continuing widespread influence of what I came to call "Judaic Family Values" maintained a loathing of any hint of the androphilic associations that were characteristic of Aryan cultures and essential to the creation and preservation of those cultures.

As for the more moderate, traditional Right of the "conservatives" or Republicans, it was flawed as well; supposedly pragmatic and practical, their even more entrenched Christian homophobia prevented them from accessing the culture-creating and sustaining talents of the androphiles, leading to the Right's perennial status as "beautiful losers."[7]

Even Steve Sailer, one of the sharpest knives on the right side of the drawer, seems nonplussed:

> As I've mentioned before, the inner elite of the celebrated Black Lives Matter movement is heavily homosexual. I think that was part of BLM's appeal to political, NGO, and corporate elites: BLM seemed safer than the typical black agitators. These weren't ex-con hard men like the

---

[5] See *Androphilia* (2007; expanded edition, Milwaukee, Or.: Dissonant Hum: 2012 — hey, that's five years!) and of course jackdonovan.com.

[6] See Kris Kershaw, *The One-Eyed God: Odin and the (Indo-) Germanic* Männerbunde (Washington, DC: Journal of Indo-European Studies Monograph No. 36, 2000).

[7] Sam Francis, *Beautiful Losers: Essays on the Failure of American Conservatism* (Columbia: University of Missouri Press, 1993).

Black Panthers of yore, these were irate lesbians and peevish gays. How much damage could they do? Well, judging from the extraordinary increase in black-on-black homicides since Ferguson, a lot.[8]

Contrarywise, the Left had reaped nothing but benefits from the perception of being the "natural home" of these confirmed bachelors, who contributed their unsurpassed talents in symbol manipulation, along with their disposable income and all that non-family time on their hands to the cultural triumph of the Left; while their contrived "gay" identity caused them to "swerve"—to use Camille Paglia's term—from their role as guardians of traditional Western culture into lives of empty promiscuity and consumerism.[9]

And yet, as I recalled from dim memories of New York club-land (as they say, if you remember Limelight, you weren't there),[10] there was no more "implicitly White" an autonomous zone than a gay dance club, especially on Tuesday nights.[11]

---

[8] "Black Lives Matter Signs in Canada: 'May We Never Again Need to Remind You That WE Built This'" by Steve Sailer; Unz Review, July 8, 2017, https://www.unz.com/isteve/blm-signs-in-toronto-may-we-never-again-need-to-remind-you-that-we-built-this/#comment-1929103.

[9] Thus differing from the Left's partnership with Islam, which is based on Islam's *inherent* hatred of the West.

[10] See "Fashion Tips for the Far-from-Fabulous Right," herein, and "From Ultrasuede to Limelight: Halston & Gatien, Aryan Entrepreneurs in the Dark Age," in my later collection *Green Nazis in Space! New Essays on Literature, Art, & Culture*, ed. Greg Johnson (San Francisco: Counter-Currents, 2015).

[11] I actually "noticed" this due to the "gay" press periodically recycling articles deploring "racism in clubland" from the '80s onward; an early example of virtue-signaling. "A profound streak of racism ran through the club-kid scene, which was made up largely of the pampered offspring of middle-class whites . . . 'We don't want any stupid niggers or lowlife spics coming to the club' . . . Michael Alig said. 'Black people aren't cool. When the niggers start showing up, you know your club is over.'" Frank Owen: *Clubland* (New York: BroadwayBooks, 2003), p. 159. For more on Alig's role as Loki, see

While some, like Paul Gottfried, have noted the rise to dominance of the originally and still predominantly Jewish Neo-Cons, (almost?) no one had sussed out that the rot had set in long before, in the open-air insane asylum of First Century Palestine.[12]

I don't recall if Alisdair brought up the idea of developing these ideas myself, or if I was only inspired by his own blog (a new tool for dissemination of ideas at the time), but it seemed unusual enough and important enough that I decided to get this down in writing.

Since all this was taking place in the intersection of art, religion, and politics, it occurred to me that the best vehicle would be a Manifesto, as favored by groups ranging from the Rosicrucians to the Communists to the Surrealists and Futurists (Aryan Futurism, indeed!)[13] Something along the lines of de Sade's

---

"From Ultrasuede to Limelight," *loc. cit. Plus ça change*: "Let's start with the epicenter of your problematic behaviors towards my kind: your dating app profile. . . . To be clear, you're allowed to describe the kind of guy you're looking for and the things that turn you on, but specifying the race of your desired partner is a line that is not to be crossed. It comes off as racist, and that's because it is." Donovan Trott, "An Open Letter To Gay, White Men: No, You're Not Allowed To Have A Racial Preference," *HuffPost*, June 19, 2017, http://www.huffingtonpost.com/entry/an-open-letter-to-gay-white-men-no-youre-not-allowed_us_5947f0ffe4b0f7875b83e459.

[12] Though Gottfried's contributions are immense, he is, perhaps, handicapped by his ethnic identity; he still seems to think "gay marriage" is the ultimate abomination of desolation, rather than simply the method used by the Judaic Left to forge the manacles of matrimony and replace the warrior band with the wedding band. See his "Yes, Virginia (Dare) There Is a Cultural Marxism — And It's Taking Over Conservatism Inc," *Unz.com*, May 22, 2017, http://www.unz.com/pgottfried/yes-virginia-dare-there-is-a-cultural-marxism-and-its-taking-over-conservatism-inc/.

[13] The proximate influences were the "Broadsheets of Ontological Anarchism" and "Communiques of the Association for Ontological Anarchy," later reprinted as *T.A.Z.: The Temporary Autonomous Zone* (Brooklyn: Autonomedia, 1991) by "Hakim Bey," aka Peter Lamborn Wilson, a private scholar whose own perverse renditions of Tradi-

"Yet Another Effort, Frenchmen, If You Would Become Republicans."[14]

Hence, the broad strokes and blunt, bald assertions, leaving the reader the task of finding cites and making connections, if he wanted to, before taking it as a guide to action. I also found this to be an excellent way to overcome a decades-long writers block.

Another influence, from student days, was Marshall McLuhan. *Wikipedia*[15] says:

> While some critics have taken issue with McLuhan's writing style and mode of argument, McLuhan himself urged readers to think of his work as "probes" or "*mosaics*" offering a toolkit approach to thinking about the media. His eclectic writing style has also been praised for its postmodern sensibilities[16] and suitability for virtual space.[17]

"Mosaic," of course, was the browser that popularized the web, and since the Manifesto was first published online,[18] I intended to make full use of hyperlinks to create an experience of what Michael Hoffman calls "loose cognition" and which he believes is necessary for grasping new ideas.[19] Again, Jack Do-

---

tionalism, Islam, and archetypal psychology were pioneering efforts to update and "make hip" these very staid realms.

[14] Marquis de Sade, "Yet Another Effort, Frenchmen, If you would become Republicans," in *Philosophy in the Bedroom and Other Writings*, trans. Richard Seaver and Austryn Wainhouse (New York: Grove Press, 1966), 296–384.

[15] https://en.wikipedia.org/wiki/Marshall_McLuhan.

[16] Paul Grossweiler, *The Method is the Message: Rethinking McLuhan through Critical Theory* (Montreal: Black Rose, 1998), 155–81.

[17] Paul Levinson, *Digital McLuhan: A Guide to the Information Millennium* (New York: Routledge, 1999), 30.

[18] In Finnish New Rightist Kai Murros' excellent but short-lived digital platform *Le Journal de l'esthétique nouvelle de la révolution nationale*, http://www.kolumbus.fi/~kf1508/journal/09c.html.

[19] "The dissociative cognitive state is highly relevant to philosophy

novan was one of the few who "got it," saying "Reading [the Manifesto] is a psychedelic experience."

Perhaps the most decisive influence, or perhaps just the most useful way to look at what I was doing, came again from Alan Watts; this time, ironically, from the period after his abandonment of Traditionalism.

Rather than seeking some supposed "transcendental unity" above, behind, or perhaps beneath the variety of religions and cultures,

> Watts . . . turned toward hermeneutical analyses exploring interconnections and disjunctions between localized narratives. Through this kind of interpretive study, one arrives at an expanded awareness and comprehension of perspectives via the dialectical rotation of differing vantage points.[20]

In *Beyond Theology: The Art of Godmanship*[21] Watts describes his technique as the "Chinese Box method" (although it sounds more like the Russian Doll method): what happens when we fit, say, Christianity into Hinduism, and—if we can—vice versa?

---

because it enables deep-level symbolic re-indexing of mental constructs. . . . Normally, for convenience, the mind uses linguistic and conceptual associations in a rigid, rutted, and repetitive way; debates are permanent standoffs, because the same cliched assumptions are carelessly adhered to every time words are used. Mastery of semantics and mental association matrixes enables one to release one's assumptions about every single word or concept in an argument, not just a key term in isolation." On the need to not give exhaustive definitions of one's terms at the start of an investigation, in order to be able to produce new knowledge, see Jason Reza Jorjani's *Prometheus and Atlas* (London: Arktos, 2016), Introduction.

[20] *Alan Watts — In the Academy: Essays and Lectures* (SUNY series in Transpersonal and Humanistic Psychology); edited and with an introduction by Peter J. Columbus and Donadrian L. Rice (Albany: SUNY Press, 2017); see my review https://www.counter-currents.com/2017/07/alan-watts-the-first-alt-academic/#more-73053.

[21] New York: Pantheon, 1964.

And so, what happens if we fit a gangster movie into the historical role of the *Männerbund*,[22] or a Henry James *nouvelle* into the metaphysics of René Guénon,[23] or Julius Evola's prehistoric history into the Cthulhu Mythos?[24]

Have I been understood?[25] Apparently, no.[26]

Most recently, and most publicly, a screed on *Slate*, which erroneously but gratifyingly dubbed me "a leader of the alt Right," asserted that my thesis was designed to "attract" gays (like some flying insects) into the clutches of the New Right. The exact opposite of my intentions, of course.[27]

Reading this perhaps deliberately illiterate piece,[28] I could only recall the scene in *Annie Hall* where Woody can conven-

---

[22] "'God, I'm with a heathen': The Rebirth of the *Männerbund* in Brian De Palma's *The Untouchables*," herein.

[23] "The Corner at the Center of the World: Traditional Metaphysics in a Late Tale of Henry James," reprinted in *The Eldritch Evola . . . & Others: Traditionalist Meditations on Literature, Art, & Culture*, ed. Greg Johnson (San Francisco: Counter-Currents, 2014), as well as in the premier issue of *Aristokratia* (Manticore, 2013).

[24] The title essay of *The Eldritch Evola*.

[25] "Have I been understood? — *Dionysus Versus the Crucified*." Nietzsche, final line of *Ecce Homo*. "None of the rulers of this age understood it. For if they had, they would not have crucified the Lord of glory" (1 Corinthians 2:8).

[26] But hope springs eternal! "Sweden far-right plans gay parade in mainly Muslim area," Fatma Naid, *Al-Jazeera*, May 29, 2017, http://www.aljazeera.com/news/2015/07/sweden-farright-plans-gay-pride-muslim-area-lgbt-150728180328656.html.

[27] "How the Alt-Right Is Using Sex and Camp to Attract Gay Men to Fascism" by Donna Minkowitz; June 5, 2017, online http://www.slate.com/blogs/outward/2017/06/05/how_alt_right_leaders_jack_donovan_and_james_o_meara_attract_gay_men_to.html (I'm a "leader" according to the URL). To see what Minkowitz considers laudable, see "I Am Helping Donna Minkowitz Hide Her Perverted Family Incest" by Gilad Atzmon, June 15, 2017, http://www.gilad.co.uk/writings/2017/6/15/i-am-helping-donna-minkowitz-hide-her-perverted-family-incest.

[28] Perhaps itself an instance of the manifesto method — keep punching away, facts be damned?

iently pull Marshal McLuhan—appropriately enough—out from behind a lobby poster to berate a loudmouth academic:

Marshall McLuhan: I heard what you were saying! You know nothing of my work! You mean my whole fallacy is wrong. How you got to teach a course in anything is totally amazing!

Alvy Singer: Boy, if life were only like this!

I despair, I really do.[29]

Nor has the response on the Right been encouraging. One blogger responded to an essay added to this edition, "This Old Gay House," a look at the role of homosexual men in historic preservation, with the laconic: "Yeah, we get it: you're gay[30] and want to be accepted."[31]

While a mere comment, calling attention to the historical

---

[29] A favorite line of BBC comedian Rik Mayall.

[30] A conclusion derived, with typical un-intelligence, from my lack of homophobia; and with such demonstrated inability to draw proper conclusions based on evidence, he purports nevertheless to instruct us in the finer points of genetic science. The idea, *mutatis mutandis*, that only black folks were, or could be, interested in desegregation, would make hash of the Right's favorite idea that the civil rights movement was a "Jewish conspiracy."

[31] "O'Meara again," June 18, 2016, https://eginotes.wordpress.com/2016/06/18/omeara-again-61816/. This blogger, whose obsession with evolutionary psychology has apparently resulted in a Lovecraftian de-volution into knuckle-dragging "tough-guy" attitudes—see "Hard Men and Wild Boys," within—habitually refers to me as "O'Meara," *tout court*, which must surely upset Michael O'Meara. "These types can't carry out connected thought for long without the reptilian brain stem breaking through to bark an obscenity. Their grip on reasoned discourse is not strong. Self-restraint again: not always in evidence on the Right, to be sure, but well-nigh extinct on the Left, even among Ivy League law professors."—Commenter on John Derbyshire's "Like Nazis after 1945: Never Forget The Bullet We Dodged When Hillary Was Defeated," *Unz Review*, July 2, 2017, https://www.unz.com/jderbyshire/like-nazis-after-1945/.

fact of Baron von Steuben's key role in America's victory in the Revolutionary War, due to Washington's "don't ask, don't tell" policy, met with sneering sloganeering: "Must everything be pozz'd?"[32]

Indeed. I came to feel as if I had shown up at a party, laden with balloons, puppies, and ice cream—Hey, guys, we can add millions to our movement, and the best kind, with high IQs, lots of money and oodles of free time! And all we have to do is live up to our Aryan heritage!—only to have my contributions swept from my arms, hammered into the ground, and shat up-on.

But let us continue our meditations.

Let's start with the title—the only thing that most of my critics have read—and the subsequent analysis of the archetypes I call the Homo and the Negro. The choice of this nomenclature I call, without false modesty, sheer genius; and like all such strokes of genius, it seems, subsequently, to be only inevitable.

The rhythm, the rhyme; perfect.

And what else could I have used? If I had wanted to be purely offensive, I would have said *The F*g and the N*gger*, but that kind of *Daily Shoah* vulgarity is not how I roll. The politically correct terminology—*The Gay and the Black*, I suppose[33]—would have been a betrayal of my purpose right from the start.

The Homo and the Negro perfectly evokes the pre-PC, post-War era, the crest of the wave of White Western Civilization,

---

[32] See the oddly titled "Baron von Steuben, 'Don't Ask, Don't Tell' Franklin to Washington" by Mark Segal, Gay History Project, *Windy City Times*, October 1, 2013, http://www.windycitymediagroup.com/lgbt/Baron-von-Steuben-Dont-Ask-Dont-Tell-Franklin-to-Washington/44574.html. Indeed, Washington "surrounded himself with *a group of young officers in a close-knit circle that was marked by affectionate bonds of unusual intensity*, a group Washington himself referred to as his 'family.'" A *Männerbund*, in short. See James Neill, *The Origins and Role of Same-Sex Relations In Human Societies* (Jefferson, N.C.: McFarland, 2011), p. 413; and see my review on Kindle.

[33] PC terminology likes to change frequently, so as to keep people confused and liable to "gotcha!" attacks at any moment. The LGBQT Person and the Black Body?

when such terms were perfectly acceptable; still being un-PC enough to get people's attention and set them on edge, while also being unquestionably objective (being merely the apocopations of the eminently scientific terms 'homosexual' and 'negroid').[34]

The downside, however, is that readers — or more likely, potential readers and those lazy non-readers known as "journalists" — have quite misconstrued the content. As my most perceptive reviewer on Amazon points out, "this is not a book about homos and negroes." Nor, despite what the journalists say, is homosexuality, or sexuality as such, or race, my only concerns, and certainly not my obsessions.[35]

In fact, were I to point to my "best" essay, or favorite, or most characteristic, it would likely be "'God, I'm with a heathen': The Rebirth of the *Männerbund* in Brian De Palma's *The Untouchables*," which touches the one only implicitly, the other not at all, except perhaps in terms of European ethnicities.[36]

Nevertheless, old softy that I am, and always looking to give my reader the maximum bang for his beloved buck, this "Embiggened" edition adds a few pieces of a psycho-sexual nature. *¡Disfrute!*

---

[34] For more on the importance of terminology at the start of any original investigation, see Jorjani, *loc. cit.*

[35] "Because I once wrote a story in which — for good and sufficient plot reasons — a young woman is killed an eaten by a dog, I am stereotyped by casual readers of my work as one writes nothing but stories of violence and cannibalism." Harlan Ellison, *Harlan Ellison's Watching* (Los Angeles: Underwood-Miller, 1989; New York, Open Road Media, 2014).

[36] Or perhaps "Mike Hammer, Occult Dick: *Kiss Me Deadly* as a Lovecraftian Tale, reprinted in *The Eldritch Evola . . . & Others*. From my entire oeuvre, I might point the curious to my recent Kindle essay, *"Coffee? I* like *coffee! The Metaphysical Cinema of Coleman Francis* (Amazon, 2017). It begins to seem as if I am not the "Camille Paglia of the New Right," as Andy Nowicki quipped, but the Roger Ebert (minus the race-mixing); except that honor already belongs to Trevor Lynch; see *Trevor Lynch's White Nationalist Guide to the Movies*; foreword by Kevin MacDonald; edited by Greg Johnson (San Francisco: Counter-Currents, 2012) and its sequels.

But there are limits to how much even the kindest author can be expected to spoon-feed his readers. How could I be expected to plan for a potential audience dumber than ever before, and getting dumber?[37] No wonder then that they can only crave safe spaces, and when challenged, resort to violence.[38]

The Homo and the Negro are ideal types, through which I seek to explain certain features of Western culture, especially current year America. It's just the way I think, but it does seem common enough on the Right, with such thinkers as Oswald Spengler (who spoke in his *Decline of the West* of the need for "physiognomic tact" over and above mere fact-grubbing[39]) and Alfred Rosenberg (whose *Myth of the Twentieth Century* could have profited from a snappier title, such as *The Aryan and the Judaic)*; two authors, come to think of it, rather frequently misunderstood.

The most proximate and substantive influence, though, was the *magnum opus* of old-style Lefty Camille Paglia, *Sexual Perso-*

---

[37] "Freshmen and seniors at about 200 colleges across the U.S. take a little-known test every year to measure how much better they get at learning to think. The results are discouraging. At more than half of schools, at least a third of seniors were unable to make a cohesive argument, assess the quality of evidence in a document or interpret data in a table, *The Wall Street Journal* found after reviewing the latest results from dozens of public colleges and universities that gave the exam between 2013 and 2016. At some of the most prestigious flagship universities, test results indicate the average graduate shows little or no improvement in critical thinking over four years." See "Exclusive Test Data: Many Colleges Fail to Improve Critical-Thinking Skills" by Douglas Belkin, *Wall Street Journal*, June 5, 2017, https://www.wsj.com/articles/exclusive-test-data-many-colleges-fail-to-improve-critical-thinking-skills-1496686662.

[38] And no wonder Bible-thumping conspiracy-monger Jay Dyer was so upset when I dared to point out that bragging about his "graduate studies in philosophy" was ill-advised, when he seemed unable to tell an argument from a hole in the ground. See my review of his *Esoteric Hollywood*, https://www.counter-currents.com/2017/02/pizza-a-movie-part-one/.

[39] See H. Stuart Hughes, *Oswald Spengler: A Critical Estimate* (New York: Scribner's, 1952), p. 71.

nae: Art and Decadence from Nefertiti to Emily Dickinson (New Haven: Yale University Press, 1990), a study of Western Culture that not only employs the technique of identifying the origin and historical metamorphoses of the titular personae, but also was among the first to adumbrate the idea[40] of homosexuals as an essential part of (implicitly) White culture:

> Male homosexuality may be the most valorous of attempts to . . . defeat nature. By turning away[41] from the Medusan mother, whether in honor or detestation of her, the male homosexual is one of the great forgers of absolutist Western identity. . . . Major peaks of Western culture have been accompanied by a high incidence of male homosexuality—in classical Athens and Renaissance Florence and London. Male concentration and projection are self-enhancing, leading to supreme achievements of Apollonian conceptualization.[42]

---

[40] Another, though rather a guilty pleasure than a source, is *The Pink Swastika: Homosexuality in the Nazi Party* by Scott Lively and Kevin Abrams (Founders Publishing Corp., 1995 and now in its 5th edition), where the Evangelical authors locate the sin of National Socialism in its anti-Semitism, which in turn is only a function of its homosexuality, which is a function of its paganism, which is *au fond* identical with its White racial origins; sorry, White Nationalist Christians, all of White, Western culture is merely more or less disguised sodomy, and the only hope of redemption is to worship the Jewish deity — or the Jews themselves. Obviously a farrago of nonsense, but a window into the Evangelical mentality and a striking way to state the truth—by inversion.

[41] Her key notion of "the swerve," in art and cultural history, which I assimilate to the Guénonian notion of the spiral; see, most recently, *"Coffee? I Like Coffee," op. cit.*

[42] One of the few—only?—authors to understand Paglia's influence on both myself and the New Right in general is Peter D. Bredon; see his "St. Camille of the Alt Right," https://www.counter-currents.com/2017/04/st-camille-of-the-alt-right/. Mr. Bredon, late of Trinity Coll., Oxford and part of the Metroland set, is one of the bright lights of Counter-Currents; he may be my only contribution to the movement, and if so, *Ich habe genug.*

Recently, another work has appeared on the New Right itself that appears to take the same archetypal or physiognomic approach to Western Culture: Jason Reza Jorjani's *Prometheus and Atlas* (London: Arktos, 2016) where the titular Titans of Greek mythology are envisioned as spectral presences that literally haunt or inhabit the minds of the West; I consider it the only work since *Sexual Personae* to command the same cultural heights and plunge to the same cultural depths.[43] Together, along with Spengler, they could form a concise bookshelf for the New Right autodidact.

Along with the one in your hand, dear Reader.

Rust Belt, USA
July 9, 2017

---

[43] While the content of our books is quite different, Jorjani's embrace of the paranormal no doubt makes his book as much feared and loathed as — my own. See my review https://www.counter-currents.com/2016/09/jason-jorjanis-prometheus-and-atlas/, as well as Bredon, *op. cit.,* who compares the "Promethean" endeavors of all three of us.

THE HOMO & THE NEGRO:
A MASCULINIST VIEW OF THE FUTILITY OF THE "RIGHT"

"How is it possible to brush aside entirely the intellectual and moral qualities of the ancient sages and to put oneself blithely on the other side of the balance? If a maximum of intelligence and virtue and a maximum of error could co-incide in one and the same consciousness, as the demolishers of the human spirit and its innate truths unhesitatingly take for granted, then man would be nothing, and the emergence of philosophical luminaries—supposing them to be such—would by the same token be impossible. . . . [T]his conjecture bespeaks a monstrous lack of imagination and sensitivity and is belied at every turn—we repeat—by the intellectual and moral eminence of the men at whom it is aimed. One almost feels the need to apologize for drawing attention to something so obvious."

— Frithjof Schuon[1]

For quite some time people have been writing analyses of the futility of the Right (perhaps best summarized by the title of Sam Francis's book *Beautiful Losers*).[2] How can a movement that seems so, well, right, seem to get nowhere, either losing outright or, when in power, never, as Evelyn Waugh said of the British Tories, turning the clock back one bit. Apparently none of these essays has been useful, or used, and so the self-examination has not ceased.

This essay takes a different tack; I want to locate the peculiar

---

[1] Frithjof Schuon, *Logic and Transcendence: A New Translation with Selected Letters*, ed. James S. Cutsinger, trans. Mark Perry, Jean-Pierre Lafouge, and James S. Cutsinger (Bloomington, Ind.: World Wisdom, 2009), p. 33.

[2] Samuel Francis, *Beautiful Losers: Essays on the Failure of American Conservatism* (Columbia, Mo.: University of Missouri Press, 1993).

futility of the Right, especially its American version, in a more general sexual-cultural critique. I locate the futility factor in two related areas: its Judeo-Christianity, and its consequent homophobia. Whether a movement *sans* these features could be recognized as "The Right" is not really a problem for anyone interested in *praxis* rather than mere taxonomy; for now, let me suggest that "gay Rightist" is no more absurd than "gay rabbi."

To anticipate, let me say that I agree with many on the Right that "homophobia" is indeed an absurd term; however, apart from being the most readily understandable, it does convey some truth: the Right's futility is rooted in what is, indeed, a fear of homosexuality.

In a nutshell: the American Right, or the Republican party, cannot be a vehicle for the preservation and expansion of White culture, since its Judeo-Christian element leads it to oppose the culture-creating and culture-sustaining element of homoeroticism, while ultimately embracing, in the name of equality and multiculturalism, its opposite, the Negro.

While obviously not all Aryan cultural figures are homosexual, we may take the Homosexual as the ideal type in a masculinist, homoerotic system; in the same way, not all liberals are Negroes, but for the same reasons we may take the Negro as the ideal type, which is to say, that human type to which the system inexorably leads to or valorizes.

I.
THE FRUIT OF THE POISONOUS TREE

Again, in a nutshell: once the American Right chose to base itself on Judeo-Christianity, its assimilation to the Left was a mathematical inevitability.

Why? Just as no people has reached a high level of culture without some acceptance of homosexuals in that culture, as a function of a more general cultural bias that might best be called more broadly "masculinist"; so no political movement can achieve dominance, or even influence, without a similar worldview; nor would it be worth supporting even if it did prevail.

An excellent summary of what a masculinist movement would be has been provided by Ean Frick: it would be "possessed of a heathen morality and thus certainly open to homosexuals. It would oppose the feminized, Judeo-Christian culture of being a passive viewer or consumer of life and would propose a new culture of excellence, creativity and active participation in all aspects of life."[3]

For more detail, see the works of Hans Blüher, the ideologue of the German youth movement (the *Wandervogel*) and the historical male *Männerbund*, whose influence extended even to such Rightist icons as Baron Evola and Francis Parker Yockey; original texts of the Masculinist movement can be found in *Homosexuality and Male Bonding in Pre-Nazi Germany*,[4] while the late Alisdair Clarke's blog *Aryan Futurism* contains valuable modern contributions.[5]

In short, the Right has ceded cultural domination to the Left, by leaving it to be the only place publicly tolerating and indeed welcoming what the Right perceives as "deviance." The recent takeover of the Right by the Trotskyite-Democratic-Judaics known as "neocons" is only a sideshow, interesting only as being the latest and most blatant, and thus most obvious and revealing (as in the Masonic "Revelation of the Method") form of this more basic transformation; once their Christian stooges soften things up, the Judaics can then step in to take the place of the Right's missing "intellectual elite."

In a truly diabolical "turn of the screw," of course, the welcoming Left hardly promulgates a "masculinist" mentality either. Rather than the unnatural demon of the Right's imagination, the Left first promoted the supposedly "liberating" promiscuity and general sex-obsession of certain parts of the "gay

---

[3] Personal communication.

[4] Harry Oosterhuis, ed., *Homosexuality and Male Bonding in Pre-Nazi Germany: The Youth Movement, the Gay Movement, and Male Bonding before Hitler's Rise. Original Transcripts from* Der Eigene, *the First Gay Journal in the World*, trans. Hubert Kennedy (Binghamton, N.Y.: Harrington Park Press, 1991), a collection of translations of selections from *Der Eigene*, published from 1896 to 1932 by Adolf Brand.

[5] Archived at aryanfuturism.blogspot.com

community" (the feminizing word "community" is itself revealing); when AIDS made that unfashionable, they now promote
the entirely feminized model of "I'm limp-wristed and hate
football, but you accept me!"

Where once a distorted image of the male *Männerbund* in the
form of San Francisco-style libertinage (still observable in the
infamous "Folsom Street Fair") was at least offered, now there is
the demand (on both society and gays themselves) for "marriage
equality," the ultimate capitulation to Judaic "family values." As
gay-libertarian-Buchananite Justin Raimondo has said, marriage
is for women and lesbians, who can bear children; what possible
interest could a man, straight or gay, have in it?

So while the Right deprives itself of the elitist cultural creativity of homosexuals, the Left "accepts" and thus attracts them,
but then demands submission to an anti-cultural feminist-
socialist-egalitarian "Gay" identity.

In both cases, the masculinist forces of White culture are ren-
dered inoperative.

Of course, the "choice" of Judeo-Christianity is more of an
historical inevitability, given the nature of the elements that have
made up, in varying proportions, the American Right, rather
than a literal act in time, like the convention that promulgated
what came to be known as "The Fundamentals," hence "Fundamentalism." By definition, a mass movement is made up of
average Americans, hence Christians, mostly of a dreary
Protestant type.

The best place to locate such a formal choice might be the
moment when William Buckley expelled the Randians from the
movement. Of course, Ayn Rand was a tedious nut job, but the
ground for her dismissal was her atheism. That W. F. B. was a
Catholic might have made this inevitable; that the chosen means
was a review of *Atlas Shrugged* by Whittaker Chambers, and that
the party it was meant to please was represented in America by
Archbishop Spellman, both semi-closeted homosexuals, is a de-
licious irony, emblematic of the important role of homosexuals
in the American Right, where even Buckley himself gave off a
distinctive air of epicene sophistication inconceivable in today's
Gingrich-Beck American Right. Toss in (or out) J. Edgar Hoover

and Roy Cohn, and it's hard to image what the American Right would have been or accomplished without the tacit support of the *faygeles*.

II.
HOMOEROTIC OR HOMOSEXUAL?

But what does this really have to do with masculinism? Have I simply conflated masculinism with homosexuality? While I would defend a bell curve-like distribution of cultural creativity as heavily skewed to the homosexual (even Steve Sailer called Camille Paglia's *Sexual Personae* the most important book of the last 20 years), thus explaining the Right's loss of cultural dominance, the effects of this cultural homophobia are much wider.

There is a relentless slippage between what is perceived as "gay" and all positive cultural qualities that are (1) easy to identify and (2) possessed by homos in optimum form.

Thus every culture-creating male bonding organization (the priesthood, the military, the Boy Scouts, bodybuilding, etc.) is presumed "gay" (and thus, "bad") whether or not any move from the homoerotic to homosexual occurs (i.e., whether or not one moves from masculinist to homosexual) and despite their own (Judaic-influenced) public denials. Ironically, the most officially homophobic organizations in America are widely, and correctly, treated exactly as a bunch of homos.

At a pop cultural level, consider the mainstream and Leftist mockery of the movie *300*, which (despite any number of real flaws) concentrated on "impossible six-packs" and other supposed elements of "homoeroticism." An earlier film containing masculinist themes, *Fight Club*, was met with similar smears, which were renewed more recently when the book's author voluntarily "came out," leading to his astute observation that this is "a way of negating a story that they can't be with. Things used to be dismissed as, 'Oh, that's just a black thing,' and now it's, 'Oh, that's just a gay thing.' That just kind of smacks of dismissal."[6]

---

[6] Lou Lumenick, "10 Years Later 'Fight Club' Author Still Whining About My Review," *New York Post*, Nov. 17, 2009.

Like the Jewish and Judeo-Christian authors of *The Pink Swas-tika*,[7] even liberal movie reviewers can think of no insult greater than sniggering about something being "gay" and if the targets profess no such "gayness," then it must be "unconscious" and thus even funnier.

III.
THE JUDAIC CONTAGION

The origin of the American Right's homophobia is, of course, its acceptance of Judeo-Christianity.

Obviously, various approaches to homosexuality have exist-ed in various cultures, and nothing like the Liberal idea of un-limited "sexual freedom" has ever really existed. Every culture "structures" homosexuality, like everything else, in socially ap-proved ways. Still, however male-male relations have been structured—see for example Crompton's *Homosexuality and Civi-lization*[8] or Hardman's *Homoaffectionalism*,[9] which is an easier read, and more focused on "masculinist" issues, even though he doesn't seem to have heard of the concept—homoeroticism has only been entirely condemned by Judaic culture, and conse-quently by those based on it: the Christian and Islamic. Other cultures have seen Judaism as distinctly "odd" on the subject, and Judaics have been pleased to take pride in their "purity" on this matter, so I think this is a fair characterization.

Using a variation on the "one drop" definition of race in the American South, we can see that any acceptance of homosexuali-ty in a culture (only with slaves; only until the beard grows, etc.), however opposed to the "anything goes" model of "gay libera-

---

[7] Scott Lively and Kevin Abrams, *The Pink Swastika: Homosexuality in the Nazi Party* (Keizer, Or.: Founders Pub. Corp., 1995). Actually covering far more time and space than the subtitle would indicate; as usual with such polemics, everyone everywhere was (1) Gay and (2) Very bad indeed.

[8] Louis Crompton, *Homosexuality and Civilization* (Cambridge, Mass.: Harvard University Press, 2003).

[9] Paul D. Hardman, *Homoaffectionalism: Male Bonding from Gilga-mesh to the Future* (San Francisco: GLB, 1993).

tion" makes it, for our purposes, homosexual-friendly. No bish-op could get away, for example, with saying "I condemn sex be-tween men. I do, however, endorse the fine Spartan practice of kidnapping small boys and educating them in the ways of man-hood."

The implications of this, however, are seldom thought through. It is obvious, I think, that the acceptance of "one drop homosexuality" is itself merely a superficial symptom of a more important factor: these cultures are actually based on a mascu-linist ethos. Again, it is obvious that these cultures are the ones that have produced the great moments of civilization that "The Right" seems to laud, such as Athens and Florence, causing and being caused by such masculinist elements as hierarchy, elitism, and striving for personal greatness.

And it is obvious that they stand in stark contrast to Judaic civilization, which, at least after the Babylonian disaster, has been family-and-reproduction oriented, conformist, repressive, uncreative, and parasitic on those who are.[10]

What then, does Judeo-Christianity "contribute" to the Amer-ican Right along with its "superior" anti-homoerotic moralism? (For anyone who is still inclined to accept that cliché, I recom-mend re-reading the passage from Frithjof Schuon quoted above.) Exactly the anti-cultural doctrines of "equality," "love thy enemy," etc. that the Right supposedly opposes, which are destroying our culture, and whose secularized counterparts make up the even more virulent doctrines of the Left.

Thus the American Right presents a false and therefore futile opposition, whose doctrines, superficially "opposed" to the Left, make it an enticing stopping point on the way to the Left.

These secularized versions of these Judeo-Christian doctrines found on the Left are, admittedly, more "liberal" but not in any way that makes them less harmful to White culture, just as some

---

[10] For an excellent account of the real history of Judaic "culture" and the myths of "Jewish" love of scholarship/science/ humor/free-thinking/enlightenment etc., see Israel Shahak's *Jewish History, Jewish Religion: The Weight of Three Thousand Years* (London: Pluto Press, 1997).

Jews are "more strict" than others, while remaining Jews.

For example, while the Judeo-influenced American Right demonizes homosexuals as unnatural monsters of sexual appetite, the Judeo-influenced Left initially agreed as well; homosexuality was "bourgeois decadence" for Marxists while the lunch-bucket Old Left hated "da fags." Then, after Stonewall, the Lifestyle Left promoted the same model of animalistic sexuality, only presented as positive "sexual freedom." When AIDS caused that to go tits up, they regrouped and now promote gay marriage (significantly, now marketed as "marriage equality" to make it isomorphic with its other causes) because "gays are just like everyone else" (leveling equality again). This, in turn, is more easily sold to the "Right" as a compassionate compromise (Andrew Sullivan's muscular glutes are the main transmission belt) which everyone can join in on; after all, we all endorse "family values," right?

On every issue, the American Right not only demonizes its own elite, but presents traditional Right positions (say, from the Conservative Revolution of pre-war Germany) only after they have been run through the Judaic Family Values machine, emerging in grotesque, distorted, and unusable forms, not unlike what happens to anything that goes through Judaic scientist Jeff Goldblum's teleporter in *The Fly*.[11]

For example, think of "really Right-wing" ideas like the "Right to Life." This is a function of the "every sperm is equal" mentality of Judeo-Christianity. No attempt to genetically improve or even protect the White race is allowed, while lesser races are allowed to breed freely. The same with opposition to birth control and capital punishment. The "conservative" Catholics are the best gift the Judaics ever gave the Left.

Civil Rights? Well, this has already been lost, with the neocon takeover and the resulting compulsory adulation of Martin Luther King as the Greatest American/Christian/Compassionate Conservative of all time. Sam Francis was among the Real Right figures who were sacrificed to the mob for this one, while the Republicans proudly point to their African-American party

---

[11] See the Wikipedia account at http://tinyurl.com/82le9eu

leader as a kind of Shadow Obama.

Immigration? An interesting opportunity to see a real-time example of the Marxist idea of "unequal development of the base and superstructure" (i.e., economics determines culture, except when it doesn't). The conservative masses aren't buying it yet, but all the "respectable" conservatives are on board: George H. W. Bush and his "little brown grandkids," John McCain on "reform," the *Wall Street Journal* on "open borders," etc. Once again, to hell with tradition, culture, the White race; we're all equal in God's sight, right?

To quickly grasp the Masculinist position on these issues, consider the response of Leonidas to the Persian ambassadors in *300*.

IV.
THE NEGRO

This anti-homosexual, thus anti-masculinist, thus anti-White culture bias, explains another troubling cultural trend: the ever-increasing influence of the Negro on American, and thereby world, culture.

The Homo (that is, the Masculinist) and The Negro are polar ideal types.

This arises from material facts: differences in IQ, impulse control, and other psychological factors make the Negro an unsuitable host for masculinist idealism (where achievement requires modesty, restraint, asceticism, though not to be confused with Judeo-Christian "work ethic" or "unworthiness"). Thus, the well-known but un-PC fact of the inferiority of Negro societies, or even Negro parts of otherwise White societies.[12]

If the homosexual is the most extreme form of the masculinist, then the Negro homosexual is almost a contradiction in terms, and at least is subject to considerable cognitive dissonance. Thus, Michael Jackson's pursuit of whiteness, along with his mental instability.

---

[12] See the evidence presented at the invaluable *Stuff Black People Don't Like*, http://stuffblackpeopledontlike.blogspot.com/

On the other hand, the heterosexual, nominally Christian, family values Negro, and especially the young "gangsta," is the most purely anti-masculinist, and thus the well-known hatred of "acting White" (intelligent, well-spoken, hard-working, etc.) which as we have already pointed out easily shades off into "acting gay."

Again, this is the factually material basis of The Negro as the symbol of all things non-masculinist, and thus non-homosexual; one "stereotype" they would no doubt welcome.

However much the American Right may bemoan the decline of culture and indeed of basic social livability, it cannot finger the Negro as the culprit (that would be "racist" and hence anti-Christian), however much the remnants of Traditional cultural criticism it still tolerates may inexorably point that way.

Moreover, the American Right is defenseless from a relentless process of its own negrofication. It not only has no intelligent or creative leaders or members (intelligence and creativity being "gay"), but its acceptance of Family Values Machismo implicitly commits it to valorizing The Negro as the syncretic combination of all that is non-gay (the white man is always a doubtful entity, suspected of being "secretly gay" due to his intelligence, beauty, etc., as in the expression "Not gay, just British").

Thus, the American Right was completely helpless to resist the influx of the neocon (step one, lack of an elite due to anti-homo stance) and the resulting canonization of MLK (step two, positively pro-Negro), now a litmus test for "decency." The end result: the complete demoralization before the meme that "even Republicans must vote for Obama," since only a racist would oppose this "historic opportunity," and the subsequent (typically futile) response of anointing a Negro party head: "See! We like Negroes too!"

CONCLUSION

As Julius Evola and René Guénon knew, nothing was more useless, or positively dangerous, than "conservatives" that merely seek to preserve some old institutions, without asking what principles they were grounded in—the principles themselves being the only thing there was any point in "preserving," and thus the necessity not of stupidly preserving "what was" but rather of finding the right principles in the first place.

If the "Right" had any intelligence, they would be resolutely stripping themselves of any traces of Judeo-Christian inspired negritude, and encouraging masculinist forces whatever their possible homoerotic content, asking themselves: "Who is smearing this cultural element as 'gay'? Our Negro, Judaic, and Christian enemies, that's who!"

HOMOSEXUALITY, "TRADITIONALISM," & REALLY-EXISTING TRADITION

It's a rare experience to find one's self battling bourgeois "Traditionalism" at the side of Baron Julius Evola, and I gotta say, I like it!

Shortly after the war, Baron Evola found himself the target of some aspersions from self-styled "Traditionalists" which led him to these valuable reflections on:

> . . . the danger of a Guénonian "scholasticism" (in the negative sense of the term), which can *reduce everything to something which is both inoperative and abstract,* despite the claims (without a proof) advanced by many followers of Guénon, of having attained a knowledge which should be "realizing" as well. The proof that such a danger is real, is given by the orientation taken by some Guénonian cliques of "strict observance." An example is also found in Italy, by the periodical *Review of Traditional Studies,* which was started last year in Turin, and which imitates the French Guénonian periodical *Études traditionnelles* even in its editorial contents. The translations made in it of old articles written by Guénon, along with some texts or theoretical orientations, may be helpful. However the tone of this review is a pedantic one. One can frequently notice in it an academic inclination, namely the style of *speaking* ex cathedra *and* ex tripode *in a final and pedagogical tone, and with an authority which no member of the editorial staff possesses, either because of spiritual stature or because of valid works being published.*
>
> What Guénon had to say in an unfortunate essay concerning "The Need for a Traditional Exotericism," must also be rejected, since it offers *dangerous incentives and alibis to a reactionary and petty-bourgeois conformism.* The pe-

dantic representatives of Guénonian scholasticism should rather *strive to reach a deeper understanding of the true meaning of the Way of the Left Hand, which is not any less traditional than the Way of Right Hand*, and which has the advantage of emphasizing the transcendent dimension proper of every truly initiatory realization and aspiration. *An abstract and intellectualizing Guénonian scholasticism, typical of "research institutes,"* may well ignore the real meaning of the Way of the Left Hand.[1]

The Timeless Relevance of Traditional Wisdom purports to "rediscover the sacred worldview of Tradition, governed by truth, virtue, and beauty, as [it] addresses some of the most pressing issues today, including fundamentalism, gender and sexuality, religious diversity and pluralism, faith and science, and the problem of evil."[2] And while there is much good here (and well worth the $3.00 it's going for on Amazon.com, such is the modern world's disinterest), I find it discouraging, though predictable, to find this quote from the august Whitall Perry: "The homosexual error is, among other things, that of isolating one pole of a binary cognate and treating it as an absolute, which does violence to the imperatives of the cosmic order" (p. 76).

Well!

This sort of flummery posing as profundity (what is a "pole of a binary cognate," and how does a limp-wristed queen "do violence" to imperatives of no less than a "cosmic order"?) happens too often when Traditionalists attempt to pontificate ("*ex cathedra*" indeed) on subjects without, as Guénon would say, the proper data. The data, in this case, being knowledge of traditional societies, and knowledge of homosexuality. How then can they apply Traditional principles to either, or especial-

---

[1] "René Guénon and the Guénonian Scholasticism" from "René Guénon: a Teacher for Modern Times," available online at http://web.mac.com/juliusevola/iWeb/excerpts/Rene%20Guénon%20and%20the%20Guénonian%20Scholasticism.html

[2] M. Ali Lakhani, *The Timeless Relevance of Traditional Wisdom* (Bloomington, Ind.: World Wisdom, 2010).

ly to their supposed interaction?

A conclusion is reached, supposedly by long and profound meditation of "principles" but really based on caricatures and stereotypes ("dangerous incentives and alibis to a reactionary and petty-bourgeois conformism"), and then merely dressed up, *post hoc*, in "deduction from principles." Reading such comments, I am reminded of Peter Damian, the "inventor" of the concept of "sodomy," which has had a peculiar quality through centuries of discussion: it cannot be described, because though "unnatural" it is so delectable that a description would increase its occurrence—especially among the clergy themselves! By the 19th century, this theological scruple would produce "the Love that dare not speak its name."[3]

This is all the more unfortunate, and unacceptable, since a man with the requisite knowledge of Tradition, and experience living in a traditional society, and experience of homosexuality, is available within the Traditionalist fold, indeed, among the very First Generation, a friend and correspondent of Guénon himself, and published alongside Evola by Inner Traditions: Alain Daniélou.

Daniélou, unlike any other Traditionalist, actually lived, "full time," in a traditional society, the rural India of the 1930s, where he became fluent in Sanskrit and Hindi, was initiated into several local cults, attended the lectures of authentic traditional teachers, and, in short, acquired a knowledge, unavailable to Westerners or from "anglicized" Brahmins, of Indian art and philosophy that, unlike the "cult" status of Guénon's work, was recognized by the scholarly world as unsurpassed.

He did all this while traveling the back roads of India in a Gulfstream trailer with his "long time companion," as we would say, Raymond Burnier. While this lifestyle would have had him arrested in England, and even today in parts of the USA, he found that in India it was a non-issue: his French birth made him an outcaste, and since marriage was out of the ques-

---

[3] See Mark D. Jordan, *The Invention of Sodomy in Christian Theology* (Chicago: University of Chicago Press, 1998), especially chapter 3 on Peter Damian.

tion, his private life was ignored.[4]

Eventually, Daniélou learned that even theoretically (or "principially" as Traditionalists might say) there was no "objection" to homosexuality; quite the contrary:

> Homosexuality is recognized (in the Hindu tradition) as a biological fact, given the necessity for all the intermediate degrees between masculine and feminine, and has never been persecuted. Its various practices are described in the classical treatises on the art of love, which every young scholar must study in just the same way as the other traditional sciences. Even today, boy prostitutes have their niche in society and certain privileges, in particular, that of playing female roles—dressed as women—at major religious performances, organized by the temples in each town or village, and representing episodes in the epics that recount the lives of the divine heroes Rama and Krishna.[5]

Such passages occur throughout his writing, but this one is interesting for containing both points I want to draw attention to. Traditionalists, by and large, are born and raised in modernized Western societies, and acquire their knowledge of Tradition largely through books. Daniélou is unique in having, admittedly at a later age, undergone the education of a traditional young man, and lived in a traditional society. He is thus fully aware of both the actual role played by homosexuals in such societies, as well as the objective, technical knowledge of it possessed by every educated man. (He is also the author of the standard modern English translation of the *Kama Sutra*.)

Even on a "principial" level, Daniélou has no patience with

---

[4] See his autobiography, Alain Daniélou, *The Way to the Labyrinth: Memories of East and West*, trans. Marie-Claire Cournand (New York: New Directions, 1987).

[5] Alain Daniélou, *India, A Civilization of Differences: The Ancient Tradition of Universal Tolerance*, ed. Jean-Louis Gabin, trans. Kenneth Hurry (Rochester, Vt.: Inner Traditions, 2003), p. 11.

such simple-minded shuffling of "archetypes," pointing out that if there are two basic principles, light and dark, male and female, etc., then there must be many "resultant intermediate states." Shiva, for example, is not merely paired with Shakti, but manifests in many forms, some bisexual or hermaphroditic, which are the subject of numerous homosexual cults.[6]

All this is in contrast to say, Guénon, who learned his "Eastern Metaphysics" in Paris, from some traveling Hindus. The dangers of this were immediately apparent in his condemnation of Buddhism as a heresy in his early works (unlike Evola, whose *Doctrine of Awakening* promoted Pali Buddhism as a true Aryan path).

Just as Guénon learned his anti-Buddhism prejudice from bigoted Hindus, and then "derived it from the Principles of Tradition," so Perry and company read their Western, Semitic prejudices into their discussion of homosexuality.

Daniélou reveals that when Guénon eventually felt the need for some "hands on" experience, and wanted to settle in India, the British refused him a visa. Thus his "seeking refuge in traditional Egypt" was actually his second choice. Daniélou regrets that Guénon was unable to avail himself of living Hindu traditions, which might have lent more nuance to his overly intellectual and abstract works.[7] Indeed, how different the overly-Islamized world of "Traditionalism" would be had he been able to join Daniélou in India; and how uncomfortable the "Traditionalists" must be today, stuck with their "last valid revelation" in post-9/11 America.

But perhaps they have only their *petty-bourgeois conformism* to blame. For what kind of world would Guénon have actually found in Cairo? Fortunately, we have the more recent work of John R. Bradley[8] to set the record straight on homosexuality

---

[6] See Alain Daniélou, *Virtue, Success, Pleasure & Liberation: The Four Aims of Life in the Tradition of Ancient India*, trans. Anonymous (Rochester, Vt.: Inner Traditions, 1993), pp. 95–96.

[7] Evola makes a similar criticism of Guénon, in the article cited, and elsewhere.

[8] John R. Bradley, *Behind the Veil of Vice: The Business and Culture of Sex in the Middle East* (New York: Macmillan, 2010).

and traditional Islamic societies. His journalistic account of re-ally existing traditional Arab societies (where boys proudly seek wealthy patrons, and gay-bashing is as unknown as "Gay Pride" parades) parallels Daniélou's account of how reasonable and homo-friendly Tradition was[9] until challenged by import-ed notions of "vice," first Victorian, then "modernist" (and now, perhaps, "Traditionalist").

For a more "academic" perspective, Ziauddin Sadar surveys the Qur'an and *hadith* and concludes:

> Given the Qur'an's emphasis on diversity, it seems strange to me that the sacred text would not recognise sexual diversity. When we are asked, in 17:84, to "Say, 'Everyone does things in their own way, but your Lord is fully aware of who follows the best-guided path,'" should we not include homosexuals in "everyone"?
>
> It seems that the Prophet Muhammad did. One reason the Qur'an mentions "men who are not attracted to women" is that such men existed in Medina during the time of the prophet. They lived outside the dominant pa-triarchal economy but moved freely amongst the women. *The prophet accepted these men as citizens of the diverse socie-ty that was Medina with the usual stipulation that they should not break the ethical and moral codes of society.*[10]

Apart from ritual abjuring of any approval of "negative treatment" of homosexuals (viz., murdering them on sight)

---

[9] Islam, though an "Abrahamic" religion, purports to "correct" the distortions and lies that the Jews and Christians have added to Al-lah's pure revelation; rather than wallowing in smug "folly" like the Christians, the Arabs preserved and developed Greek wisdom; rea-sonably enough, they took over Greek pederasty as well as pedagogy. See William Armstrong Percy III, *Pederasty and Pedagogy in Archaic Greece* (Champaign, Ill.: University of Illinois Press, 1998).

[10] http://blogs.guardian.co.uk/quran/2008/09/homosexuality_p art_1.html. See also Ziauddin Sadar, *Reading the Qur'an: The Contem-porary Relevance of the Sacred Text of Islam* (Oxford: Oxford University Press, 2011).

there is still much of substance that we agree with in the rest of the essay by Ali Lakhani, from which the Perry quote was extracted, such as the absurdity of "gay marriage" and the evils of the consumerism that "the gay lifestyle" seems to bring with it. However, this all is covered by our distinction (first adumbrated by the late Alisdair Clarke on his blog, *Aryan Futurism*), between the Leftist-concocted "gay" identity and real homosexuality as it has existed throughout history. The later, much to the chagrin of the Leftist, has been largely on the side of the Right, from the ancient *Männerbund* (to which Evola traced the origins of Aryan culture) to the pre-war "Masculinist Movement" of Germany to William Burroughs' Wild Boys and pirate utopias. His comments on modesty and consumerism recall Sardar as well as Bradley:

> Reading the Qur'an in terms of contemporary circumstances, is it not right to question whether the commodification of sexuality, the constant bombardment with sexualised images in advertising, for example, as well as the insistence on explicit display of sexual behaviour on tv and in the movies, has taken things to absurd limits and got the balance totally wrong? The pressure such commodification puts on people, especially young girls, to conform to the current fashion in body form, behaviour and acquisition of male company, *far from being a "liberation," can be a nightmare. It is the kind of waking nightmare that far from encouraging personal fulfilment of the whole of our being emphasises one aspect of our nature to the detriment of all others.* So, it seems to me modesty and privacy would have a large role to play in countering the excesses of consumer culture while they present no impediment to fulfilling our sexual nature in the privacy of our own homes.[11]

You would think that after the revelations about Schuon's later

---

[11] http://blogs.guardian.co.uk/quran/2008/09/homosexuality_2. html

activities, and even Evola's remarks on whipping and deflow-ering virgins, the Traditionalists would steer clear of offering advice on sexuality.[12]

Still, we find much wisdom in an argument Schuon used in a different context, and with suitable though slight modifica-tions, it can serve as our warning to Traditionalists[13] who would enter these topics:

> [H]ow is it possible to brush aside entirely the intellectual and moral qualities of the ancient sages [who treated homosexuality as unimportant or even as particularly sa-cred] and to put oneself blithely on the other side of the

---

[12] Leaving aside the charges of child molestation, as "unproven," Schuon on his own evidence seems almost to have, after moving to Indiana, come under the influence of fellow Midwesterner William Burroughs, devising a synthesis (despite Guénon's condemnation of such "syncretism") of Islam and Native American rites, which among other things required him to dance about clothed only in a "specially designed mini-loincloth." One might even welcome him as a proto-typical Wild Boy were it not for the hypocrisy of his animus towards homosexuality.

[13] Is Whitall Perry "unqualified" as Evola calls his tormentors? Perhaps not; he is the author of some incisive essays, reprinted in Whitall N. Perry, *Challenges to a Secular Society* (Oakton, Va.: Founda-tion for Traditional Studies, 1996), as well as the editor of the monu-mental and invaluable *Treasury of Traditional Wisdom: An Encyclopedia of Humankind's Spiritual Truth* (New York: Simon and Schuster, 1971; Louisville, Ky.: Fons Vitae, 2000). In the latter work, the titular ex-cerpts of wisdom are arranged by topics, within an overall structure, not unlike Mortimer Adler's *A Synopticon: An Index to The Great Ideas*, vols. 2 and 3 of *Great Books of the Western World*, 54 vols. (Chicago: Encyclopædia Britannica, 1952), while modern Traditionalists are quoted in the introductions, really mini-essays, to each topic, thereby avoiding the danger of seeming to elevate them to the level of revela-tion. However, curiously enough, Perry chooses to quote, along with the expected Guénon, Schuon, and Coomaraswamy—Daniélou! Thus, if Perry is qualified, then so is Daniélou, with the latter having the additional qualification of actual experience, of both traditional socie-ty . . . and homosexuality.

balance? If a maximum of intelligence and virtue and a maximum of error could coincide in one and the same consciousness, as [Perry and company] take for granted, then man would be nothing, and the emergence of [these traditional sages and societies]—supposing them to be such—would by the same token be impossible. . . . [T]his conjecture bespeaks a monstrous lack of imagination and sensitivity and is belied at every turn—we repeat—by the intellectual and moral eminence of the men at whom it is aimed. One almost feels the need to apologize for drawing attention to something so obvious.[14]

[14] Frithjof Schuon, *Logic and Transcendence: A New Translation with Selected Letters*, ed. James S. Cutsinger, trans. Mark Perry, Jean-Pierre Lafouge, and James S. Cutsinger (Bloomington, Ind.: World Wisdom, 2009), p. 33.

A Band Apart:
Wulf Grimsson's *Loki's Way*

Wulf Grimsson
Loki's Way: The Path of the Sorcerer in the Age of Iron
Second Edition
Lulu.com, 2011

A few weeks ago I was privileged to receive this unsolicited review copy, "the result of over 30 years of research, study and practice," by Wulf Grimsson. I've been trying to read, and then review, the contents ever since, but found it difficult. Not because of the writing—Wulf is admirably clear and free of both "scholarly" stodginess and "occult" rigmarole—but precisely because of its dense content of interesting and important ideas. Almost every page gives one something to think about, a source to look up and perhaps reconsider, an inspiration to a new connection made for one's self.

Why I should have been selected for this privilege is plain from the contents. *Loki's Way* covers the whole range of topics I've explored on my blog, outside of the more pedestrian political and economic ones, from the *Männerbund* to mystery traditions to runes, from Nietzsche to Evola to Colin Wilson. I am above all grateful for Wulf's freeing me from the mild guilt I have felt about all the topics I haven't done to adequate length, as well as my regret that the late Alisdair Clarke did not live to produce a similar treatise from his path-breaking blog, *Aryan Futurism*. My Constant Readers will find *Loki's Way* to be essential reading.

But first let Wulf define his subject: "Loki's Way is an adaptation of the Left Hand Path or sorcery for the Kali Yuga. This tradition has taken many forms throughout the centuries, in the modern age it must be updated to deal with new discoveries in science and psychology" (p. 62).

The last part there also brings up another reason I've had trouble writing about this book. I have grave reservations about

much of the material in the first third, and thus, as Wulf express-
es it here, in a sense his whole project. I would prefer that he
take Guénon's advice and forget about "reconciling" science and
Tradition and especially "updating" the latter by the former. Not
only should the process be reversed, judging Science by the
timeless principles of Tradition, but the process is necessarily
unending, as Science by contrast is the realm of the amorphous
and ever-changing, requiring the "synthesis" (really, as Guénon
would point out, syncretism) to be redone over and over—
although I'm sure the publishers appreciate that!

In particular, I think that Wulf's claim that "the esoteric is the
physiological," i.e., the "discovery" that what esoteric Tradition
has been talking about in guarded language can "now be revealed" (as the New Age publishers would shout) as being techniques for manipulating the endocrine and other bodily systems,
is really just a misreading of what Evola among others has described as the starting point that remains when all dogmas and
theories have been tested and abandoned, in the alchemical
abyss:

> But then the individual finds himself confronting his body,
> which is the fundamental nexus of all the conditions of his
> state. The consideration of the connection between the ego
> principle in its double form of thought and deed and cor-
> poreality . . . and the transformation of said connection by
> means of well-defined, practical, and necessary acts, even
> though they are essentially interior, constitutes the essen-
> tial core of the Royal Art of the hermetic masters.

Evola adds:

> The latter will be directed first of all to the conquest of the
> principle of immortality, and then to the total stable na-
> ture, no longer transitory or deteriorating . . . by which the
> human manifestation is established within the realm of
> becoming.[1]

---

[1] Julius Evola, *The Hermetic Tradition: Symbols and Teachings of the
Royal Art*, trans. E. E. Rehmus (Rochester, Vt.: Inner Traditions, 1995),

Immortality! Yes, indeed:

> Loki's Way gives us the opportunity for individual immortality. It means using the very structures that are in place to satisfy the replicators and which sustain collective immortality for our own benefit. We are literally making a u-turn; the very things that sustain the immortality of the collective must be used against the norm to achieve a permanent, discrete and individual self.
>
> This, of course, is extremely difficult and confronting and accordingly the path to immortality is one that only a few will attempt and less will achieve. It is hard to conceptualize just how radical such a process must be. The best way is to seriously consider that absolutely everything you believe, feel and think could be wrong. Your tastes, choices, preferences, likes and dislikes are all conditioned. Nothing about your life is authentically real. It is as though you were conditioned as a government agent and everything you believe to be true about yourself, your life, your career even your family is simply brainwashing. The truth about the human condition is really that terrifying. Most will find such a scenario so frightening and so personally confronting that it is easier to look away and find fault with this book than to wake up and smell the coffee. (p. 58)

What Evola calls alchemy or The Royal Art, Wulf calls . . . sorcery:

> What is sorcery? Sorcery is a means by which an individual is able to wrench control of the evolutionary processes to become individually aware and immortal. He or she becomes a discrete, isolate intelligence which exists beyond the confines of the collective processes of eternal reoccurrence. . . . Within Loki's Way this change is the transformation of human to post human through the focusing

---

of the Will. (p. 61)

The bit about the Will reminds us that Evola was compelled to treat Crowley with some respect, despite his deplorable life and personality, as someone who Knew Things. Wulf goes Evola one better and brings in Crowley explicitly.

Another thing he brings in explicitly, and much to my heart, is the *Männerbund*, which Evola only relatively briefly discusses. Wulf connects the dots between the historical *Männerbund* and the esoteric path to individual immortality followed by the elite—in contrast to the common fate in store for the followers of the Vedic "path of the fathers," Evola's realm of society beneath the State, my own contrast of Family Values and Wild Boys. For Wulf it's replicators versus Sorcerers.

The *Männerbund* or Warrior Band is the origin of the esoteric path, because the latter is, *au fond*, a battle; which Wulf explains, typically, in equal parts Sufism and Dawkins:

> Memetic eugenics is the process whereby we weed out unworthy memes and replace them with memes which will help us evolve. This is what Loki's Way is all about. We dissolve conditioning and replace it with memes which are conducive to our own process of godmaking. This book is a meme, bringing esoteric traditions in line with science and hopefully awakening the small number of people with the potential to become more than what they are.
>
> Sorcery is found in many ancient traditions. In the Norse we can see that the warrior ethic was an expression of the battle against the flawed aspects of the emotions and psyche to achieve a true Self which would enter Valhalla. The berserker or warrior is a great "type" of the seeker for the Overman. An even more intriguing example is in Sufism where the concept of Jihad is interpreted in a unique way. The outer form of Jihad is a just war but the inner form of Jihad, the more significant, is against the false and flawed aspects of the personality. This model of the internal battle where we wage a sacred war against

genes, memes and frames to achieve a Self is an expressive and poetic way to represent our sacred quest. (p. 66)

So, paradoxically, only the Warrior Band, the Group, can provide the context for true individuation:

This is one of the reasons cell, unit or *Männerbund* work is so significant, it keeps you grounded and stops the fragments of the ego from influencing your worldview. A good group of fellow working sorcerers can bring you to earth quick smart! (p. 95).

We might also suggest, this self-selected group that never the less valorizes individual male excellence — thus, androphilic if not homosexual — is the solution to the paradox that Michael O'Meara has observed: the White race contains an overemphasis on the individual against society, which, while contributing to our creative dynamism, can be exploited by our enemies to render us uninterested in or even hostile to concern for our own race.

This warrior elite, devoted to realizing a higher principle, is the origin of the Traditional Aryan State, which is oriented to a transcendent principle, in contrast to the common herd and its promiscuous "wants" and "needs" (think: peasant frivolity vs. the Templars) and thus also the social stratification characteristic of Aryan society (p. 72):

The sorcerer and warrior both have the potential to become Overman via different means or by combining paths. Loki's Way is the modern equivalent of [Georges Dumézil's] first function combined with a warrior ethic. It can be applied via the mode of the lone wolf, with a blood brother or in a *Männerbund*. The teaching level of the sorcerer and warrior is esoteric and left hand path. (p. 74)

At this point, the story takes a turn that may give the average reader a turn himself, but not our Constant Readers:

As organic and social memes are dissolved new forms of sexuality and emotional bonding needs to be created. Every man has androphilic potential, it just has to be activated and directed. Since the transition to the Overman is unnatural and works against the normal evolutionary process which favours reproduction then the focus must be on same-sex bonding. (p. 112)

I am not suggesting that every screaming queen or muscle-mary is a spiritual warrior or engaged in Platonic love. I am suggesting that to cultivate a unique form of androphile friendship based on esoteric ideas is the highest form of relationship and for the Overman naught else will do. (p. 109)

Which leads to chapters discussing both historical traditions from India to the Norsemen, and modern theorists from Edward Carpenter to Hans Blüher to Jack Malebranche. Especially important are his careful dissection of the various "models" of homosexuality that have gone into creating the modern notions of "homosexual" and "gay," and analyzing their usefulness for the Left Hand Path.

The [Uranian] model was popularised by both Ulrichs and Hirschfeld and ultimately proves wanting. It confuses intersex and transgenderism with homosexuality. While this is not surprising due to the early period of their work it is still a view popular today. It seems an ongoing slur in a culture which devalues women and sees them as "less than men" to associate men who take the passive sexual role as female. It could be argued that this identification has its roots in misogyny and was later fed by Judeo-Christian thinking. Many also believe that the idea of seeing a homosexual as a woman in a man's body led to the medicalization of homosexuality which continued right through to the 1960s.

The Intermediate Sex model [Carpenter] is significant as the shaman, priest and androphile warrior existing outside the normal structures of the society. At the same time I think we need to be careful using the term third or intermediate sex as it infers a state which is not quite one or the other, rather than as one which is both. The masculinist model of Brand and others (it is also found represented in the work of Jack Malebranche today, *Androphilia*) is appealing and certainly relevant.

Personally I we think we need to develop a new model for our sexuality hence terms like Androphilia and the *Männerbund* need to be understood in a new way. This is especially significant since we are talking about same-sex relations in terms of a unique goal not as an everyday preference. For the *Männerbund* androphilia is a special form of "sacred" bond which is expressed between warriors; it is also initiatory.

All comrades have a male and female side and clearly since they are working to transcend human restrictions would have no problems exploring passive or active sex roles. The genders within us, so to speak, represent a great source of power and we may use cross dressing or passive techniques for Seidr work but also have no issue with being warriors for Galdr (active runic sorcery) or even in battle. (p. 129)

I think Wulf is on to something important here. All of the existing "scientific" and especially "historical" models seem skewed against the correct understanding of the *telos* of esotericism being to transcend by uniting male and female, active and passive, etc.

[P]rohibitions against same-sex relations hence the fear of homosexuality comes from an alien desert religion and has little to do with our traditions. . . . Many of these same phobias were passed down into Christianity and Islam. Many traditions had a very different attitude to same-sex relations prior to their infection by Christianity. Japanese Buddhism had a strong homoerotic element as did the Samurai, it was only Christian missionaries that did away with such traditions. Sadly many of the Eddic references to same-sex relations are negative but that is to be expected considering they have come down through the hands of Christian scribes! (p. 219)

One could add here Daniélou's similar comments on the importation of Victorian and modernist prejudices into Hinduism, as quoted in chapter three above.

A careful reading of Guénon would lead one to infer that all "Traditions" are products of the Kali Yuga, early, to be sure, but still of the Dark Age. Therefore one might well find some misunderstandings of the wisdom that was being recompiled after the chaos of the last cyclical turn. Combined with the necessarily elite and secret nature of the esoteric path, it should be no surprise that there should be no adequate understanding of male bonding publicly available even in Traditional sources. Here, at least, we find ourselves agreeing with Wulf's project to "make anew" Tradition: "Each form of the modern world represents a degeneration of the Perennial Tradition . . ." (p. 168).

And quoting Crowley:

Behold! the rituals of the old time are black. Let the evil ones be cast away; let the good ones be purged by the prophet! Then shall this Knowledge go aright. — *Liber AL vel Legis* II:5.

In this verse we are given clear instructions about how to deal with the old schools of magic, esotericism and their formulae. The "old time" are the Older Aeons. These rituals are black, that is they should not be used until reassessed by New Aeon formula. Since most are based on the sacrificial image of the Dying God they must be purified and cleansed.

Those which cannot be changed will be disposed of, those that can be purified can be adapted. As discussed throughout this book, Traditional forms of spirituality must be radically re-examined both in terms of Loki's Way. Old age fertility rites must be cast away, let the blood brotherhood of Set and Horus Reign!

A close reading of the passages in Evola's *Hermetic Tradition* mentioning "androgyne" would show that the process involves the male becoming and then dominating, becoming so as to dominate, the feminine energies, a process he gives the provocative name "philosophical incest."

Also useful would be a reading of the essay from UR, "Serpentine Wisdom," reprinted in his *Introduction to Magic*,[2] in which Evola, under a pseudonym, mocks those with a "muscle-bound" understanding of power, and advises them to take on the "power of the feminine" (yes, Evola!).

Later chapters feature a fascinating discussion, new to me, of occult warfare via Aeonic Magick and Time Sorcery and the attempts of Evola, Crowley, and even H. P. Lovecraft to tap into eternal principles in order to literally re-create the conditions of the primordial state in our modern age.

The reader may find himself feeling a bit overwhelmed with all this somewhat theoretical discussion. The last third of the book balances this out with several chapters of "Sorcery in Practice," the "many forms of sorcery and many models for recognizing the associations between our own inner world and that which is beyond" (p. 205) ranging from runes to sexual sorcery.

The reader must have realized by now that no mere review could do justice to the contents of this rich and important book. I hope they will have also realized that the solution is to get their hands on this book for themselves. It is essential reading for those in the modern world who would "decide whether to be a *nithing* or coward or nothing, a member of the herd or crowd or a hero, a warrior, a comrade of the *Männerbund*" (p. 240).

Counter-Currents/*North American New Right*
September 23, 2011

---

[2] Julius Evola and the Ur Group, *Introduction to Magic: Rituals and Practical Techniques for the Magus*, ed. Michael Moynihan, trans. Guido Stucco (Rochester, Vt.: Inner Traditions, 2001), pp. 318–23.

Sir Noël Coward, 1899–1973

Noël Coward
The Noël Coward Reader
Ed. Barry Day
New York: Knopf, 2010

> "The only thing that really saddens me over my demise is that I shall not be here to read the nonsense that will be written about me and my works and my motives. . . . There will be lists of apocryphal jokes I never made and gleeful misquotations of words I never said. What a pity I shan't be here to enjoy them."
> — *The Noël Coward Diaries*, March 19, 1955[1]

> "White"
> — from a list of things with "style," solicited from Sir Noël for an ad by Gillette razor blades.

One is so used to today's notion of the artist as an outsider, tortured or haughty as the case may be, or perhaps proudly degenerate, that it can come as a shock to find, or recall, that the artist has usually been, and more importantly seen himself as, a productive and grateful member of society, whatever its flaws; even a patriot.

Ah, but what of the homosexual artist? Surely here we can find a true outsider. According to the victimology of the Left, life "before Stonewall" was one long uncut period of gay-bashing and oppression, subtle or overt.

The point of such a mythology is to convince the homosexual that by accepting the manufactured "gay" identity, and thus contributing to the Left's project of destroying and reconstructing Western civilization, he will be rewarded with both vengeance now and a bright future in an entirely new gay-friendly world.

---

[1] Noël Coward, *The Noël Coward Diaries*, ed. Graham Payn and Sheridan Morley (New York: Da Capo, 2000).

Well, it wasn't that way, and it needn't be that way. As the late English New Right theorist Alisdair Clarke put it:

After the 1967 de-criminalization in the UK, homosexuals faced a choice between re-integrating with European civilization in a way not possible for 1,500 years (i.e., since the Jewish heresy of Christianity infiltrated the Roman Empire), or siding with the Marxist, Maoist, New Left enemies of European civilization, the ones who brought "Gay Liberation" from Manhattan to London. Instead of taking up our traditional responsibility of defending and glorifying our civilization, as did so many homosexuals in the past like Frederick II and von Humboldt, we supported of those who would destroy that very same civilization.[2]

In this context, it may be instructive to examine the case of Sir Noël Coward, "The Master," who practically invented the idea of "The Englishman" in the 20th century, as an example of such full-hearted, un-ironic "defending and glorifying our civilization."

Was Coward a "conservative"? It seems odd to those who remember him, if at all, as the campy cabaret entertainer of the '50s and '60s. When Coward's *Diaries* were published in 1982, *Variety* was puzzled: "It's a bit startling to discover that Coward was a 'political reactionary,'" quoting his views on Suez: "The good old imperialism was a bloody sight wiser than all this woolly-headed, muddled 'all men are equal' humanitarianism which has lost us so much pride and dignity and prestige in the modern world."[3]

Rather than accepting such loaded terms as "reactionary," we can certainly designate Coward as a "conservative" or "man of the Right" as Paul Gottfried has recently defined the term:

---

[2] Alisdair Clarke, "Paris Shockwaves" at *Aryan Futurism* http://aryanfuturism.blogspot.com/2006/08/paris-shockwaves.html

[3] Philip Hoare, *Noël Coward: A Biography* (Chicago: University of Chicago Press, 1998), p. 521.

The Right by its nature is anti-egalitarian and favors hierarchy over the idea (or chimera) of universal individual equality. It is also committed to preserving organic institutions in which families and communities can survive. It is profoundly skeptical of any scheme that seeks to advance some notion of human perfection, and especially in the modern world, the Right should be fighting doggedly against social engineering and leveling.[4]

Jere Real reviewed the work of Coward back in 1976 and came to the same diagnosis, but with this useful caveat:

[A] conservative may desire simultaneously order in society and the toleration of personal non-conformity, he can doubt the existence of equality in the abstract but hope for the greatest variety in human experience. This combination — the orderly society combined with considerable expression of individual eccentricity — exists in our time, almost as nowhere else, in the England of a writer such as Noël Coward.[5]

With the publication of *The Noël Coward Reader*, which chronologically mixes excerpts from his public work and private diaries and letters, we can now take a synoptic look at six decades of artistic public work and private rumination and not only see that Coward deserves, as Real suggested, Russell Kirk's sobriquet, Bohemian Tory, but also some idea of how he came to be that way.

The *Reader* is a big, well-organized, finely-produced volume, but it suffers from a couple of odd flaws. First, it claims that "to date, there has never been a Noël Coward reader; this is the

---

[4] Paul Gottfried, "Cannon Fodder," http://www.unz.com/gottfried/canon-fodder/

[5] Jere Real, "The Playwright as Bohemian Tory," *Intercollegiate Review* vol. 11, no. 2 (Winter–Spring 1976). Available online at http://www.firstprinciplesjournal.com/print.aspx?article=487&loc=b&type=cbtp

first"; in fact, *The Cream of Noël Coward* was published in 1996 by the Folio Society.[6] One might claim this was a "limited edition," but it is still easily available online for half the price of the *Reader*. More importantly, although the *Reader* is three times larger, it ignores *Not Yet the Dodo*, which as we will see is Coward's most explicit discussion of homosexuality, the artist, and society; it even claims that *A Song at Twilight* from the previous year is "the only time he touched upon the subject of homosexuality in his work" (*Reader*, p. 546). What could explain this curious omission?

Despite Coward's reputation, and carefully constructed pose, as the quintessence of high-class sophistication and airy panache, his biographers have shown how the man was shaped by his distinctly unglamorous childhood, what the *Reader* calls the "refined suburban poverty" and proud of it to the end of his life:

> How fortunate I was to have been born poor. If Mother had been able to send me to private school, Eton and Oxford or Cambridge, it would probably have set me back years. I have always distrusted too much education and intellectualism. . . . My good fortune was to have a bright, acquisitive but not, *not* an intellectual mind, and to have been impelled by circumstances to get out and earn my living.[7]

He earned that living as a hard-working child actor, which he considered to have taught him quite a lot about the "basic facts of life by the age of fourteen."

What were those facts of life? Here is John Simon's summary of them:

> Yet no one loved England (climate apart) and its common people more than Coward, as his friend the Queen was first to acknowledge. "England may be a very small is-

---

[6] Noël Coward, *The Cream of Noël Coward*, ed. Michael Cox (London: The Folio Society, 1996).

[7] *Diaries*, December 21, 1967.

land, vastly overcrowded, frequently badly managed," he wrote, "but very much the best and bravest in the world." Repeatedly he flaunts his pride in the Scottish and English blood to which he owes his success.[8]

That success, early on, came from work that, though superficially as "decadent" and "modern" as the Bright Young Products of Oxbridge, was actually bringing the critical eye of a practical, working-class mind to their intellectual pretensions.

Like his contemporary Evelyn Waugh, Coward created a character, what Kenneth Tynan later called his "protective pose" (*Reader*, p. 522), which made him seem to be of that very milieu, while employing a subtle wit to create aesthetically pleasing and enjoyable works that also mockingly expose the flaws in "the modern age."

As Guillaume Faye advises, "It is mocking and 'eccentric' brainwaves that should lay the foundations" for any critique, a principle also well known to the Surrealists ("Gravity lies in what does not appear serious" — André Breton) and the Situationists ("subversive ideas can only come from the pleasure principle" — Raoul Vaneigem).[9]

Coward was far from a flapper or a toff, but rather an honest and sympathetic participant-observer and conservative critic, in the same way Burroughs played with crime and drugs and Kerouac with irresponsibility, but were not themselves "Beat" as that "lifestyle" was distilled from their works by the mass media. In the same way Coward writes of hopelessly romantic couples while privately, in his letters and diaries, disdaining the very idea of "love."

The pose was solidified for all time after his first major success, his play *The Vortex* (which was almost banned until a sur-

---

[8] John Simon, "Sir Noël's Epistles," *New York Times*, November 25, 1967, a review of Noël Coward, *The Letters of Noël Coward*, ed. Barry Day (New York: Knopf, 1997), available online at http://www.nytimes.com/2007/11/25/books/review/Simon-t.html

[9] Quotes in Guillaume Faye, *Archeofuturism: European Visions of the Post-Catastrophic Age*, trans. Sergio Knipe (London: Arktos Media, 2010), p. 57.

prisingly perceptive civil servant noted that this mélange of drugs and incest served a serious aim, and observed that "if we ban this we shall have to ban *Hamlet*") when he allowed himself to be photographed in Chinese garb, in bed, with a look of "advanced degeneracy" caused (he later said) by the flashbulb. But his teasing interviews were designed to leave the same impression: his mind is "frightfully depraved" and "a mass of corruption" due to incessant visits to "opium dens, cocaine dens" (*Reader*, p. 103).

There is certainly no attempt to advance any kind of "gay agenda." The "camp" of *Demi-Monde* was a serious attempt to explore morality that had been shattered but not destroyed by the First World War (as he says quite openly in his Preface) and *Bitter Sweet* is intended as parody of Wilde, not hagiography.

Eventually real or affected decadence led to a nervous breakdown, where his treatment involved composing a list of good and bad qualities — among the former: "common sense."

Gradually, his "exploration" of modernity modulated to an open disillusionment with this life of bobbed hair and cigarettes; were people *really* happy?

By dancing
Much faster
You're chancing
Disaster
Time alone will show
("Poor Little Rich Girl")

"These words from me may surprise you" indeed; and three years later, in 1928, Coward is even more emphatic, and specific:

But I know it's vain
To try to explain
When there's this insane
Music in your brain . . .
Nigger melodies
Syncopate your nerves . . .
And when the lights are starting to gutter

Dawn through the shutters
Shows you're living in a world of lies.
("Dance Little Lady")

Indeed, as Spengler observed five years later (in a book published by same house as *The Noël Coward Reader* today), "jazz music and Negro dancing [are performing] the Dead March for a great Culture."[10]

All this subtly subversive work culminated in 1931, when encapsulating the "essential psychology" of his time in the classic song "Twentieth Century Blues."

One might think, if one were under the "general perception" of him, that the ensuing Depression and war would leave a campy social critic like Coward without a subject. But what was called for was patriotism and belief in the British spirit, and these were hardly alien.

And while it would be inaccurate and even absurd to think Coward welcomed the war, it did give him the opportunity to exercise his profoundly conservative instincts in a more open, as it were out of the closet, fashion.

Coward's patriotic work was on two fronts; one was more public than ever, to buck up British spirits with a play, *Blythe Spirits*, a song, "London Pride," and a movie, *In Which We Serve*. "To make that film he had to overcome extraordinary opposition from high up, only to have it turn into a major artistic and morale-building hit."[11]

The other was more secretive: undercover work promoting, among other things, US involvement in the war. Though some conservatives might prefer the "isolationist" side from today's perspective, Coward, like Lindbergh after Pearl Harbor, was simply defending his homeland from attack by outsiders.

This is again consistent with Gottfried's notion of "conservative":

---

[10] Oswald Spengler, *The Hour of Decision, Part One: Germany and World-Historical Evolution*, trans. Charles Francis Atkinson (New York: Knopf, 1934), pp. 227–28.

[11] John Simon, "Sir Noël's Epistles."

[F]riend/enemy distinctions are natural to how people live. The way out of this situation, even when it becomes heated, should not be through international administrative regulation of individual human lives for the sake of perpetual peace and brother- or sisterhood. Such utopian efforts can only lead to tyranny and the utter destruction of traditional ways of life. The best we can do in dealing with conflict is to control and channel violence through timely diplomacy and only if absolutely necessary, military interventions.

Rooted in real connection to his country, Coward's patriotism did not entail any ideological demonizing of the German enemy, or a demand for "unconditional surrender" (the typical motive of the modern war of "humanism" versus "enemies of humanity"), and certainly no dream of a post-war "world administration," whose actual manifestations, displacing the beloved Empire, he despised. As Guillaume Faye has said:

It is possible to be a "patriot," someone tied to his subcontinental motherland, without forgetting that this is an organic and vital part of the common folk whose natural and historical territory . . . extends from Brest to the Bering Strait.[12]

No modern neocon or liberal ideologue could have the sense of his enemy's humanity that would allow him to see the ironic humor in a song like:

Don't let's be beastly to the Germans
When our victory is ultimately won,
It was just those nasty Nazis who persuaded them to fight
And their Beethoven and Bach are really far worse than
    their bite
Let's be meek to them —
And turn the other cheek to them

---

[12] *Archeofuturism*, p. 20.

And try to bring out their latent sense of fun.
Let's give them full air parity
And treat the rats with charity,
But don't let's be beastly to the Hun.

Certainly the BBC didn't appreciate it.

Oddly enough, Churchill loved the song; but maybe he just loved forcing Coward over and over to jump up and sing it on command. In any event, Coward's authentic patriotism was miles from the war-mongering ideologue Churchill, and the two hardly saw eye to eye on anything involving the war. Churchill rebuffed his offer to work for the war effort, disparaging his talk of "intelligence" (though Coward pointed out that he was talking of his own talent, not "Intelligence" in quotes, *à la* James Bond) and suggested he "sing to the troops while the shooting goes on" ("not practicable," Coward later sniffed).

Churchill was no doubt part of the "higher authorities" who didn't want him involved with the film *In Which We Serve*, and Coward, rightly as later documents showed, suspected Churchill had personally torpedoed his knighthood for the ensuing film.

For his part Coward hardly granted Churchill the reverence today's neocons demand; he considered him "a spoiled petulant gaga old sod."[13]

Coward was hardly committed to idolizing the Yanks (who still seem to think that "the war" began in January 1942, by which time Britain had been in action for three years).

In Coward's *Middle East Diary*, he made several statements that offended many Americans. In particular, he commented that he was "less impressed by some of the mournful little Brooklyn boys lying there in tears amid the alien corn with nothing worse than a bullet wound in the leg or a fractured arm."[14]

Tame, it would seem, but one can sense the sneer underlying

---

[13] Graham Payn, *My Life with Noël Coward* (New York: Applause Books, 2000), p. 135.

[14] Robert Calder, *Beware the British Serpent: The Role of Writers in British Propaganda in the United States, 1939–1945* (Montreal: McGill-Queen's University Press, 2004), pp. 102–04.

"mournful little Brooklyn" and "the alien corn" and the corresponding -witzs and -steins it implies. After protests from both the *New York Times* and the *Washington Post*, the Foreign Office urged Coward not to visit the United States.

One is also reminded of a similar incident, around the same time, involving General Patton and an apparently malingering soldier. Coward and Patton (who once proposed a tank uniform of green leather jumpsuit and gold helmet) belonged to an earlier generation that expect soldiers to get out there and get results, whatever their taste in haberdashery; today's macho commanders worry about "gays" but haven't won a war since, well, Patton.

And speaking of "macho," the incident also gave him an opportunity to demonstrate the usefulness of his "campy" persona, when backed by genuine physical courage. As fellow spy David Niven tells the story:

> Now [on the day that *Stars and Stripes* headlined "Kick this bum out of the country"], Noël opened in Paris with Maurice Chevalier, whom the American soldiers were sure was a collaborator, and with Marlene Dietrich, whom they were sure was a German spy. . . . I went to see Noël before the performance, and I said . . . what are you going to do about it? Sir Noël said, "First I shall calm them, and then I shall sing some of my very excellent songs." So I went out and stood at the back by the exit, and Noël came on to a deathly hush, which he's not used to. A deathly hush. And then he looked at them and said, "Ladies and Gentlemen, and all you dear, dear, sniveling little boys from Brooklyn . . ." And they fell down and absolutely loved it.

But the Navy was his true love:

> I love the Navy, I inherited my affection for it, all my mother's family were Navy. Admirals and Captains. I love everything to do with the Navy. To start with they've got the best manners in the world and I love the sea and Navy discipline, which is very hard. It wouldn't have frightened

me because I'm quite disciplined anyway, and I'm used to accepting discipline. I would have loved to have been in the Navy.[15]

The combination of pride in family heritage and personal predilection for self-discipline are expressed honestly, while in these days of "gay sensibility" as well as official "don't ask, don't tell" policies they seem almost "camp."

Even Churchill's opposition couldn't stop his writing and acting in the classic film, *In Which We Serve*, a tribute to his friend, Lord Mountbatten, as well as to the regular sailors, whom he demanded be detailed to the production instead of actors. That confidence in the "ordinary man" was rewarded by performances that led the Admiralty Head of Personnel to exclaim: "By Jove, Coward, that convinces me you were right to ask for a proper ship's company, *real* sailors. No actors could have possibly done that" (*Reader*, p. 432).

Although it must be said that when he gave his patriotism too free a hand (in the wartime isolationist-bashing *Time Remembered*, the pre-war *Post-Mortem*, or the post-war *Peace in our Time*) it tended to become strident and a bit hysterical, forgetting his first rule of the dandy's pose: "The greatest thing in the world is not to be obvious—over ANYTHING."

If the early Coward developed an aristocratic veneer for solidly working-class values, and the wartime Coward was a simple spokesman for a patriotism considered old-fashioned if not criminal, the post-war Coward now became the "surprisingly" reactionary. Coward hadn't changed; what had changed was England. Having won the war, would it now win the peace?

Coward had his doubts; the post-war "Festival of Britain" was like Britain itself: "the last word in squalor and completely ungay" causing him to riposte with the lugubriously conservative, almost Guénonian "Bad Times are Just Around the Corner":

---

[15] Charles Castle, *Noël: Biography of Noël Coward* (New York: Doubleday, 1973), p. 173.

There are bad times just around the corner.
There are dark clouds travelling through the sky.
And it's no good whining
About a silver lining.
For we know from experience they won't roll by.

The '50s were indeed a bad time for Coward, who was put on the shelf by critics who found him, and his work, terribly old-fashioned, though the public never deserted him.

His send-up of "modern" art, *Nude with Violin*, based, of course, not on rival "theories" but his own experience as an amateur painter, ran for over a year but was ignored by the critics.

> **Sebastien**: I don't think anyone knows about painting anymore. Art, like human nature, has got out of hand.

Since he wasn't taken seriously in the theatre anymore, Coward even tossed aside the pose and began to speak over the heads of the critics, directly to the public, in a serious of articles for the *Sunday Times*, "Consider the Public." Here he diagnosed and rebuked the bad new playwrights, who were:

> [B]igoted and stupid to believe that tramps and prostitutes . . . are automatically the salt of the earth [or] that reasonably educated people who behave with restraint in emotional crises are necessarily "clipped," "arid," "bloodless," and "unreal."

Coward also lambasted the bad new actors who use a pretentious and unreliable "Method" to justify an inflated sense of their own "intellects" as well as a contempt for audiences, actors of the older generation, and the theatre itself, expressed mainly through coprophiliac stage business, slovenly dress, and dirty fingernails; and above all, the bad new critics, whose "old-fashioned class consciousness and inverted snobbism" (the Leftist as the true reactionary!) leads them to assume that any successful West End play is "automatically inferior" to a shoestring production in the East End, and who mislead the actors and writers by over-praising anything that "happens to coincide with the racial, political and social prejudices of a handful of journalists."[16]

Against all this Coward praised simple, unpretentious craft — "You must have the emotion to know it, then you must learn how to use the emotion without suffering it" — which he had honed the hard way entertaining troops; "Noël distrusted every emotion on stage and dealt solely in the illusion."[17] And above all, respect for theatrical tradition, and the audience itself, without which there would be no theatre at all.

The critics sneered, but as usual the public applauded Coward's common sense, and the *Times'* letters column had to be cut short.

Sadly, not much would have to be rewritten for publication in, say, *The New Criterion*; today actors like De Niro and Theron undergo grotesque physical metamorphoses for roles (satirized in the recent *Tropic Thunder* by Robert Downey's character who preps for a role "by working in a Beijing textile factory for eight months"), writers seek only to shock and disgust their passive audiences, and critics impose a rigid, class-conscious code of political correctness and crap-Freudianism.

And there was bad politics as well; here comes that "reactionary" stuff, though confined to his *Diaries*:

> The British Empire was a great and wonderful social, economic, and even spiritual experience and all the parlour pinks and eager, ill-informed intellectuals cannot convince me to the contrary.[18]

Bad actors and bad critics were one thing he could "rise above," to use his characteristic expression, but not the parlor pinks. The tax-happy welfare state drove him out of his native land; at a professional ebb and subjected to scorn for leaving, Coward typically replied: "An Englishman is the highest exam-

---

[16] Payn, pp. 322–37.

[17] Payn, p. 42.

[18] *Diaries*, February 3, 1957.

ple of a human being who is a free man. As an Englishman I have a right to live where I like." That turned out to be Jamaica, where he was indeed able to "conserve," as the *Reader* puts it, a little bit of the old England. By 1963 he had concluded that "the England we knew and loved was betrayed at Munich, revived for one short year in 1940 and was supreme in adversity, and now no longer exists."[19]

The next year, with the Beatles, the '60s began in earnest. As Philip Larkin put it in *"Annus Mirabilis"*: "Sexual intercourse began/In nineteen sixty-three/(which was rather late for me)—/Between the end of the *Chatterley* ban/And the Beatles' first LP."

In "Swinging London," along with a new freedom of expression in the theatre, there was a perhaps surprising Coward renaissance. Coward now began to openly discuss homosexuality; first, in a one act play, *A Song at Twilight*, where letters revealing a homosexual affair threaten an elderly, knighted writer living in Switzerland (where Coward now lived, but still without the knighthood). Here the homosexual angle anchors a fairly conventional melodrama, based on Max Beerbohm but with a bit of Maugham tossed in. Certainly "today's youth" is not courted:

> **Sir Hugo**: I detest the young of today. They are grubby, undisciplined and ill-mannered. They also make too much noise.

But there were also hints of a libertarianism that Coward would soon present explicitly:

> **Carlotta**: To outside observers my way may seem stupid and garish and, later on perhaps, even grotesque. But the opinion of outside observers has never troubled me unduly. I am really only accountable to myself.

Or simply:

---

[19] *Diaries,* 1963.

Sir Hugo: My inner feelings are my own affair.

But he chose verse, always the home of "his secret heart," to once and for all address the question of the homosexual and society; or rather, typically, the homosexual and his everyday family.

While Britain's Wolfenden Report, a decade before Stonewall, may have brought the issue to society's attention and thus on Coward's agenda, for Coward the '60s promised not the chance to overthrow or otherwise remake society in some utopian formula for absolute "freedom" (the "freedom" of those grubby, undisciplined, ill-mannered, and noisy youths, actors, and critics) but rather a chance for good old English common sense (always to be distinguished from media-programmed proles) to be heard from on such issues as homosexuality.

In the title piece of *Not Yet the Dodo*, common sense is expressed by the family maid to her employer, a mother of conventional middle-class morals who has finally realized her son is a theatrical homosexual:

> "If you want my opinion," she said, "I think
> We're both of us wasting our breath,
> You can't judge people by rule of thumb
> And if we sit gabbing till Kingdom Come
> We'll neither one of us sleep a wink
> And worry ourselves to death.
>
> People are made the way they're made
> And it isn't anybody's fault.
> Nobody's tastes can quite agree
> Some like coffee and some like tea
> And Guinness rather than lemonade
> And pepper rather than salt."

Here Coward had the opportunity, towards the end of a long, professionally successful but, the Left ideologues would imagine, privately thwarted and persecuted life (nursing perhaps a grudge at the knighthood that would be denied him until the last moment in 1970), to pen an explosion of rage and expose society's rottenness, like the "kitchen sink" dramatists he had deplored (but, typically, personally befriended) in the '50s. Instead, Coward delivered a paean to the common sense, live-and-let-live conservatism of his working-class roots.[20] As he wrote in his diary at the time: "I have always distrusted too much education and intellectualism. Always dead wrong about things that really matter."[21]

This is one of the passages where Real locates his fundamental conservatism:

> [It] lies, I think, in the manner in which these acts are presented. In every instance, such nonconforming behavior is shown to be individualized; true, it is the individual's right, but it is also his or her responsibility. In other words, the problem — if there is one — is the individual's, not society's. Coward may seem to endorse a "new morality," but he also implies that personal morality is ultimately just that, personal. . . .
>
> In summary, therefore, it might be said that Coward's attitude was one of maximum toleration of independence and non-conformity for the responsible individual. However, on larger societal issues of order, patriotism in times of crisis, tradition, national loyalty, skepticism about man's perfectibility, and the inherent flaws of human nature, he was consistently conservative. Because of these views and his accompanying total trust in the intelligence of many average men, he qualifies, perhaps as much as any literary figure of our time, for that appellation Russell Kirk so frequently invokes, the Bohemian Tory.

---

[20] Faye describes his view, opposing not only "repression (or) banning" of homosexuality, but also homosexual "marriage," as "*common sense,* a notion with which the French Left — the most stupid Left in the world — has been in conflict with since 1789 thanks to its ideological hallucinations" (*Archeofuturism*, p. 107).

[21] *Diaries,* December 21, 1967.

One might find this redolent of the kind of vulgar libertarianism that is anathema to many conservatives, including Kirk. Rather, I suggest it has its analogues in an almost Nietzschean recognition of different moralities for different people (without his anti-social bias), or rather, for those who can make themselves different people, and thus be worthy of their own morality.

It may also suggest the Absolute Individual of Baron Evola (and who was more of a "Bohemian Tory" than the Baron, at least in his younger, Dadaist days, or when he toured Soviet Russia in white tie and tails to annoy the commissars?) or the four castes and differentiated ethics of Traditional India (and it is interesting that other than Guénon, the only Traditionalist who actually lived in a traditional society was Alain Daniélou, who roamed pre-war India with his lover in a silver motor home and reports that it was being a European that made him outcaste, and as a result his sexuality was of no interest to anyone).

The editors of the earlier anthology, *The Cream of Noël Coward*, were correct to include *Not Yet the Dodo* as "a fitting capstone" to the book and his life's work, "because it celebrates the people and the country which Coward knew so well and the values which he always stood for: loyalty, courage, and good manners."

Counter-Currents/*North American New Right*
December 7 & 8, 2010

ACCOMMODATE THIS!
BRUCE JENNER & THE HERMETIC REBIS

"Never let a good crisis go to waste"

> —Winston S. Churchill (supposedly)

"You don't ever want a crisis to go to waste; it's an opportunity to do important things that you would otherwise avoid."
> —Rahm Emanuel, 2008

"Never waste a good crisis . . . Don't waste it when it can have a very positive impact on climate change and energy security."
> —Hillary Clinton, 2009

After my recent discussion of "manspreading,"[1] in which I deplored the knee-jerk of the man-o-sphere ("Womens be talkin' too much!") and contrasted the true politeness, the *noblesse oblige* of the Aryan Male, I have been led to some more abstract and more generally applicable reflections.

Now, the whole point of politeness is to spare the feelings of the other person. I recall, for example, hearing this tale many years ago:

> According to the account, Queen Victoria was once at a diplomatic reception in London. The guest of honor was an African chieftain. All went well during the meal until, at the end, finger bowls were served. The guest of honor had never seen a British finger bowl, and no one had thought to brief him beforehand about its purpose.[2] So he

---

[1] "Mad Manspreading," reprinted in *The End of an Era: Mad Men and the Ordeal of Civility* (San Francisco: Counter-Currents, 2015).

[2] "As with most formal customs of etiquette, there are considered to be right and wrong ways to present and use a finger bowl, and these

took the bowl in his two hands, lifted it to his mouth, and drank its contents down!

For an instant there was breathless silence among the British privilege guests, and then they began to whisper to one another. All that stopped; however, when Queen Victoria silently took her finger bowl in her two hands, lifted it, and drank its contents! A moment later, 500 surprised British ladies and gentlemen simultaneously drank the contents of their own finger bowls.

It was the queen's uncommon courtesy that guarded her guest from certain embarrassment. This is a very rare but very effective human trait which only true leaders can demonstrate![3]

Although entitled "A True Story," this appears to be an urban myth; the role of the African chieftain has also been taken by South African Paul Kruger on his first visit to England in 1877, while more recently Nelson Mandela has been inserted, with Victoria, of course, updated to Elizabeth.[4] All of which only underscores its archetypal wisdom: this is how people with class act.[5]

Now, when it comes to those who do not seem to immediate-

---

can differ. The acceptability of floating lemon or of using the finger bowl to wet the mouth, for example, are disputed. Unfamiliarity with this custom has led to many common *faux pas*, including drinking the water, eating the flower, or failing to move the doily with the bowl when shifting it off of the dessert plate." Wikipedia, http://en.wikipedia.org/wiki/Finger_bowl.

[3] From WonderfulInfo.com, http://www.wonderfulinfo.com/inger-bowl-true-story/.

[4] "Legends of Mandela #2: Rugby legend revived," by Arthur Goldstruck, 22 October 2007, http://thoselegends.blogspot.com/2007/10/legends-of-mandela-2-rugby-legend.html.

[5] The scene is recreated in *Scarface* (Brian de Palma, 1983) when Tony and Omar visit the Columbian drug lord Sosa. Tony is momentarily nonplussed but decides to eat the lemon. Omar pays no attention and uses it properly; I'm not sure if there was a point to this, but we already know Omar is a jerk-ass, and we are not surprised when he is soon hanging by his neck from Sosa's helicopter.

ly or obviously fit into our social norms,[6] what has traditionally been expected in polite societies—as supposed to the stereotypical "You ain't from around here, ain't yah, boy?" situations[7]—is some level of, ah, "accommodation." The word is still used in such contexts—"special accommodations" for religious holidays, etc.—but it's become something of an anachronism, if not a sick joke.

As it said on a poster popular in the '60s,

I do my thing and you do your thing.
I am not in this world to live up to your expectations,
And you are not in this world to live up to mine.
You are you, and I am I,
and if by chance we find each other, it's beautiful.
If not, it can't be helped.[8]

Supposedly, this is the "Gestalt Prayer" authored by that fat, hairy, disgusting slob Fritz Perls, no doubt composed while— and useful for—seducing naïve *shiksas* in his hot tub. But the joke on the poster was the picture, and attribution, to Adolf Hitler.

This was more appropriate than the poster designers could know. For you see, the goal is no longer, and hasn't been for quite a while, to simply accommodate the Other—to not insist the Jew sing along with your Christmas carols—but rather to recut society's cloth to fit the Other's shape—only government approved nondenominational holiday jingles allowed.

As Greg Johnson has observed, when told that "Merry Christmas" is "insulting" to Jews,

---

[6] "Your uncle Billy Costigan—you named after him?—got busted selling machine guns to federal officers. Among many other departures from, ah, 'normative behavior.'" —Sgt. Dignam, *The Departed* (Martin Scorsese, 2006).

[7] Such as rural Wisconsin: Cousin Billy at the Rock Shop: "It's a geode. It's not from around here." Crow: "Let's beat it up!" —MST3k, Episode 810— *The Giant Spider Invasion* (Bill Rebane, 1975).

[8] http://en.wikipedia.org/wiki/Gestalt_prayer

I thought to myself, "I would not be offended if a Jew wished me a Happy Hanukkah. That would be small-minded. So why should a Jew be offended if I wished him a Merry Christmas? What makes Jews different? Why do people cater to such small-mindedness?" . . . I also thought to myself, "Wouldn't a pluralistic, liberal attitude imply many different holiday greetings, rather than one bland, characterless, homogeneous one?"[9]

Indeed, it would. The demand that all denominationally distinct greetings be banned, and replaced with a single, state-approved one, is exactly the sort of thing you'd associate with . . . Adolf Hitler.[10]

Not for the first time do we find the Jew, in power, acting rather like the mythical Hollywood Nazi. Projection, much?

Again, it's not deemed sufficient to allow women to marry each other in peace, and go to hell in their own way;[11] no, the only "fair" thing is to force Christians to perform the ceremonies and even bake them cakes against their will.

And of course, these examples can be multiplied; I'm sure every reader has his own list of outrages. The general point here is, in case after case, we have situations that could be handled, one would think sufficiently, by simple, local, personal accommodation, where instead, the demand is made *to entirely restructure the whole of society*, for the benefit of the aggrieved party.

What's interesting in all these cases is that the proposed remedy goes far beyond anything that might simply address the

---

[9] "Merry Christmas, Infidels," an annual Christmas tradition at Counter-Currents.com and reprinted in *Confessions of a Reluctant Hater* (San Francisco: Counter-Currents, 2010; revised and expanded, 2016).

[10] For the story of how dozens of time-honored, traditional regional greetings were suppressed by the Party and replaced by the compulsory stiff-armed "Heil Hitler" see *The Hitler Salute: On the Meaning of a Gesture* by Tilman Allert, trans. Jefferson Chase (New York: Picador, 2009).

[11] "I hold it to be the inalienable right of anybody to go to hell in his own way." — Robert Frost. Perhaps alluded to here: "Enough money for you to be able to go to Hell in your own way." — *The Rebel Set* (Gene Fowler, Jr., 1959)

supposed problem.

We have completely reversed the wisdom of the old Hindu tale, of the king who wanted to slaughter tens of thousands of cows, to produce enough leather to cover the roads, until a sage suggested that he just give his subjects shoes.

One can't help but think, will such a disproportion between the goal and the means, that the goal is really only an excuse. Thus, "never let a good crisis go to waste."

Jack Donovan once did a few quick calculations about those directly affected by "gay marriage" and concluded that "all of this is about what might be good for 400,000 people out of 300 million."[12] And yet this has been the #1 issue of the entire decade. Why?

How did the simple idea of freeing homosexuals from archaic restrictions and allowing them to fully participate in society again become the demand for the redefinition of marriage, unlimited adoption, and free sexual reassignment surgery? I defy anyone to find, in public or private documents, a single closeted homosexual demanding any of that before, say, 1990; and yet these are presented as "our basic rights."

How did the simple, eminently Western idea of hey, let's not burn Moslems at the stake but let them go about their business in peace, become "Let's ban all mention of pigs or alcohol lest we offend them"?[13]

When, one wonders, will "Go ahead, let them buy and sell their kosher foods among themselves" become "All supermarkets and restaurants—and homes?—must be kosher-approved

---

[12] "Gay Marriage: 'What-The-Fuck-Ever,'" by Jack Donovan (April 9, 2013), http://www.jack-donovan.com/axis/2013/04/gay-marriage-what-the-fuck-ever/.

[13] "Oxford University Press has warned its writers not to mention pigs, sausages, or pork-related words in children's books, in an apparent bid to avoid offending Jews and Muslims. The existence of the publisher's guidelines emerged after a radio discussion on free speech in the wake of the Paris attacks." *The Telegraph*, 9 June 2015, http://www.telegraph.co.uk/news/uknews/11345369/Oxford-University-Press-bans-use-of-pig-sausage-or-pork-related-words-to-avoid-offending-Muslims.html.

lest we offend one of God's Lambs"?

There is an agenda, but it might not be as simple as you imagine. Oh, if only it were . . .

Here's the *Vigilant Citizen*, Internet scourge of the Illuminati, reflecting on the newest outrage, the Jenner Kerfluffle.[14] He starts with the Aryan live and let live:

> Before I go further (and because some people like to put words in my mouth), I need to emphasize that I do not think that all transgenders are "evil" nor that they are part of a sinister Agenda. If one feels more comfortable and happier living as the opposite sex, well that's their business and not mine. As a staunch proponent of true freedom, I will never judge a person who took a personal decision to live a better life.

But, as he goes on:

> Bruce Jenner's sex change, however, was everything but personal. *It was an orchestrated media event, blown-up to proportions so large that it has been turned into a grand ritual, a staged ceremony meant to push an agenda.*

And what might that be? The Citizen is quick to take us away from the lower depths of the media—the videodrome—and rises to the heights of metaphysics:

> In occult secret societies, the highest stage of illumination is achieved through the internalization of duality and the equilibrium between opposing forces—good and evil, active and passive, male and female. This concept is symbolically represented by the horned, hermaphrodite god Baphomet. It is also represented in alchemical symbolism such as the Alchemical Androgyne:

---

[14] "The Agenda Behind Bruce Jenner's Transformation," by VC (June 5, 2015), http://vigilantcitizen.com/vigilantreport/the-agenda-behind-bruce-jenners-transformation/.

"The . . . hermaphroditic figure [symbolizes] the accomplishment of the *magnum opus*. The active and passive principles of Nature were often depicted by male and female figures, and when these two principles, were harmoniously conjoined in any one nature or body it was customary to symbolize this state of perfect equilibrium by the composite figure above shown." (quoting Manly P. Hall, *The Secret Teachings of All Ages*).

As "Cologero" elucidates at the Traditionalist site *Gornahoor*:

The fall of the True Man from the Primordial State is the result of a decentering, a change in consciousness to exteriority from interiority. Now the Primordial State is the *Androgyne* of the Alchemists, that is, the perfect balance of the male and female principles. From the center, he is the unmoved mover, and his actions are *wei wu wei*, or non-acting activity.

We, of course, have frequently made use of the Traditional doctrines of the True Man, the unmoved but all moving *Chakravartin*, the Tree at the Center the Garden. But what possible use are these doctrines to the man in the street? The answer is, none, or rather, *only the negative effect of turbulence and confusion* — the result of throwing pearls before swine, as the New Testament warns; as Cologero says:

We see that the shift from the ordinary state to the Primordial State represents, spiritually, a transition from a passive, *yin*, or feminine state of existence to a more active, *yang*, or masculine state. This is the opposite of the "macho" man, obsessed with frenetic activity for its own sake and focused solely on material life. *Yet, when esoteric teachings enter into the popular domain, they are completely misunderstood by those at the hylic and psychic level. When such types hear of the Androgyne, they can only envision a feminization of man, that is, a[n] exterior type of man taking on more effeminate characteristics. Thus the epicene man of today, common in the West, regards himself ipso facto as an advanced spiritual being.* Unfortunately, *this occludes the true spiritual nature of man* and discourages many more masculine men from developing themselves in that direction.[15]

And that is the use these doctrines have for the media-powered elite: to sow confusion among the masses, while also vulgarizing and debasing spiritual symbols.

On the latter point, we can see the effect on the lumpenright and the man-o-sphere—the negro brute will continue to be their only safe ideal. They will be completely dumbfounded and given to clueless mockery as Evola himself extolls the Androgyne (in *The Hermetic Tradition*[16]), where the goal is not to emasculate the male, still less to create some crude physical amalgam of the sexes (another example of materialistic science aping metaphysical principles) but for the male to submit to the female and then, *and in order to*, overcome the female and reaffirm the male in turn at a higher level: the so-called "alchemical resurrection" or "philosophical incest."[17]

In another place—the essay "Serpentine Wisdom" (i.e., Taoism)—after describing the Man of Tao who "'acts without acting" as Cologero says, Evola already dismisses these current year Men of Game with some preemptive mockery of his own:

How disheartening to those who uphold the myth of manhood based on muscles and metallic strength: this [the Androgyne] alone is the TRUE man, the ABSOLUTE man. *He absorbs within himself the ambiguous virtue of the female . . .'* The Way that is the Way is not the ordinary way' indeed . . .[18]

[15] Cologero, "The True Man," http://www.gornahoor.net/?p=1039.

[16] Julius Evola, *The Hermetic Tradition: Symbols and Teachings of the Royal Art* (Rochester, Vt.: Inner Traditions, 1995).

[17] As we have also frequently emphasized, the true metaphysical principle is the spiral, not the circle; the turn of the screw.

[18] Julius Evola and the UR Group, *Introduction to Magic: Rituals and Practical Techniques for the Magus* (Rochester, Vt.: Inner Traditions, 2001).

But all this is not a proper activity for the masses; as Evola says when discussing Nietzsche in the first part of *Ride the Tiger*,[19] one must be worthy of such freedom, else one destroys oneself in futility, as the masses do with their endless pursuit of pleasures and distractions. Nor is it even the media-elite's intention that the masses should try to become free individuals; far from it.[20]

As the *Citizen* says:

Of course, the concepts above are meant to be interpreted in an esoteric and spiritual context where the human soul transcends its physical shell. However, *today's elite is bent on twisting and corrupting occult concepts, using its inherent powers for sinister purposes.* Therefore *the concept of equilibrium has turned into a[n] unhealthy obsession on transgendered media pawns. . . .*[21]

---

[19] Julius Evola, *Ride the Tiger: A Survival Manual for the Aristocrats of the Soul* (Rochester, Vt.: Inner Traditions, 2003).

[20] It is interesting to compare what might be called the Family Values quotient represented by Jenner and, say, Baron Evola. Jenner, having married and fathered children, would seem to have fulfilled his duties to society, like any ancient Greek or Roman, and as with them any personal hobbies of his would not be any concern of the state. Evola, on the other hand, never married or, as far as we know, fathered any children. In fact, in his later works he heaps an elitist scorn on the whole idea (or "obsession," he would say, thinking of Mussolini's population policies) that a large and rising population is essential to, or a sign of, a rising and dynamic state; the examples of 19th century Britain and India should be enough to make his point. Jenner can also be seen to fit with the transition from the Householder stage to a — as we've said somewhat misunderstood and dangerously misapplied — version of the Forest-dweller stage of the Hindu tradition, where those who have married and raised children are allowed to abandon them and pursue ascetic disciplines (as opposed to the vulgar post-war American Dream — now inoperative anyway — of endless rounds of golf or whittling on the porch.

[21] For example, "Liberals Worship Caitlyn Jenner as Transgender 'Goddess'; Cult-like adulation is downright creepy," by Paul Joseph Watson (June 2, 2015), http://www.infowars.com/liberals-worship-

The Caitlyn Jenner story was orchestrated to bring specific concepts to the forefront, notably the complete reversal of gender roles. Although the elite's occult teaching are about complete equilibrium, *they want the masses to be completely out of balance. That's how you keep them confused and malleable.*[22]

Now, you don't have to go all the way with the Vigilant Citizen's idea of an "occult war" being fought against society through media indoctrination,[23] to see that something is going on here. Non-conspiratorially, it may simply be that the liberal mind has a vector to "social" causes and "social" solutions — hence, for example, the refusal to consider genetics to explain black pathology, preferring to fall back on the search for increasingly subtle and attenuated forms of racism such as "white privilege" or "structural racism."[24] A truly degenerating research project,[25] but when you only have a hammer, everything looks like a perfectly lacquered nail.

Counter-Currents/ *North American New Right*
June 11, 2015

---

caitlyn-jenner-as-transgender-goddess/.

[22] Vigilant Citizen, *loc. cit.*

[23] "The battle for the mind of North America will be fought in the video arena — the *videodrome.*" — Brian O'Blivion, *Videodrome* (David Cronenberg, 1983).

[24] "Why is the Stretch from Baltimore to Newark called "The Corridor of Pain," Mr. Charlie LeDuff? The Same Reason Detroit Collapsed: Blacks" by Paul Kersey, June 7, 2015, http://stuffblackpeopledontlike.blogspot.com/2015/06/why-is-stretch-from-baltimore-to-newark.html. A commenter adds: "Charlie LeDuff, you douche, examine the negro genome and find the epic fail . . . THERE'S your story! Lower IQ, lower impulse control, poor future time orientation, lower threshold for violent behavior = inability to assimilate into a First World society!! Enough fist bumping with the soul brothers — study some science . . . hipster doofus!"

[25] See my review of Nicholas Kollerstrom's *Breaking the Spell*, https://www.counter-currents.com/2015/03/dachau-blues/.

MILO & THE *MILES*[1]

"'Garçon' means boy." — Waitress in *Pulp Fiction*

There's a reason you're not supposed to use the Devil's name. No sooner does *Counter-Currents* publish a review[2] dealing with the Great Purge-Meister Buckley than the MSM, including outlets like *Salon* that are happy to publish outright defenses of pedophilia,[3] was shocked, just *shocked*, to discover some interviews in which Milo made some comments about pedophilia which, when stripped of their obvious intent to offend, reduce to these anodyne propositions:

❖ it seems pretty reasonable to set 16 as the age of consent, and
❖ his own experiences, at a slightly younger age, were not traumatic and actually rather interesting.

Now, in the first he is merely agreeing with the British Parliament (he is a Brit) and the majority of American states,[4] while the second is a subjective report, which if true is interesting and if false is delusional. Understandably, though, people don't relish stories of pedophilia with a happy ending.

What struck me about the dust-up was that, having recently begun to reacquaint myself with the New Testament, it seemed a perfect opportunity to explore what conservatives are always claiming they care about: what would Jesus do?

Because, unlike the necessarily *ad hoc* and arbitrary results of an attempt to obtain contemporary advice from an ancient book

---

[1] Latin noun, third declension, masculine: soldier.
[2] https://www.counter-currents.com/2017/02/where-conservatism-went-wrong/
[3] https://www.counter-currents.com/2015/11/the-coming-pedophile-rape-epidemic/
[4] Long before "gay marriage," the Commonwealth of Massachusetts decided to let girls marry *at 12*.

of fairy tales, here we have a pretty clear incident to go on.

I refer to the incident of the Centurion and his Servant. In Matthew, we read:

> When Jesus had entered Capernaum, a centurion came to him, asking for help. "Lord," he said, "my servant lies at home paralyzed, suffering terribly." Jesus said to him, "Shall I come and heal him?" The centurion replied, "Lord, I do not deserve to have you come under my roof. But just say the word, and my servant will be healed. For I myself am a man under authority, with soldiers under me. I tell this one, 'Go,' and he goes; and that one, 'Come,' and he comes. I say to my servant, 'Do this,' and he does it." When Jesus heard this, he was amazed and said to those following him, "Truly I tell you, I have not found anyone in Israel with such great faith. I say to you that many will come from the east and the west, and will take their places at the feast with Abraham, Isaac and Jacob in the kingdom of heaven. But the subjects of the kingdom will be thrown outside, into the darkness, where there will be weeping and gnashing of teeth." Then Jesus said to the centurion, "Go! Let it be done just as you believed it would." And his servant was healed at that moment. (Matthew 8:5-13, NIV)

As is so often the case, there is a parallel account in Luke:

> When Jesus had finished saying all this to the people who were listening, he entered Capernaum. There a centurion's servant, whom his master valued highly, was sick and about to die. The centurion heard of Jesus and sent some elders of the Jews to him, asking him to come and heal his servant. When they came to Jesus, they pleaded earnestly with him, "This man deserves to have you do this, because he loves our nation and has built our synagogue." So Jesus went with them. He was not far from the house when the centurion sent friends to say to him: "Lord, don't trouble yourself, for I do not deserve to have you come under my roof. That is why I did not even consider myself worthy to

come to you. But say the word, and my servant will be healed. For I myself am a man under authority, with soldiers under me. I tell this one, 'Go,' and he goes; and that one, 'Come,' and he comes. I say to my servant, 'Do this,' and he does it." When Jesus heard this, he was amazed at him, and turning to the crowd following him, he said, "I tell you, I have not found such great faith even in (((Our Greatest Ally)))." Then the men who had been sent returned to the house and found the servant well. (Luke 7:1-10, NIV)

I quote both because there is a very interesting sleight-of-hand going on in most modern translations, including the NIV used here.

Christians usually take offense at being referred to as endorsing a "slave religion," but the fact is that the early Christians, at least, were quite happy with the idea of slavery, at least metaphorically. Paul is proud to call himself "a slave of Christ" repeatedly, for example. The basic idea is that one has ceased to be a slave . . . to sin, and instead moved into the higher (though perhaps not comfier) realms of a slave to Christ or God.

On the other hand, modern PC Christians also find the word uncomfortable. And indeed, antique slavery was rather different from the sort of *Roots* image it calls to mind today. And so the tendency has been to use the rather anodyne word "servant."

In Luke, the word translated as "servant" is *entimos doulos,* which means "honored slave," a sort of "house Negro." Matthew uses *pais,* which Matthew Nederlanden notes "produces a nice play on words with the Greek word for paralysis." He then says that:

At the time, *pais,* a term of endearment, could mean one of five things:

❖ "son or boy"
❖ a "special servant" who lorded over other servants and cared for his master's children
❖ a particular type of servant—one who was "his mas-

ter's male lover"
* ❖ an endearing term for the junior partner in a homosexual relationship
* ❖ an attractive young male[5]

I think you see where this is going. Although there are tamer
connotations, James Neil has pointed out that it would seem odd
for a Roman centurion, the very model of a Tough Guy, to be so
concerned about a mere slave (remember all those bad connotations of slavery, right?) as to seek out a Jewish miracle worker to
cure him.[6]

So, here we have Jesus confronted with a pagan, a blood-
thirsty soldier, a Roman oppressor, and quite likely (as they so
often seem to go together) a practitioner of pederasty.[7]

What does Jesus do?

It would be useful to contrast this with the Woman Caught in
Adultery. We often hear it said, more or less disingenuously,
that one must "love the sinner but hate the sin." Thus, Jesus tells
the woman's would-be punishers that the one throwing the first
stone must be without sin. As they slink away, Jesus tells the
woman "Go, and sin no more." He's pretty clear: adultery *is* a
sin, and she *is* a sinner; going forward, she must sin no more.

With the centurion, however, Jesus' attitude might be called

---

[5] http://www.matthewnederlanden.com/bible-
commentary/jesus-heals-the-centurion-matthew-8.php

[6] James Neill, *The Origins and Role of Same-Sex Relations In Human
Societies* (Jefferson, N.C.: McFarland, 2011), p. 216. See my review on
Kindle.

[7] More likely, ephebophilia, which is well within the 16-year limit,
but since no one wants to bother with such distinctions, we'll let it
stand. That a Roman pederast at this time would be romantic enough
to be distraught at his boy's illness is consistent with a shift in Roman
culture under the influence of the Greeks. Conservatives and Traditionalists who purport to revere the Romans should take into consideration that traditional Roman culture really was essentially what
feminists today call a "rape culture," in which male citizens could
basically do anything they wanted with women, slaves, or children.
See Neil, *op. cit.*

sovereign indifference. There is not a word about the sin or sinner, if such they be. Instead, Jesus marvels at *the faith* held by the man. Throughout the New Testament, Jesus is stymied by Jews who are uncomprehending or hostile; even his own disciples betray him (Judas), deny him (Peter), and doubt him (Thomas). And yet here is a Roman, a *goy*, who gets it!

Jesus is not the Jewish Messiah, come to overthrow the Romans and establish the *Pax Judaica*.[8] As Max Stirner says, he is not interested in revolution, but insurrection; not external change, but change that at least starts from within.[9] He associates with gluttons, drinkers, tax collectors, and whores, much to the disgust of the (literal) Pharisees. The physician (like Luke himself) must go where the sick are to be found; what matters is that they *have the faith* with which anything is possible.

And so the centurion's words become the faithful's formula of contrition: the priest and the congregation together respond to the invitation to "Behold the Lamb of God" with these words: "Lord, I am not worthy that you should enter under my roof, but only say the word and my soul shall be healed."

My moral being that Milo is someone who *gets* it. What's

---

[8] Of course, Luke was himself likely a gentile, and was writing for a gentile audience soon after the Neronian persecutions, so he is likely to be emphasizing the non-treasonous aspects of the religion. See *The Human Bible New Testament*; translated and introduced by Robert M. Price (Cranford, N.J.: American Atheist Press, 2015); reviewed https://www.counter-currents.com/2015/05/lovecrafts-bible/.

[9] "He was not a revolutionary, like Caesar, but an insurgent: not a state-overturner, but one who straightened himself up . . . [Jesus] was not carrying on any liberal or political fight against the established authorities, but wanted to walk his own way, untroubled about, and undisturbed by, these authorities . . . But, even though not a ringleader of popular mutiny, not a demagogue or revolutionary, he (and every one of the ancient Christians) was so much the more an insurgent who lifted himself above everything that seemed so sublime to the government and its opponents, and absolved himself from everything that they remained bound to . . . precisely because he put from him the upsetting of the established, he was its deadly enemy and real annihilator . . ." — Max Stirner, *The Ego and Its Own* (London: Rebel Press, 1982), pp. 280–81.

"it"? They hate us, and want us to die, and we will, if we don't stop Them.

Rather than virtue signaling and morally panicking at the slightest lifting of an eyebrow by Those who are themselves hardly paragons on the subject (indeed, "first stone," MSM?) but are certainly mortal enemies of our side, we should in such circumstances rather be "as wise as serpents." Let us make common cause with those who *share the faith*. Sufficient unto the day is the evil thereof.

After all, if They do take over, the children will hardly be any safer, right?

Of course, as with all Biblical exegesis, your mileage may differ.[10] Since we started with the opening of *Pulp Fiction*, perhaps it would be best to let Jules have the last word, as he usually does; here he is, at the end, after his own conversion experience:

> Now . . . I been sayin' that shit for years. And if you ever heard it, that meant your ass. You'd be dead right now. I never gave much thought to what it meant. . . . But I saw some shit this mornin' made me think twice. See, now I'm thinking: maybe it means you're the evil man. And I'm the righteous man. And Mr. 9mm here . . . he's the shepherd protecting my righteous ass in the valley of darkness. Or it could mean you're the righteous man and I'm the shepherd and it's the world that's evil and selfish. And I'd like that. But that shit ain't the truth. The truth is you're the weak. And I'm the tyranny of evil men. But I'm tryin', Ringo. I'm tryin' real hard to be the shepherd.[11]

Counter-Currents/*North American New Right*
February 28, 2017

---

[10] Try Dr. Jorg Lanz von Liebenfels, *Theozoology, or the Science of the Sodomite Apelings and the Divine Electron* (1905) sometime to see how far out this stuff can go. Woo-hah!

[11] *Pulp Fiction* (Tarantino, 1994). For more on Jules as (relative) moral exemplar, see the review reprinted in *Trevor Lynch's White Nationalist Guide to the Movies*; Foreword by Kevin MacDonald; edited by Greg Johnson (San Francisco: Counter-Currents, 2012).

WILD BOYS VS. "HARD MEN"

Many of today's "alternative" Rightists aspire to a pre-modern, even Traditional worldview that they hope will return us to the vital sources of our civilization. But that is just a castle on a distant hill. In the meantime, we still live in the subdivisions of bourgeois conservatism, where all intellectual progress can be undone with a single wrong turn in a labyrinth of mental *cul-de-sacs*.

Issues touching on sexuality, family life, and economics particularly seem to set us off, for most American conservatives inherit their ideas of healthy Traditional society from the profoundly modern and anti-traditional heresy of Calvinism, which imprisoned *eros* within marriage and formerly free men, women, and even children in mines, factories, and workhouses.

When one looks through these lenses, the real sources of our civilization become invisible, for civilization begins not with the nuclear family, but the *Männerbund*; not with work, but with play; not with necessity but with luxury; not with modesty but with display. Thus I wish to deploy the phenomenon of dandyism to shock the bourgeois blinders off would-be Traditionalists.

I.
ARE WE MIDDLE CLASS CONSERVATIVES?

At *The Occidental Observer*, Elizabeth Whitcombe in "The Difficult Class"[1] lauds the supposed "strength" of the middle class, epitomized by its supposed "individualism," and laments how global elites have tried to undermine it. Of course, one might question how "individualist" the middle class is, or

---

[1] http://www.theoccidentalobserver.net/2009/08/the-difficult-class/

whether, if so, that is a strength. Kevin MacDonald, for one, argues that the alien elites (you know who They are) are precisely promoting individualism itself to undermine White societies.

Whitcombe, however, has an odd idea of "individualism" since she thinks that, "In his *Republic* Plato recognized the power of middle class principles. Family loyalty, community participation, self-reliance, and prizing education are all things that help the individual resist the will of the State. Plato knew that a class of virtuous citizens needed these qualities in order to prevent the state from slipping into tyranny."

I'm not sure any of this is particularly "individualist" or "middle class" as opposed to archaic Greek warrior virtue, promoted by pederasty and represented in public art by statutes of invincible male friends who resisted tyranny to the death, but whatever; at least she seems to admit that Plato must be pretty smart, since she wants to draft him for her cause.

Alas, our trust is misplaced; apparently, Plato is an untrustworthy ally, and reveals himself as . . . wait for it . . . "naïve": "Plato naïvely thought that he could get rid of internecine conflict by extending the family relationship across an entire class — in other words, communal property and no nuclear family."

Somebody is "naïve" here, but I don't think it is Plato. Rather, Plato is quite aware of what he is about. In this "class" of Guardians, he is attempting to recreate the features, and thus the benefits, of a *Männerbund*, the male warrior groups that split away from exactly the "nuclear family" Whitcombe naïvely eulogizes, in order to create the higher institutions of the state and culture.

Ironically, many of the institutions that one thinks of as "middle class," such as the Boy Scouts, the Little League, the Armed Forces, and the Church, etc., are in fact vestiges of such bands; that's why women are obsessed with "gaining entrance" or, like Ms. Whitcombe, naïvely ignoring them and promoting the female cults of Family Values. That's also why they are subject to Christian-inspired witch hunts for "homos." (Why there, rather than in banks or hardware stores?)

At one time, Rightists from Hans Blüher to Julius Evola knew of such things, but today it's all about Judaic Family Values.[2]

These are the Wild Boys that William S. Burroughs mythologized, which I have taken as my blog's emblem; indeed, Burroughs' mythology will crop up again in our examination of the next offending article.

II.
KURTAGIĆ'S "HARD MEN"

The very next day at TOO, Alex Kurtagić contributed "They Don't Make Them Like They Used To."[3] Here Alex treats us to a visit to a local exhibition, where photographs of some Olde Tyme factory workers (a pencil factory, if you will) produce an odd effect on our correspondent. Whitcombe's middle class likely leaves him cold, but these filthy old codgers set his mind athinking in odd, unwholesome ways. He calls the Wife over and she concurs; these chaps, with their "hostile frowns, ice-cold blue eyes, and troglodytic beards and angrily scowling moustaches" are Real Men, and are sadly lacking today. In another article, Kurtagić pays tribute to the industrious Quakers, who played a prominent role in creating the kinds of factories that produced pencils, matches, and "Hard Men."[4]

Right off, I have some questions here. For all their beards and stares, these are after all pencil factory workers, not coal miners. Secondly, would these Hard Men be spending their precious "free time" gazing nostalgically at old photographs, and even if so, would the Wife be along? It seems to me that when Men were Men, Women were Wives, and stayed home

---

[2] For the real history, see the works of Alisdair Clarke and Wulf Grimmson cited above in Chapters One and Two, as well as Wulf Grimmson, *Male Mysteries and the Secret of the Männerbund*, available at http://www.lulu.com/spotlight/lokisway.

[3] http://www.theoccidentalobserver.net/2009/08/they-don%e2%80%99t-make-them-like-they-used-to/

[4] http://www.theoccidentalobserver.net/2009/07/black-metal-lord-attends-quaker-meeting-and-discovers-the-victorian-capitalists/

mending and birthing and boiling tripe.

Unhindered by such negativity, Kurtagić continues to drift in his vaguely erotic reverie about the days when factory labor made men Hard, and even waxes nostalgic for the "muscular Christianity" and the Cult of Work that served as ideological cover for the mechanized enslavement of the English yeomanry.

Orwell already made similar observations on the degeneracy of British manhood in *The Road to Wigan Pier*, but formed a rather different, and more plausible, diagnosis. Observing the sorry specimens arrayed under a dreary sky for the funeral of King George (the only color supplied by the pink bald heads revealed when hats were doffed), he lays it first to the sacrifice of the physical best of a generation in the Great War, and thus the loss of their progeny; and moreover, the appalling conditions (filth, hard work, poor nutrition, overcrowding) of the Industrial Revolution that Kurtagić lauds!

The futile evil of WWI, and the evils of the factory system: more evidence that Orwell and Waugh were, as a recent dual biography argues, *The Same Man*? Certainly he's more of a "conservative" here than Kurtagić.

III.
TRADITIONALISM VERSUS CAPITALISM

Is this what the Right has become? Eulogizing Victorian factory slavery and the twisted troglodytes it produced? At one time, English Traditionalists saw these men as "a ruined race" (Tolkien), and thundered against the system that produced it. That Christianity produced and defended it is hardly a positive feature of the religion, as Kurtagić thinks, and most English Traditionalists who stayed Christian (Chesterton, Belloc, Gill, Eliot, etc.) fobbed it off on the Protestant deviation.

The medieval Church, steeped in Aristotle, was part of a continuous Western tradition, going back to the Greeks, which condemned work and promoted leisure as "The Basis of Culture," in the words of Thomist philosopher Josef Pieper, whose *Leisure: The Basis of Culture,* was a surprise bestseller in the

1950s when T. S. Eliot prompted his publisher Faber & Faber to put it out. Imagine, a Catholic bestseller!

Non-English, non-Christian Traditionalists such as René Guénon and Julius Evola were even more scathing. And why not? Modern "work" is the satanic parody of traditional craft, which, before it was destroyed by Protestant "work," was an integral part of traditional society, each vocation appropriate to elicit the perfection of the laborer's own nature (hence, caste) as well as to serve as a "support" for metaphysical and initiatory knowledge. The factory system, by contrast, treated "all men as 'equal'" and interchangeable units to be worked at the stupidest tasks until the last ounce of strength was gone, and then tossed on the scrap heap.

Evola devoted two chapters of his post-war manifesto, *Men Among the Ruins*, to "the demonic nature of the economy" and its tin idol, work. As Troy Southgate summarizes it in his book *Tradition and Revolution*:

> The emergence of capitalism has often been equated with the Protestant work ethic, and is here dismissed by Evola for the simple reason that labor has been transformed from a means of subsistence to an end in itself. It is not only the Right who are obsessed with work, of course, it is the Left too. One thinks of endless marches organized by the likes of Militant Labour and the Socialist Workers Party, during which the only objective is to enslave the proletariat to the employment system: "The most peculiar thing is that this superstitious and insolent cult of work is proclaimed in an era in which the irreversible and relentless mechanization eliminates from the main varieties of work whatever in them still had a character of quality, art, and the spontaneous unfoldment of a vocation, turning it into something inanimate and devoid of even an immanent meaning." Evola sees this process as the very proletarianization of life itself.[5]

---

[5] Troy Southgate, *Tradition and Revolution* (Aarhus, Denmark: Integral Tradition Publishing, 2007), p. 209.

But what is all this to Kurtagić? Who cares for waxing airy-fairy about medieval crafts and vocations? Protestantism and Capitalism (the original "PC"?) produced these deracinated pencil-making Hard Men. Chesterton, Eliot, Guénon, Evola; not a beard among them! Nothing to tickle his fancy here!

IV.
THE WILDE WILDE WEST

Many Rightists are surprised to learn that Evola admired the works of Oscar Wilde, at least in his youth, but it's not hard to see why. Evola despised Whitcombe's bourgeoisie, and Wilde was their great tormentor. And Wilde's social thought, as epitomized in "The Soul of Man Under Socialism," was part of the same "work should ennoble or not be done at all" tradition that would later be mined by such Traditionalists as Ananda Coomaraswamy and Guénon as well as Evola himself.

As someone once said about Ayn Rand's idealized portraits of industrialists, "she writes about industrialists as if she had never met one," so with Kurtagić and his Hard Men, whom he only knows from photographs; one can only imagine what he would think of Wilde's idea that work must be abolished because it is ugly and *makes men ugly*.

Interestingly, Wilde, unlike Kurtagić, actually met with miners, along with cowboys and other Hard Men of the West during his famous American tour. A fascinating article by Jan Wellington[6] gives an account of the remarkable encounters, where "Wilde both advertised and embodied the aesthetic movement with its *scorn for middle-class Victorian life* and *the uglier effects of the Industrial Revolution*," a perfect summary of what Evola hated, while also summarizing what Whitcombe and Kurtagić want to preserve in the name of the Right.

Since Kurtagić extends his admiration to "the frontiersmen of American Old West," let's see what happened when The

---

[6] Jan Wellington, "Oscar Wilde's West," *Literary Traveler* Aug. 2007; available online at http://www.literarytraveler.com/authors/wilde_west.aspx

Aesthete met The Hard Men.

> From the time Wilde disembarked in New York, Americans were surprised to observe that, despite his elegant hands and languid gestures, the Aesthete was a strapping young man who, offstage, ate and drank with gusto and spoke with genial frankness. They learned that even his oft-ridiculed stage dress of black velvet jacket, lace cravat, silk knee breeches, and patent leather pumps could be understood in terms of pragmatics. As Wilde explained, "When a man is going to walk or row, or perform feats which require a display of strength and muscle, the trousers are done away with and knee breeches are worn."

The Hard Men or Wild Boys of the West were not bowed down under the twin curses of work and muscular Christianity that Kurtagić wants to press down on our brows. Indeed:

> [T]hat quintessential westerner, the cowboy, enjoyed freedoms unique in Victorian America: intimacy with women outside of marriage, intimate (though not necessarily sexual) relationships with men, and even the playful donning of women's garb. To this alternative masculine subculture, their eccentric trans-Atlantic visitor would have seemed uncannily familiar, and thus it is no surprise that at least some Westerners found space in their tradition of individualism for one whose masculinity was complicated by a "feminine" aesthetic and appearance.

This, of course, is the West that served William Burroughs as the basis for his *Dead Roads* trilogy. These Wild Westerners sound like they could just as well be called the Mötley Crüe or the Guns N' Roses Gang.

Indeed, one aspect of that free Hard Man culture that Kurtagić, and his Victorians, might have found hard to swallow: the men took Leif Garrett (a relation to Pat Garrett?) as their model, not Thomas Arnold:

> In truth, Wilde's long tresses and outsized hats were not
> all that eccentric, for Americans had come to associate
> long hair on men with boldness and adventure. In the
> West, long hair distinguished masculine men like Wild
> Bill Hickok, George Armstrong Custer, and Buffalo Bill
> Cody. . . . The *Denver Republican* declared approvingly
> "that if placed in a mining camp dance hall, [the Aes-
> thete] would pass for a real bold, bad man."

Wellington notes that the Hard Men placed value on three
things, and they were not high in the value system Kurtagić
promotes: fighting, drinking, and cards. This allows us to get
an idea of how Wilde would score on the Hard Man meter (I
suggest we designate the units as Kurtagićs, or Ks).

Fighting? Wilde? Sure, he was huge man in real life, although later some described him as resembling a "fat, white
slug." The lecture tour did not give any opportunities for fisti-
cuffs, although he did make "a promising impression": a reporter noted that he "stumbled onto the stage with a stride
more becoming a giant backwoodsman than an aesthete."

Drinking? "In San Francisco, he foiled an attempt by the Bohemian Club to ply him with liquor and prove him a 'Nancy
boy'; after out-drinking (and out-talking) them all, he was giv-
en a proud place in a group photograph of the club."

Cards? "In the same city, he thwarted another attempt on
his manhood by professing his ignorance of poker, bluffing
bafflement, and then beating all challengers at the game."

In short, "when I lit a long cigar," he reports, "they cheered
till the silver fell in dust from the roof . . . and when I quaffed a
cocktail without flinching, they unanimously pronounced me
in their grand simple way a bully boy with no glass eye —
artless and spontaneous praise which touched me more than
the pompous panegyrics of literary critics ever did or could."

As for the miners' own opinions, the Leadville miners
"cheered as Wilde drove a silver spike into the lode that would
bear his name. Years after his visit, they recalled their guest

with affection, one reportedly declaring, '[t]hat Oscar Wilde is some art guy, but he can drink any of us under the table and afterwards carry us home two at a time.'"

Driving a spike? That's some real work there, Alex; I doubt your beloved pencil factory workers would find that an easy task. Twenty years making the same tiny motions with your hands is likely to leave you with a mean, suspicious visage, but isn't really good for developing the biceps. No wonder they wore long pants; breeches would have revealed their pitiful shins!

What was the basis of this evident kinship of Oscar Wilde, the dandy and aesthete, with these Wild Boys of the Wild West? Simple: no matter how hard they may have worked, they did not allow their souls to be subjected to bourgeois economic necessity. Instead, their lives were dedicated to ideals and actions that transcended economic necessity: aesthetic appreciation and display, games and contests, chivalrous behavior, the unfettered imagination — in short, the wellsprings of real culture. The West is where the freest spirits in America escaped from the creeping blight of factories and tenements — until they hit the West coast, and modernity finally caught up with and consumed them in the end.

V.
BUNNY ROGER

Speaking of hard men and revealing outfits, consider one final example of the Homo as Hard Man: Bunny Roger. Reading Nicky Haslam's memoir, *Redeeming Features*,[7] I was delighted to find out about this actual gun-toting Wild Boy, Bunny Roger, described by Clive Fisher as "Erstwhile couturier, wit, dandy, landowner, and social ornament, Bunny Roger was what obituary in its obliquer days styled a lifelong bachelor and what gossip columnists knew as a flamboyant homosexual."[8]

---

[7] Nicky Haslam, *Redeeming Features: A Memoir* (New York: Knopf, 2009).

[8] Clive Fisher, "Bunny Roger," *The Independent*, 1997; available at

But what interests us right now is Bunny's military career, and the Traditionalist character behind it. As Haslam says, "His legendary parties, his houses, his dandified approach and outré taste were but a soufflé. They masked an encyclopedic mind, a sense of history, nerves of steel, passionate loyalty, deep patriotism, and the most patrician of values."

Not only was Bunny a standing rebuke to post-Stonewall, Leftist, "gay," "queer," "adversary," "transgressive" nonsense, his service in WWII should put paid to any nonsense about "gays in the military"; not because of some Leftist whining about "we wanna be equal" (and so hypocritical, given the Left's pacifism and anti-Americanism), but precisely because, as the pagan world has known since Plato, homosexuals (or rather, as Ean Frick suggests, masculinists) are better soldiers, naturally:

> Bunny himself was made of burnished metal. Physically very fit—I saw him run up mountains in Scotland, at the summit adjusting his makeup from a compact kept in his sporran—he was also fearless. As a captain in the Italian campaign, even if his tent was lined in mauve with gilt chairs, and his army overcoats altered to look like Garbo's redingotes, he was revered by his men for the number of Germans he shot—"some right up the arse"—and after the war even refused ever to set foot in Germany.

Bunny, apparently, could give the Bear Jew a run for his money. Here's more of Bunny's War:

> After Anzio, while surveying a bombed-out village, he ran into a friend who greeted him: "Bun! What're you doing here?" Bunny looked at the destruction around them, "Shopping," he replied. Although appalled and incensed by what he had witnessed during the war, he had the good taste to make light of it. "Now that I've shot so many Nazis," he observed, "Daddy will have to

buy me a sable coat."[9]

The greatest generation indeed. Of course, now the American army is fully Judaized, doing "God's work" in the Near East with no homos. How's that working out for you, boys?

Kurtagić's beloved beaten-down proles, or Bunny Rogers, leading a battalion of Wandervogel: Which is the face of our White Future?

Counter-Currents/*North American New Right*
September 20, 2012

---

[9] Haslam, *Redeeming Features*, p. 79.

FASHION TIPS FOR THE FAR-FROM-FABULOUS RIGHT

Patsy: [nervous on TV] You can never have enough hats, gloves, and shoes.
Edina: Darling, even Amanda de Cadenet would remember the word "accessories."[1]

I.
THE NOT-SO FABULOUS RIGHT

The Right can make even Patsy Stone seem like Karl Lagerfeld.[2]

Alex Kurtagić, despite his miserablist glorification of pencilworkers, at least sees the problem. In several essays at various "New Right" websites, he's observed, all too truly, that the Right is losing, has lost, the "cultural war" not because the Left has better arguments, but because no one wants to be seen with us.[3]

What has happened over the last 50 years or so has been the systematic removable of status—basically, chicks and money—from White cultural expressions, ranging from rebellious rockers in spandex pants to authors speaking correct English, which are one and all systematically denigrated as "white" and—therefore—"gay."

As Antonio Gramsci told us long ago, in the contemporary words of Pierre Krebs, "To be precise, it is impossible to overthrow a political apparatus without previously having gained

---

[1] *Absolutely Fabulous*, Season One, "Magazine."

[2] Lagerfeld is something of a Wild Boy himself, as I observed after watching his bio-flick, *Lagerfeld Confidential* (2007), at
http://jamesjomeara.blogspot.com/2010/05/holiday-homocon-heroes-karl-lagerfeld.html

[3] See "It's Not the Arguments," at *The Occidental Observer*,
http://www.theoccidentalobserver.net/2010/02/it%e2%80%99s-not-the-arguments/

control of cultural power."[4]

Or, as the protagonist of *Bright Lights, Big City* says, as he wistfully gazes at a Talmud-reading Hasid on a New York subway:

> This man has a God and a History, a Community. He has a perfect economy of belief in which pain and loss are explained in terms of a transcendental balance sheet, in which everything works out in the end and death is not really death. Wearing black wool all summer must seem like a small price to pay. He believes he is one of God's chosen, whereas you feel like an integer in a random series of numbers. Still, what a fucking haircut![5]

"Why?," whine the Rightists, "why? We are so brilliant, so cutting edge. Why are we so ugly?"

The answer is simple: as Kanye says, "No Homo."

First, the homos themselves get excluded, taking with them style, ideas, etc. They, by a natural process of cognitive drift, anyone and anything that seems homo-like comes under suspicion, and is then thrown out or self-censored.

First, manicures are scorned as "metrosexual"; then washing altogether, until the ideal "rightist" resembles Khrushchev's father, who boasted of having taken two baths in his life, once when he was baptized, the other on the day of his wedding.

Gradually, a sort of Gresham's Law of Fabulosity comes into play, and thus the "movement" moves from epicene, hand-waving fancy-talkers like William F. Buckley to Real American Guys like paunchy, cigar-puffing Rush Limbaugh: "The 'face' of White Rage has become the big, flabbily White behind of the thousands of porcine nitwits marching to Sean Hannity's drums."[6]

---

[4] Pierre Krebs, "The European Rebirth," trans. anonymous, http://www.counter-currents.com/2011/12/the-european-rebirth/

[5] Jay McInerney, *Bright Lights, Big City* (New York: Vintage Books, 1984), pp. 56–7.

[6] See, for instance, "March of the Fat, Old, Angry White People,"

See, the problem with the "man of the Right" is that he thinks he's Euro-American, and maybe even anti-Joo, but he's also a Christer, which of course means he's really just a self-hating semi-Semite. And along with the Christing, of course, comes a big heaping helping of homo-hate.

Failing to see the root connection of masculinism or homoeroticism (not necessarily "homosexuality" as defined by 19th-century Judaic "scientists") with Aryan culture, they merely try to turn the clock back a couple of minutes; nor can they even accomplish that, since they fail to meet the opponent at his strongest point.

He's has been thoroughly fooled by the Judaic Two-Step, the one-two punch of always being on top by covering both sides of every bet. He's bought into both the Right-Wing satanic sex maniac stereotype, along with the Left-Wing fabulous sex maniac stereotype.

Thus, he's completely oblivious to the fact that White Civilization was created and sustained by androphiles, not Judaic "family values."[7] That's why, to paraphrase that icon of the Old Right, Albert Jay Nock, White Americans think the summit of Western Civilization is Kansas City, not Athens or Florence. No Homo!

In fact, where would the American post-war Right of Mr. Buckley have been without Whittaker Chambers, Roy Cohn, J. Edgar Hoover, or Cardinal Spellman?[8]

Mr. Kurtagić, in short, has merely inverted the basic thesis originally formulated some years ago by the late Alisdair Clarke. Rather than asking "where will the White Right find the style it needs to compete," he had better ask, "what were

---

http://unrepentantoldhippie.wordpress.com/2009/09/13/march-of-the-fat-old-angry-white-people/ at the appropriately named Unrepentant Hippie blog. Indeed, the Liberal can never refer to Whites without heaping scorn on their obesity, even though Negro obesity is double the White rate.

[7] See http://jamesjomeara.blogspot.com/2009/08/decline-of-occidental-review-or-against.html

[8] Who, according to Nicky Haslam, had an amazing closet stashed out at a friend's place in the Hamptons.

we thinking when we kicked out the homos?"

Homosexuals are by nature—elitism, style, exclusivity, etc.—of the Right. Their identification (in several senses) with the Left is a function of Christian-inspired stupidity on the Right, and clever propagandizing on the Left.

It should come as no surprise that the Right has lost the Semiotic War. As long as the White Right bows to the alien contagion of Christianity, the Left (itself a product of Christianity) will continue to win.

I hope it doesn't upset the Right's crypto-Judaic sensibilities too much, but the homoerotic Wandervogel were the last successful, decades-long White Consciousness movement, and it sure looked more like a Gay Pride parade crossed with a hippie sit-in or Occupy Somewhere, than either a Skinhead convention, a Teabagger rally, or a buncha "real men" sitting around the sports bar moaning about "them welfare queens bleeding us dry."

II.
THINK RIGHT, DRESS WHITE

Men always seem to need advice on how to dress, but it's usually funny, though sometimes creepy, when "conservatives" start bloviating about how to dress like "real men."

Feet, for some reason, always seem to come up (as it were). Yeah, I get it, the dirty hippies got all the hot chicks in the '60s, right, Mr. Boomer Conservative? Jealous, much? I remember years ago reading, in something like *American Spectator* or some "conservative" columnist, someone, a P. J. O'Rourke wannabe or himself, going on and on about a man wearing sandals at some town meeting. He kept referring to such people as "foot fetishists," but it occurred to me then, and still does, that the fetishist is the one so upset that he writes a column about it filled with references to feet, not the man wearing the sandals without a second thought; just as men are the fetishists, not the women wearing leather or stilettos.

And so, at the appropriately named TakiMag:

9. COVER YOUR MAN TOES The first thing I always say about mandals is, "What if someone slaps your girl and you have to chase them?" Nobody's saying you have to be Randy "Macho Man" Savage and pile-drive everyone who doesn't open the door for your lady, but flip-flops render you incapable of physical combat. Shit, I don't even think mandals should be allowed on the beach. Wear your sneakers to the beach. When you get to your towel, you can leave them there before swimming or, if the sand is hot, wear them to the tide's edge and leave them there. Men are wearing flip-flops to work, parent-teacher interviews, apartment closings, and the dentist. Wearing mandals reveals a level of shameless self-love that reminds me of a baby playing with his penis while he gets his diaper changed. I barely want to look at a woman's hideous black toenail polish on the filthy city streets. Seeing your mangled foot-claws flip and flop through dog crap is like forcing us to watch you masturbate.

There's actually nothing particularly wrong with the peroration:

Here is the fundamental point behind all these rules: A grown man is meant to be prepared for conflict and provide for his wife and family. Indulging oneself like a gay teen on vacation is not only abandoning your post, it's leaving women to pick up the slack. And nobody wants a world like that—especially women.[9]

Except, of course, it leads to easy rebuttal: You want a "grown man . . . prepared for conflict and provide for his wife and family"? OK, buddy, here you go; one be-sandaled, world-dominating Roman centurion coming up.

---

[9] Gavin McInnes, "The 12-Step Program to Restore American Machismo," http://takimag.com/article/the_12_step_plan_to_restore_american_machismo/print#axzz1xNA990Rv

We have frequently been puzzled at the complete lack of historical awareness among modern "conservatives," who keep mistaking their current fashion phobias for timeless truths about manhood.

Consider the portrait by Anthony van Dyck (no jokes, please) of Lord John and Lord Bernard Stuart ca. 1638. These two long-haired, be-rouged poofters died fighting to restore Charles I to the throne. A lot harder work, and more usefully "conservative," than blogging about the "feminizing" attire of Winter (i.e., Nordic) Olympic athletes, eh, Steve Sailer?

Faced with such indisputable historical evidence, the "conservative" will usually respond: "So what? Times change, fashions change. We must be modern, etc."

So, the acceptance of anything that modernity throws up, the acceptance of the dictates of fashion, the imperative of modernity, makes you a "conservative," or perhaps even "manly," how, exactly?

The more sophisticated, or at least better read, "conservative" will cite Chesterton on the Medievalism (or Mediaevalism, as we were taught at the Pontifical Institute) of "William Morris and His School":

When he was denouncing the dresses of modern ladies, "upholstered like arm-chairs instead of being draped like women," as he forcibly expressed it, he would hold up for practical imitation the costumes and handicrafts of the Middle Ages. Further than this retrogressive and imitative movement he never seemed to go. Now, the men of the time of Chaucer had many evil qualities, but there was at least one exhibition of moral weakness they did not give. They would have laughed at the idea of dressing themselves in the manner of the bowmen at the battle of Senlac, or painting themselves an aesthetic blue, after the custom of the ancient Britons. They would not have called that a movement at all. Whatever was beautiful in their dress or manners sprang honestly and naturally out of the life they led and preferred to lead. And it may surely be maintained that any real advance in the beauty of modern dress must spring honestly and naturally out of the life we lead and prefer to lead.[10]

Indeed. But if one were to dress "honestly and naturally out of the life we lead and prefer to lead," then what would be more honest and natural than the bare-chested, shrunk skintight, wild-haired working class teens of the MC5's White Panther Party? Or their spandex-clad musical idols?

No, TakiMag prefers our White Youth to emulate the hang-dog faces of the latest round up of redneck "militias" infiltrated or instigated by the FBI.

That's the "conservative" movement, for yah. No metrosexuals, no homo, just a bunch of pasty, overweight patsies. You know, "Real Americans."

III.
STEVE SAILER'S FEAR OF SPANDEX

It might be helpful to remind, or inform, those living in the almost totally judeo-negrified world of America Today (Post Obama) what was once (in Pre-Obama America) considered perfectly normal, indeed, expected, attire for proud young Aryan males.

Consider three young performers, at the peak of their popularity, in three related genres of what was known as "rock" music, then the most popular form of, well, popular music. (Of course, it still is, but this fact is hidden by the deliberate promotion of judeo-negroid [c]Rap music). There's Jim Dandy, Black Oak Arkansas, "Southern Rock"; Rod Stewart, "FM Rock"; Leif Garrett, "Teen Idol" (remember the hair on that guy on *American Idol* that time?); and of course, more generally, the Rock God himself, Robert Plant.

The preachers were righter than they knew; this wasn't merely "jungle music" but a pagan rite (a modern mystery religion, as we have explained on several occasions), and this is

---

[10] G. K. Chesterton, *Twelve Types* (London: Humphreys, 1906), pp. 23–24.

how proud Aryan youth celebrate their shameless bodies with long, flowing blond hair, bare chests, and tight, often leather or spandex, pants.

Today, such men would be considered "fags," and Jim Dandy would be a "redneck" as well; his presence here suggests that "NASCAR America" is not that alien from that other form of "implicit whiteness," Heavy Metal.

Of course, even "da fags" are Judaic these days, so the first squeal of the gay gang on *Queer Eye* is always "His hair is so long! Cut it!" What's with the Judaic obsession with cutting off male parts?

Anyway, one similarity with today is that stage attire is only an exaggeration of the fans' street attire. Growing up in Detroit, spandex pants would have been a bit outré, unless you were Iggy; however, the standard uniform was long hair, bare chest, impossibly tight jeans shrunk by wearing them in a bathtub, no underwear, and what we still called "gym shoes."

The MC5's "we are the people" ideology meant that they looked like their fans, which looked like one of Steve Sailer's "feminized" Olympians, such as Shaun (note the surname) White.[11]

The point of all this is not (entirely) to take a nostalgic trip down Plum Street to the Grande Ballroom, but rather this: the idealization of the male form is a function of the broader instinct for excellence in general that, nurtured by the *Männerbünde* that were the primitive forms of the modern "rock band" and its fans, produced the heights of Western, White, culture.

When not under the thumb of the judeo-protestant—for even the Roman Church, as Roman, is scandalous for its beautiful boys and attire—the Aryan seeks excellence in all areas of culture—and that includes manly adornment—and does not sink to the baggy-panted depths of the primitive Negro.

As the latter has increasingly been promoted as our new "ideal," so all forms of excellence have been stigmatized as first "acting White," and ultimately "being a fag." No homo!

[11] See http://isteve.blogspot.com/2010/02/outfits.html

The results — America negrified — are all around us, and the "white nationalists" or "cultural conservatives" who decry the results are all too usually in the forefront of enforcing the cultural prejudices — viz., "masculine" means stupid, ugly, and dirty; hence, Shaun White is a fag, while Fitty is "manly" — that make them possible

IV.
THE DANCE CLUB AS WHITE AUTONOMOUS ZONE

Rather than relying on historically uninformed, covertly pro-Negroid guesses as the only alternative to the poisonous suggestions of the MSM, the Right would be well advised to acknowledge the gratuitous and symbolic — not utilitarian — role of dress, and use it to further its avowed aims.

They might, in fact, do well to consult the legendary weekly dress codes of the equally legendary New York nightclub, Jackie 60.[12]

During the last great period of NYC nightlife (i.e., mine) the immortal Jackie 60 not only had a theme that changed weekly[13] but also a corresponding "dress code" that supplemented its standing code, prominently displayed at the door by a Victorian-typeface sign, listing, among other peeves, "No Baseball Caps: Jackie is not a team sport."

Not only did these themes display a casual but intense grasp of modern intellectual movements as well as the news of the day,[14] far beyond what one might expect at, say, a Libertarian Party fundraiser, thus exemplifying the White Spirit at its most intense; by demanding creativity and demonizing the easy and "popular" — "Jackie is not a team sport"; "No banjy clichés and as always, no ski wear!" — they created a White-only Temporary Autonomous Zone, as neatly and legally as the price of a place in the Hamptons.

Forget Occupy Wall Street clichés. Think how much more

---

[12] See: http://www.mothernyc.com/jackie/60.html
[13] http://www.mothernyc.com/jackie/60archive/dresscodes.html
[14] Situationism! JonBenet Ramsey! Tallulah Bankhead!

effective Tea Party rallies would be, if they adopted the "Bleak House Night" code:

> Dickensian beggar-wear, gruel bowls and utensils, Cruikshank glamour, bonnets, shawls, black cockney caps, Vivienne Westwood urchin looks, ragged short pants and ill-fitting short jackets, grime smudges, top hats, period tight-lacing (1840s), Fagin cloaks, stolen wallets, cravats.

Or a meeting of the Latin Mass Society attired in the spirit of the "Night of a 1000 Stevies":

> Fringed shawls, velvet hooded cloaks, baby's breath with ribbons, ruched boot covers, Victorian coke spoons, tambourines, best hair in rock and roll, seventies gypsy, pre-Raphaelite, handkerchief hems, Lindsey Buckingham drag, Edwardian bustiers, leather and lace.

Although classically, suits and ties were also forbidden (except on women) if Jackie were still around "Mad Man Realness" would no doubt be given its own night.

Which is not even to say there were no Negroes at all; a handful were to be found, even on the event staff, but these were of the advanced, Michael Jackson's Queer Eye[15] sort, rather than the Michael Jordan, or Michael Thomas, sort.[16]

---

[15] See the YouTube video at http://youtu.be/KKJVSMT1OsI.

[16] At some point someone will bring up the Negro's "bling" and "pimp daddy" style. But it should be noted that such styles are never presented as something to be emulated, to say nothing of embraced by whiggers. Rather, they exist only as styles to be mocked or used ironically, from Dave Chappell's "Rick James" to Kramer's pimp cane, to the "pimp and ho" parties thrown by fraternity "racists."

Speaking of Rick James, it should also be noted that mulatto musicians who find themselves more comfortable in rock usually take on the tight, colorful clothing and long, flowing hair aesthetics—Jimi Hendrix, Prince, even Michael Jackson, who though not technically mulatto desperately wanted to be White.

See, it's not at all about "skin color," as the straw-man-making Liberal would have it. At Jackie 60 you were not judged by the color of your skin, but by the contents of your closet.

Usually, of course, the effect is too garish and OTT, due to the Negro's over-theatricality and lack of self-control, as in Evola's comparison of the Roman and Mediterranean strains of the Italian character in *Men Among the Ruins*.

This Old Gay House

Will Fellows
A Passion to Preserve: Gay Men as Keepers of Culture
Madison: The University of Wisconsin Press, 2004

"Ever wonder who was the first guy to put pineapple on pizza? I bet he was gay. No straight guy is gonna say: 'You know what this pizza could use? A pineapple ring!' But God bless 'im, it's good!"[1]

I sit in my house for days on end and stare at the roses in the closet. . . .
I'd better get right down to the job.
It's true I don't want to join the Army or turn lathes in precision parts factories, I'm nearsighted and psychopathic anyway.
America I'm putting my queer shoulder to the wheel.[2]

Everyone knows about the role of homosexuals in the creation as well as preservation of culture, especially that of the Aryan race. Well, maybe not. Other than James Neill's vast survey

---

[1] *Two and a Half Men*, Season 2, Episode 14, "Those Big Pink Things With Coconuts." An interviewee in the book under review recalls his father making a similar comment about prehistoric cave paintings: "It had to be the fags. All the other men are out hunting and killing. There's a bunch of fags sitting in the back of the cave, complaining about how ugly it is, wondering what they can do to make it look better. So they decide to paint some bison on the walls." For more on cave paintings see Collin Cleary "The Stones Cry Out: Cave Art and the Origins of the Human Spirit," in his *What Is a Rune?*, ed. Greg Johnson (San Francisco: Counter-Currents, 2015). Greg Johnson takes Camille Paglia to task for failing to include cave paintings in her recent survey of images, https://www.counter-currents.com/2012/10/camille-paglias-glittering-images/.

[2] Allen Ginsberg, "America."

The Origin and Role of Same-Sex Relationships in Human Societies,[3] most people with any positive interest in the topic are content to just compile lists of "famous queers." Then there are snarky works with titles like *How Homosexuals Saved Civilization.* Even Louis Cramford's magisterial survey *Homosexuality and Civilization*[4] is just an erudite variation, showing the interaction of its two titular topics without exploring the connection or interconnection.

It's common enough on the Right to somewhat grudgingly acknowledge their role in the re-homesteading and revitalizing of blighted (usually by blacks) urban areas. The Right ruefully admits that for some reason, these limp-wristed sissies are able to resist the Black Undertow that drove out all those manly Olde Tyme White families.

As the writer Alan Gurganus is quoted in the work under review, "You can always tell an urban[5] neighborhood in transition by that harbinger of change—the corner Art Deco shop opened by two gentlemen friends."

Indeed, one need only spend an idle weekend or two viewing the plethora of cable channels devoted to house-hunting or home-improvement to notice the "over-representation"—as the Steve Sailerites like to say—of male couples, to the extent that the introduction of "my partner" is less likely to reveal a business partner than what the *Times* used to call a "life partner."[6]

---

[3] McFarland, 2008. Neill is focused mostly on the role of homosexuals, and homosexuality, in providing a biological-evolutionary advantage to primates and their descendants, primitive human tribes, although he does not neglect the cultural role as well; he even finds the need to compile his own "famous queers" list. See my Amazon Kindle *A Review of James Neill's* "The Origins and Role of Same-Sex Relations in Human Societies."

[4] Harvard, 2003.

[5] You know what *that* means, of course.

[6] I suspect this is why I now find people online complaining that even the grandfather of them all, PBS' *This Old House* has "gotten too gay," though usually blamed on recent new host Kevin O'Connor (like the Joel vs. Mike battles of MST3k fans), it's more likely just contamination from the "all these shows are gay" feeling.

One might dismiss this as another example of PC-casting, as in the even more obvious and unlikely number of intact black families with enough cash flow to buy a big new house or need help purging and organizing all their stuff.

On the other hand, if it reflects reality, the Sailerites are ready with a slew of easy explanations, revolving around "high net worth" and "no kids." Here, they prefer amateur sociology to their favored biological explanations.

Our author, Will Fellows, confronts this meme right at the start, and dismisses it as a best inadequate. His research "provided me with so much—admittedly anecdotal—evidence to help dismiss some of the rather clichéd explanations as to why gay men are extraordinarily involved in the preservation arena."

> There are arguments along the lines of 'no children, so they don't have to live in safe neighborhoods with good schools,'[7] or 'no children so they have more income'. And even an argument that I heard that gay men are marginal creatures in the culture, or have been historically, and so they are inclined to take on marginal enterprises like preservation.[8]

In his Conclusion, Fellows gives his "answer":

> Gay men make extraordinary contributions in historic preservation, an arena well populated by straight women, because the mix of things that preservation is about strike many of the same psychologic chords in gay males as in straight females. These chords cluster around a number of themes: domophilia, romanticism, aestheticism, and con-nection- and continuity-mindedness.

Making things a bit more concrete, these "themes" are explicat-

---

[7] And you know what *that* means, too.

[8] Author interviewed here: "There Almost Went The Neighborhood: Gay Men and Preservation," http://indianapublicmedia.org/arts/confronting-stereotypes-preserving-culture/.

ed as a "cluster of concerns" such as:

> Creating and keeping attractive and safe dwelling spaces; restoring and preserving wholeness and design integrity; valuing heritage and identity; nurturing community relationships; fostering continuity in the midst of incessant change.

In short, the basic values of the New Right. In fact, Fellows later provides a quote from Jung (the Aryan Freud) which is very interesting in this context:

> Since a "mother-complex" is a concept borrowed from [Judaic] psychopathology, it is always associated with the idea of injury and illness. But if we take the concept out of its narrow psychopathological setting and give it a wider connotation, we can see that it has positive effects as well. Thus a man with a mother-complex . . . is likely to have a feeling for history, and *to be conservative in the best sense and cherish the values of the past.*[9]

Even further, Fellows insists historic preservation is far from "marginal work" fit only for people on the sidelines of "real work," but is "a job that is at the very center of their society's life, akin to religious work." As he explains elsewhere:

> In a certain sense I see historic preservation as a religious act, religious in the original meaning of that word, having to do with putting back together something that is broken.

> There's this whole phenomenon growing out of the human soul that resonates more powerfully for some people than for others that has to do with identifying things that are in need, things that are broken, things that are not whole, not complete, and restoring them to a state of

---

[9] Carl Jung, "The Mother Complex" in *Archetypes of the Collective Unconscious*, pp. 85-91.

wholeness. So in a certain sense I do see historic preservation as a religious act, religious in the original meaning of that word, having to do with putting back together something that is broken.[10]

We'll return to those religious dimensions, but first, let's go back to those "themes," which are not entirely self-explanatory. Domophilia is a "neologism" and rather unfortunate, as it sounds like a sexual aberration. In fact, it's nothing scarier than "an exceptional love of houses and things homey, this deep domesticity, which often emerges in childhood."

Romanticism is not a neologism but is also unfortunate, being so polyvalent. Fellows calls it "romanticism with a small r, the exceptionally romantic and emotional ways in which many gay men relate to the past, to old buildings and the places, and to the lives and possessions of their previous occupants." In short, what New Rightists will recognize as what we call "hauntology."[11]

Rightists might also think of H. P. Lovecraft as a non-homosexual, but distinctly odd, example of this trait—"I am Providence" and all that—but Fellows throws us a wonderful curveball here; Lovecraft is never mentioned in the book at all, but Romanticism is immediately exemplified by August Derleth, Lovecraft's executor and posthumous collaborator, who set up Arkham House (note the name!) to preserve Lovecraft's weird *oeuvre*. Lovecraftians, led by S. T. Joshi, have long given Derleth a hard time, but here he's lauded for his "quintessentially queer romanticism" as exemplified in such novels as *The Atmosphere of Houses*.[12]

---

[10] Fellows, *op. cit.*

[11] See, for example, Christopher Pankhurst's "Towards a Right-wing Hauntology," https://www.counter-currents.com/2014/06/toward-a-right-wing-hauntology/. "In contradistinction to overt contemporary culture which endlessly recycles and repeats the past as a commodity for the present, hauntology seeks to reinstate the melancholy fact that the past is lost, and to imbue its unknowableness with a bittersweet taste of mortality."

[12] The implication that Derleth was homosexual is news to me, and

By contrast, Aestheticism is fairly straightforward, having for a long time "served as a code word for gay." It refers to "the emergence in childhood of [an] artistic eye and aptitude, [an] extraordinary visual understanding of the world, [a] design-mindedness." In short, to refer to the cable metaphor again, a "queer eye."

Connection- and Continuity-mindedness is perhaps the most self-explanatory, but it's also the most ironic, since it presents gay men as more conservative than most so-called "conservatives."[13] Fellows delineates them thus:

> As a connection with the past is central to the definition of culture, so is a concern with connection and continuity vital to culture keeping. . . . Like [E. M.] Forster, these men cherish tradition, family, community, a feeling for place, a sense of flowing history. They are enchanted not by the modern but by "something older, something slightly mysterious yet powerful," as Nicholas Fox describes it.

Fellows then quotes the marvelously named James Van Trump, who seems to be a closet Heideggerian or archeofuturist: "We live in a kind of cultural continuum, like a chain . . . We need a constant going back and forth from the present to the

---

Fellows has not provided any evidence; is it common knowledge?

[13] Fellows quotes Philip Gambone, who lived on Boston's Beacon Hill in the '70s and attended the Anglo-Catholic Church of the Advent: "The Advent's congregation was made up almost exclusively of gay men and Boston Brahmins, a strange and tenuous coalition at best. What brought these unlikely factions together was a shared passion for the Mass, and for its high church aesthetic." The coalition may have been strange but hardly tenuous; it dates back to the 19th century. See Douglass Shand-Tucci, *Ralph Adams Cram: Life and Architecture*, especially vol. 1, *Boston Bohemia* (Amherst: University of Massachusetts Press, 1994). The afore-mentioned James Van Trump explains that, like Cram and other Boston Bohemians, becoming a High-Church Episcopalian allowed him to "have all the lights, incense, color, flowers, and music without subscribing to the rigid doctrines of Rome." I think you know what *those* are.

past. We have to have the past from which to move on."

The bulk of Fellows' book is both a history of historical preservation and an oral history of the gay men involved in it—to the extent that one can separate the two.[14] Some men are well known in their professions, some are not. Some places are obvious—Provincetown, New Orleans—others are outliers—Red Cloud, Nebraska, or Cooksville, Wisconsin. As you can tell from the quotes I've sprinkled here and there, they're a fascinating group, well worth your time to visit.

After all this Fellows has to face up to the meta-issue: how come? Here Fellows is boldly un-PC, driven by the data, anecdotal though it may be: "'Artistic,' 'musical,' 'nervous,' 'sensitive,' 'sophisticated,' and 'temperamental' have served as euphemism or code words for gay. They are all based in the reality of gay men's lives." Score one for the Sailerites—some stereotypes *are* based on reality! In this case, "based on the reality of gay men's lives."

Fellows comes down on the un-politically popular side of nature, not nurture; quoting interviewee Richard Jost: "[The numbers of men involved in historic preservation] 'would seem to argue for the existence of a preservation gene, which I would guess is located very near the Broadway show-tune gene.'"

But no sooner does Fellows take his stand on empirical reality than he moves, even more boldly, from cliché to "archetypal truth," bringing in the big guns: Camille Paglia herself: "Gay men are aliens, cursed and gifted, the shamans of our time . . . caught midway between the male and female brains."[15]

Shamans! Male and female brains! In more traditional societies, from the shamans of so-called "primitive" tribes[16] to the monks of mediaeval Christendom, these men who "partake of

---

[14] "No, indeed. It is hardly possible to separate you, even when he is summoned to a secret council and you are not." *The Fellowship of the Ring* II.2, "The Council of Elrond."

[15] Quoting from her collection *Vamps and Tramps*.

[16] See Wulf Grimmson, *Loki's Way: The Path of the Sorcerer in the Age of Iron* (Second Edition, Lulu.com, 2011) and my review, "A Band Apart," above.

the ambiguous virtue of the feminine," as Evola says,[17] have largely been drawn to perform religious functions.

In the last two hundred years, however, the speed of change has accelerated to such an extent that preservation of the built environment has itself taken on the trappings of a religious calling.[18] Indeed, clergy took a leading role in the beginnings of the preservationist movement.

As Fellows quotes another wonderfully named-interviewee, Richard Wagner, a Wisconsin preservationist, "It's a priestly role, in the sense of the shamans."

If all this talk of "brokenness" and healing and religion—shamans, even!—seems a bit much, consider some evidence from those interested in preservation as such. For example, New York's official real estate curmudgeon, "Jerimiah" (a pseudonym[19]), gathers some evidence of his own in a rare moment of meta-reflection on his task:

> You can like those towers or hate those towers. But here's the thing: All the glass boxes around the city are making us sick—mentally and physically. They are literally killing us as they hasten our deaths.

Cognitive neuroscientist Colin Ellard studied what hap-

---

[17] "How disheartening to those who uphold the myth of manhood based on muscles and metallic strength: this [the Androgyne] alone is the TRUE man, the ABSOLUTE man. He absorbs within himself the ambiguous virtue of the female. . ." "Serpentine Wisdom" in Julius Evola, *The Hermetic Tradition: Symbols and Teachings of the Royal Art* (Rochester, Vt.: Inner Traditions, 1995). This is an essay on the *Tao Te Ching*, which also provides an epigraph for Fellows' book: "Knowing the masculine and nurturing the feminine become the river of all beneath heaven."

[18] "In normal times, evil would be fought with good. But in times like these, well, it should be fought by another kind of evil." *The Chronicles of Riddick* (Twohy, 2004).

[19] Update: Apparently not; Jeremiah Moss, described as "a Jane Jacobs for the digital age," now has a book out: *Vanishing New York: How a Great City Lost Its Soul* (New York: Day Street Books, 2017).

pens to people on the sidewalk when they stand in front of a bland glass façade. In one study, he placed human subjects in front of the Whole Foods grocery store on the Lower East Side, strapped skin-conducting bracelets to their wrists, and asked them to take notes on their emotional states.

He reported, "When planted in front of Whole Foods, my participants stood awkwardly, casting around for something of interest to latch on to and talk about. They assessed their emotional state as being on the wrong side of 'happy' and their state of arousal was close to bottoming out. The physiological instruments strapped to their arms showed a similar pattern. These people were bored and unhappy. When asked to describe the site, words such as bland, monotonous and passionless rose to the top of the charts."

In his book *Happy City*,[20] Charles Montgomery calls this "an emerging disaster in street psychology." The loss of old buildings and small businesses, the homogenization from suburban chains and condo boxes, is more than an aesthetic loss. It is damaging us both psychologically and physically.

Writes Montgomery, "The big-boxing of a city block harms the physical health of people living nearby, especially the elderly. Seniors who live among long stretches of dead frontage have actually been found to age more quickly than those who live on blocks with plenty of doors, windows, porch stoops, and destinations."

In a city where people are reconceived as consumers, not citizens, it is best to keep everyone moving and disconnected.[21]

---

[20] *Happy City: Transforming Our Lives Through Urban Design* (New York: Farrar, Straus and Giroux, 2013).

[21] A post on the destruction of the Market Diner on *Jeremiah's Van-*

Disconnected! There's that word again.

And lest your cold, libertard heart thinks that all this, despite references to Heidegger and archeofuturism, is really just hippie airy-fairy nonsense, consider how our white homelands, which are very popular on the New Right as examples of How to Live, handle this sort of thing; Jeremiah again:

> Change, for its own sake, isn't necessarily a good thing. In New York, "change" means eradication. There is no effort to blend the new with, and into, the old. It's all or nothing, no compromise, no desire in preserving the past in the present to be appreciated in the future. It's funny that *Europeans understand that preserving the past, in historical and cultural contexts, is a way of maintaining a continuous link between what came before, what is now and what will be in the future.* Warsaw, Dresden and Nurnberg for example, were obliterated during WWII. *They were rebuilt, combining old and new (which included painstakingly recreating historic structures) because the people understood the importance of being able to connect with their past.* Unfortunately, preserving and acknowledging New York's history doesn't exist in the minds and actions of developers. A dystopian city, *à la* "Blade Runner" is something we all should fear since that seems to be the direction New York is heading.

Fellows even finds himself drifting further into the vortex of Traditionalism, quoting from John Brinckerhoff Jackson's *The Necessity for Ruins* to the effect that the preservationist "sees history not as a continuity but as a dramatic discontinuity,[22] a kind of cosmic drama," involving a necessary plunge into chaos and decay (as in the *nigredo* stage of alchemy?) before the work of restoration can return us to "that golden age of har-

---

ishing New York, http://vanishingnewyork.blogspot.com/016/04/market-diner-demolished.html.

[22] Evola gave grudging praise to Spengler for having overturned the idea of one, rising and progressing civilization and replacing it with the idea of discontinuity among types of civilizations; see *The Path of Cinnabar* (London: Arktos, 2009), pp. 203–204.

monious beginnings."

This is how we *reproduce the cosmic scheme* and correct history.[23] Are we perhaps trying to reenact some ancient myth of birth, death and redemption?[24]

Gosh, could the "conservatives" be wrong? Perhaps all those childless men do have some role to play in reproduction and survival, at least in the reproduction of the past into the future and the survival of cities, not global consumerist playgrounds?

I suspect that at this point Fellows' readers in the architecture[25] or "gay studies" shelves may have started to bleed from the ears as he hits these levels. Nevertheless, it is a rare and valuable empirical supplement to the more abstract works alluded to above (as well as some of my own) that strive to remind us of role of the non-family man in the creation and preservation of Aryan culture.

Counter-Currents/*North American New Right*
June 17, 2016

---

[23] I think he means "reverse or annihilate history" not the Judaic idea of *tikkun olam*.

[24] Fellows quoting from J. B. Jackson, *The Necessity for Ruins* (Amherst: University of Massachusetts Press, 1980).

[25] Painful as it may be to those whose ideas of architecture arise from the work of Ayn Rand, Fellows notes along the way that architecture has long been a similarly respectable refuge for the homosexual male. See my "Ralph Adams Cram: Wild Boy of American Architecture" in *The Eldritch Evola … & Others* (San Francisco: Counter-Currents, 2014), and "A Waste of Space: Some Thoughts on the Fabulous Career of Philip Johnson, Architect," https://www.counter-currents.com/2015/12/a-waste-of-space/. Alas, Cram get only one brief mention, but it has a good, Ignatius Reilly-an quote: "Between the years 1000 and 1500 life was in certain fundamental respects, more right than at any time before or since . . . Back to medievalism we must go, and begin again."

THE GILMORE GIRLS
OCCUPY WALL STREET

"These ladies were so much of the place and the place so much of themselves that from the first of their being revealed to me I felt that nothing else at Brookbridge much mattered. They were what, for me, at any rate, Brookbridge had most to give: I mean in the way of what it was naturally strongest in, the thing we called in New York the New England expression, the air of Puritanism reclaimed and refined."

—Henry James, "'Europe'"

What passes for "the Right" in America, having first been seduced by apologists for Capital like Ayn Rand and William F. Buckley, then subjected to a *coup d'état* by the neo-con *junta*, is in no position to support, approve, or even understand the "Occupy Wall Street" movement. The Bourbons may have, as Talleyrand supposedly said, learned nothing and forgotten nothing, but the gleaming, streamlined Neo-Right (not to be confused with the European or North American New Right) has forgotten everything the Right used to stand for, and "leaned" one thing—"Lower tax rates solve everything!"— which isn't even true.[1]

Fight Wall Street? What sense is there in that, when the "official" conservative talking heads are all employees of Murdoch or GE, and think, and look, more like Patrick Bateman than George Bailey. As Oliver Stone realized to his horror, he gave

---

[1] As House Majority Leader Tom DeLay recently declared, "Nothing is more important in the face of a war than cutting taxes." See "How the GOP Became the Party of the Rich: The inside story of how the Republicans abandoned the poor and the middle class to pursue their relentless agenda of tax cuts for the wealthiest one percent," by Tom Dickinson (*Rolling Stone*, Nov. 9, 2011, http://www.rollingstone. com/politics/news/how-the-gop-became-the-party-of-the-rich-20111109#ixzz1eAJd0btL).

Gordon Gekko a speech that could have come from the pen of William Jennings Bryan, to say nothing of William Pierce:

> The richest one percent of this country owns half our country's wealth, five trillion dollars. One third of that comes from hard work, two thirds comes from inheritance, interest on interest accumulating to widows and idiot sons, and what I do, stock and real estate speculation. It's bullshit. You got ninety percent of the American public out there with little or no net worth. I create nothing. I own. We make the rules, pal. The news, war, peace, famine, upheaval, the price per paperclip. We pick that rabbit out of the hat while everybody sits out there wondering how the hell we did it. Now you're not naïve enough to think we're living in a democracy, are you buddy? It's the free market. And you're a part of it.

And people's reaction was "Fuck yeah! Where do I git onea them MBAs?"

One theme from the dull contempt with which the Official Right greeted OWS that struck me as more true than either side may realize was something like this, which you've heard versions of time after time:

> This isn't a serious political movement worth our notice. It's just a bunch of sociology majors who can't get jobs and want the whole world to be like college again.

There's something to this, but probably not what O'Reilly's viewers think is there. First, though, let's back up a bit.

For a while I was merrily documenting each of Jim Kunstler's weekly tirades against the White People on his eponymous Peak-Everything blog, www.kunstler.com, as evidence of the White-hate that simmers just beneath the "thin veneer" (as his co-ethnic, Freud, would say) of criticism of our gas-guzzling society,[2] which is often the true motive behind all this

---

[2] A phrase coined, be it noted, by Mitt Romney's father, Michigan

"green" blather. However, it just got too boring, the same pre-
dictable rant, even the same stomach-churning metaphors—
pus, bacteria, rancid lard—for the White Plague, the same "just
wait for it" as the price of oil rose only to then fall as life went
on, until finally I called it quits.

So it's good to see Edmund Connelly taking up the torch.
His whole article is important reading, but the quote from Jim
is worth reproducing here, as it contains a very excusable mistake, worthy of further consideration.

> In his recent blog "Our Turn?," he begins with a familiar
> Jewish obsession:

> "Nations go crazy. It's terrifying when it happens, espe-
> cially to a major nation with the ability to project its cra-
> ziness outward. We look back on the psychotic break of
> Germany in 1933 and still wonder how the then-best-
> educated population in Europe could fall under the sway
> of a sociopathic political program. We behold the carnage
> and devastation left in the wake of that episode, and dec-
> ades later you still can do little more than shake your
> head in bewilderment."

> Readers of Kunstler's blogs will know of his fear and
> contempt for Americans who do not live in big cities and
> who are not reflexively liberal in their politics. These are
> the infamous "cornporn Nazis" [*sic*] of Kunstler's night-
> mares.[3]

The first thing one notices, of course, is the typical Judaic
myopia: history is all about Jim's little tribe, and it's the story of
the innocent Jews being constantly oppressed and murdered by
the *goyim*, who can't possibly have any reasons to hate Jews,
and so must be completely insane. And indeed, who but the

Governor and AMC President George.
   [3] Edmund Connelly, "Take the Money and Run,"
http://www.theoccidentalobserver.net/authors/Connelly-
Money.html

crazed could possibly want to harm God's Little Pets?

Since the Judaics, from Freud, or perhaps Moses Mendelssohn, up to the latest po-mo clown, are always boasting about how their "outsider status" allows them a privileged objectivity about the general culture, you'd think then that they'd acknowledge being a little bit of an interested party in this matter. One might think "sociopathic political program" might refer to the Bolshevik revolution, inspired by the Judaic Marx and implemented and sustained by Russian Judaic terrorists, sustained for over 70 years, and involving the imprisonment or murder of tens of millions; how's that for "carnage and devastation"?[4]

Some might suggest the original "mad nation" was France in 1789. To some other "outsiders," the "psychotic break" might be better known to them as the European Revolution of 1933. What could be crazier than that last attempt by the "best educated" of Europe to "break" the power of Finance Capital? Kinda sounds like "Occupy Wall Street," now, don't it?

But for now I want to focus on the small but interesting factual error: Jim is no fan of the big cities. Of course, it's easy to make that assumption, even apart from his liberal-Judaic background. He hates the Suburbs, as the epitome of our Easy Motoring Culture of cheap oil and plastic, and jobs for rednecks above their proper station, and of course he hates the Rural areas, being a Judaic and all—as Israel Shahak pointed out, Judaism is the only culture that has never idealized the worker of the land, from Greek pastoralism to the Prussian Junkers, British "country life," and the Jeffersonian yeoman[5]—but he loathes the energy-wasting, gentrifying Cities almost as much.

Jim, as you can see, is a very hard man to please.

See, Jim has his own version of the country squire going on, up in the Capital District, although his contempt for the proles

---

[4] See Kevin MacDonald's "Stalin's Willing Executioners," in his *Cultural Insurrections: Essays on Western Civilization, Jewish Influence, and Anti-Semitism* (Atlanta: The Occidental Press, 2007).

[5] Israel Shahak, *Jewish History, Jewish Religion: The Weight of Three Thousand Years* (London: Pluto Press, 1994).

makes him incapable of the gently amused appreciation Bill Kauffman—"The Sage of Batavia" as Gore Vidal calls him—brings to the same area. Still, Jim is very much the "country gentleman" in his own way, or rather, a way that hasn't been noticed very much—hence Connelly's natural error—and to which I want to pay some attention here, in the context of Occupy Wall Street.

I even have a name for it: the Neo-Rural Liberal.

Ever notice that despite their contempt for rednecks and Babbitts, the liberal prefers to live in a small town or village? Martha's Vineyard, Fire Island, Hampton Bays, you get the picture? Hell, even the Big City Liberal lives in a village, whether historically rooted (Greenwich Village) or just a realtor's marketing ploy (The East Village). Berkeley itself is just a village compared to San Francisco (where evil Bankers and the maids live).

Obviously, liberals prefer to live with other liberals; we all prefer to live with our own kind. One only needs to point this out because liberals themselves vociferously deny it they have any such atavistic tendencies, and deny the privilege to Other Whites, who get forced busing and integration, and a sneer if they still contrive (as most do, even now) to escape to those terrible Auto Suburbs or NASCAR Towns that the Jims hate so much.

Those that didn't grow up among Their Own soon acquire the taste when they go away (and they have to, to Get Away from Them) to college. The "college town" is the classic example of a small town filled for some reason with flaming liberals; in fact, most of them will never be as liberal as they are now, as they act out against parents, teachers, society, "townies," etc.

Even the aforementioned big cities have their college towns: Columbia is located on the Upper West Side—the White part, of course, that George Carlin's teen gang preferred to call "White Harlem"—NYU in the Village.

This was the crystallization point of the film, *The Big Chill*. The eponymous chill is the cold world outside of Ann Arbor, Michigan, home of the mighty U. of M. That was the last (perhaps only) time any of them were content, or even settled, if that doesn't seem too paradoxical a way to describe the transitory student life; now, working and living in horrifying cities (even then, before the "Black Undertow" of the last three decades) like Detroit, Atlanta, New York, and Hollywood, their lives suck.

The only reasonably grounded one lives in small town South Carolina, but he's betrayed his "radical" past and become a "businessman." His guilt is assuaged only by playing unwilling host to his college buds, and fathering a child on one of them, at his wife's suggestion. No small town prudes here!

He does have a big old Victorian house, though, so that when they all meet up for the funeral of one of their number, they decide to bag the cities for the weekend and try to re-create their student lives in one of those old Victorian student houses on Ann Arbor's Liberty Street (perhaps a few doors up from that quaint little bookstore you may have heard of, name of "Borders," which recently enacted its own cycle of boom and bust).

"You know, I live here. This place means something to me. I'm dug in." Of course, the University of Michigan sweatshirt he wears while making that "I'll take my stand" speech betrays Kevin Kline's self-delusion; he has a house full of college buddies watching the Michigan-Michigan State game (how's that for college town overkill?), and the only advantage to South Carolina, apart from cheap labor to exploit, is that as a Local Businessman, the cops don't crack his skull for smoking marijuana.

Like all Disingenuous White Liberals,[6] Motown may be "the only music in this house" but only because that's what they listened to at U. of M. (the Evil Husband who goes home to see to the kids, of course, lives in Detroit, not Ann Arbor).

Another early adumbration of the meme is found in Paul Fussell's *Class*.[7] It's pretty accurate and amusing (such as his

---

[6] See "#47" at the indispensable blog *Stuff Black People Don't Like*: http://stuffblackpeopledontlike.blogspot.com/2009/07/ 47- disingenuous-white-liberals.html

[7] Paul Fussell, *Class: A Guide Through the American Status System*

take on the reasons for the popularity of the *Preppy Handbook*, and the dreaded "one size fits all Proles" tractor hat), but Fussell just can't accept the idea that what OWS calls "the one percent" is out of his reach as well; "they have no interest in ideas" he sour-grapes (his ideas, of course), but then he reveals that some (the smart ones, of course) can drop out of the whole class system. These free spirits he dubs "Class X."

In a devastating review in *The Atlantic*,[8] authentic Top Class chronicler Wilfred Sheed pointed out that the Class X-ers seemed to be a recognizable type: tenure track academics like Fussell himself, who "never talk about the food or wine being served" not because of superior taste, as Fussell thinks, but because years of cafeteria food and jug wine "have given them palates of stone."

These are the dreary, know-it-all inhabitants of CollegeTown USA, with their Fair Trade coffee (priced out of prole reach) and solar collectors that take 10 years to "pay for themselves" (not really an option for people living on payday loans).

Of course, in itself, small town life is a natural taste. After all, small towns always score high on those "Best Place to Live" surveys. A whole cable channel, Hallmark, is devoted to hazily filmed fairy tales about big-city career women who find the secret to happiness when their car breaks down in Hooterville.[9] It's the flip side to the Lifetime channel, where the women are beaten, raped, and killed by their over-achieving big-city boyfriends. Problem is, small towns are full of White Others, who are not only non-Jewish, but even conservative. As Wallace Shawn, the WASP Woody Allen would say: Inconceivable!

Those not lucky enough to relocate to one of the Urban Villages or College Towns will work like demons at banking or law or "writing," and hopefully make enough money, mostly by ripping off the infra-dig real Main Street, to move to some

---

(New York: Summit Books, 1983).

    [8] Wilfrid Sheed, "Upward mobility: how to be an X," *Atlantic Monthly*, October 1, 1983.

    [9] http://www.imdb.com/news/ni1304529/

liberal-restricted "Main Street" inhabited by tame, amusing Vermont eccentric types and which "just happens" to exclude the Others due to lack of ready cash: the appeal of the Hamptons, Vineyard, etc.

Since Fire Island has no actual industry or economy, the vacationing Upper gets the thrill of everything he buys being a twice-as-expensive "import." Meanwhile, the handful of natives needed to run the cash registers and bus the tables lives in trailers and flee to the mainland after Columbus Day.

The Others also includes the black chappies, of course, other than a couple of IQ outliers like P. Diddy or Henry Gates, who serve as ready exhibits to show that we're not racists, like those awful Other Whites across town; no "Jim Crow" laws needed, or nasty old "traditions" or irrational "customs," just the insurmountable barriers of money and education. What could be more *fair*, as the liberal understands the word?

Even Jim Kunstler fits the picture. I've lived around there, and you've got to have some kind of money to live a decent life in a hell-hole like the Capital District. But if you do, life can be sweet; hell, if there is anything around it's cheap, and you mail order the rest, or have it delivered from the city, or custom built; even the carpenters, as Fussell already observed, are likely to be fellow Ivy grads. Money buys the private conveniences, and also the cars and air tickets that Jim uses as he circles the globe, decrying the carbon footprints of the rednecks and other Bigfoots.

Hey, the richest guys in America live in Omaha, NE and Redmond, WA.

So, after destroying the Cities with their idiotic laws and racial nonsense, the Liberal now yearns for the palmy days of ice cream socials and bandstands in the park ("Next stop Willoughby!"), recreated, Disney-like, in areas from which the twin wrecking balls of liberalism and finance capital have driven the Other Whites, leaving the Liberals, like the lucky ones in *Blade Runner*, to "live the Good Life" in what we might call the "super-Urban" colonies.

Despite all his smug superiority over "urban planners," Kunstler's vision isn't that much different than Robert Moses'.

Unlike Jane Jacobs, he has no appreciation for true diversity as manifested in the Big City, and although he wouldn't endorse Moses' techniques of political and literal bulldozing, he'd be quite happy living with his think-alike liberal peers in a devastated urban hulk, where the White Ethnics have been driven out from lack of jobs, but the Darkies are kept at bay by high rents.

This became clear to me over the last year or so, as, during an extended period of unemployment, I became hooked on the three-episode weekly marathon repeats of *The Gilmore Girls*, a show I had known only from occasional jokes and parodies during its initial run (2000–2007). Nothing I had ever heard about it had led me to consider watching it then, nor did it give me any reason to reconsider now.[10]

---

[10] For those who haven't seen it and can't bear to look, here's Wikipedia: "The pilot of *Gilmore Girls* sets up the premise of the show and a number of its recurrent themes as the audience learns that Lorelei became pregnant with Rory at sixteen but chose not to marry the father, Christopher Hayden. Instead, she moved to Stars Hollow away from her disappointed parents in Hartford and has had only irregular contact with them ever since. Later episodes reveal Lorelei and the infant Rory were taken in by the owner of the Independence Inn, Mia, where Lorelei progressed from maid to executive manager. In the pilot, Rory, who is about to turn sixteen, is accepted by Chilton Preparatory School in order to pursue her dream of studying at Harvard University. Lorelei, unable to afford Chilton's fees, strikes a bargain with her parents for a loan to cover the tuition in exchange for an agreement that every Friday night she and Rory will share dinner with Emily and Richard. The series explores issues of family, friendship and romance, as well as generational divides and social class. Ambition, education and work also form part of the series' central concerns, telling Lorelei's story from pregnant teen runaway and high school dropout to co-owner and manager of the Dragonfly Inn. Rory's transition from public school to the prestigious preparatory school, Chilton, is similarly followed by the series, exploring her ambition to study at an Ivy League college and to become a foreign correspondent. The show's social commentary manifests most clearly in Lorelei's difficult relationship with her wealthy upper-class parents, Emily and Richard Gilmore, and in the interactions between the students at Chil-

Needless to say, the show is loathsome on its own terms, but I began to find it utterly fascinating as a window onto the Liberal Mind and its Sense of Place.

Almost a decade of reviews, blogs, and forums has already established a Minority Opinion, among even Liberals, that the unintended irony of the show is that Lorelei Gilmore, rebellious child of privilege, is presented to us as supremely beautiful, intelligent, witty, and above all heroic in her struggle against her wealthy, scheming, manipulative parents, while in fact being intensely annoying, self-destructive, deluded, almost autistically self-involved in dealing with those she condescends to notice, and, above all, both spoiled and ungrateful to her long-suffering parents (the father, played by *echt*-WASP and hometown boy Edward Herrmann, was the hook that got me watching in the first place).

What particularly struck me, however, and is of relevance here, is the creation of Stars Hollow, the small town that Lorelei ran away to as a pregnant, unmarried teenager and where she has raised her daughter (also named Lorelei, or Rory for convenience — see what I mean about egotism?) over the last sixteen years, and who is also, as her namesake, supremely beautiful, intelligent, witty, but — having benefited from being raised by Lorelei and not her evil parents — is able to attend Yale and have rich boyfriends without getting knocked up.

Stars Hollow is in the television tradition of small backwaters populated by dimwitted but good-hearted folk that the main character can play against. Andy Griffith's Mayberry, North Carolina is probably the classic example. Stars Hollow is unlike Mayberry, however, not just in being in the Northeast but also by being as much a college town as one could have without an actual college; for the convenience of seven years of story arcs, it seems to be located in spitting distance of an elite girls school and Yale, and within easy commuting distance of the ritzy Connecticut suburbs (for weekly parental dinners, leading to the Airing of Grievances — yes, Lauren Graham was

---

ton, and later, Yale University," http://en.wikipedia.org/wiki/Gilmore_Girls

one of Seinfeld's ladies of the week — fueled by vast quantities of Pop's gin) and New York City (for job interviews with the *New York Times* right out of school, and perhaps to occupy Wall Street without missing Mom's home cooking).

Most significantly, Stars Hollow is brimming with small town traditions and ways that are the subject of local pride and care, but which Lorelei, despite living there almost two decades, feigns ignorance of and whose evident stupidity or outright craziness she greets with her biting "wit" and corrosive "irony" to the amusement of steadily declining TV audiences.

The town of Stars Hollow is a simulacrum, to use a word beloved by Liberals of a theoretical bent, of a small New England town but one inhabited by a multi-culti elite (well, one Korean family and a black guy who is, of course, not just hypercompetent but also FRENCH) who think like Woody Allen, while the people who built and inhabit the real Stars Hollows of the world are portrayed, if townspeople, as stupid but amusing to Lorelei (and us, of course) or else, like her parents, monsters of evil.[11]

One thinks of Henry James's description, for his English audience, of the town of Concord, Mass., in the time of Hawthorne:

It is very possible that at this period there was not (even)

---

[11] For a sample of which, consider how Lorelei explains dealing with her mother, and expects the townsperson to understand and be sympathetic: "I just imagine what my mother would do, then dial it back to Mussolini, then dial it back to Stalin, then . . ." Now, it's always tedious to explain a "joke," especially the post-modern, MST-like joke that is largely just a smart line referencing pop culture as part of a non-stop barrage of same, but notice that the "humor" here involves postulating a Spectrum of Evil, in which one's own WASP mother is the *ne plus ultra* of Evil, while Stalin is two steps away, with Mussolini in between. In the episode "But I'm a Gilmore!" the girls even get to experience the masochistic thrill of being the victims of WASP prejudice, when Rory's prospective in-laws reject her as "not suitable" for their son. The groom's family seems to be cribbed from some Henry James or Edith Wharton novel; meanwhile, in the real world, Kennedys marry Schwarzeneggers with nary an eye batted.

an Irishman in Concord; the place would have been a village community operating in excellent conditions. Such a village community was not the least honourable item in the sum of New England civilisation. Its spreading elms and plain white houses, its generous summers and ponderous winters, its immediate background of promiscuous field and forest, would have been part of the composition. For the rest, there were the selectmen and the town-meetings, the town-schools and the self-governing spirit, the rigid morality, the friendly and familiar manners, the perfect competence of the little society to manage its affairs itself.[12]

I suppose this must be what Martha's Vineyard is like: the small rural towns built by White Protestants, inhabited by Woody Allen clones.

The body snatchers came from the Levant, not outer space, and they've taken over Santa Rita! And if your town is "lucky," you're next! Tomorrow the world?

Lurking behind it all, especially the Judaic obsession with the danger of a recurrence of the German Revolution of 1933, is what we might call the Final Solution to the *Goyim* Problem. For, as no less a "genius" than Freud has told us, an obsession with the sins of others is a cover for one's own sins. The German sin was to do to the Judaics as the Judaics would do to us, before the Judaics had enough power to do so. For centuries, this has been the plan; we've seen it what happens when Judaics take power during the Russian Terror, and Palestine is only a dress rehearsal, paid for by the *goyim* themselves, for the Big Show.

As Connelly concludes, the Judaics who still form the template for "real liberals" are:

a hostile elite that fears and mostly dislikes us — people like Frank Rich, [James] Howard Kunstler, and thou-

---

[12] Henry James, *Hawthorne*, ch. 4, "Brook Farm and Concord," http://www.online-literature.com/henry_james/hawthorne/ 4/

sands of other antsy Jews like them. What will happen to us if such Jews feel so at risk that they preemptively seek to neutralize the "threatening" ones among us?

In *Homo Americanus*, as I've noted numerous times, Croatian savant Tomislav Sunić envisions such a scenario for any group in America that might be targeted: "Thus, in order for the proper functioning of future American-ized society, the removal of millions of surplus citizens must become a social and possibly also an ecological ne-cessity."

Needless to say, this is the dream of the Judaic-minded Fi-nance Capitalists as well: a global economy where the awful dirty workers are safely on the other side of the world, and some day perhaps eliminated altogether in our "virtual econ-omy," leaving them to live in peace in small towns from Jack-son Hole to Davos.

Critics like Peter Lamborn Wilson pointed out long ago that contrary to all the "cyberspace" fluff there is no "virtual" econ-omy, since we need to eat. The question is: how little food is needed? Answer: enough to feed the bosses.

And that's the ultimate appeal of Rev. Jim's Peak-Everything gospel: die-off is so much simpler, so much cleaner, even greener.[13] The ugly, fat, rural "people," who live and even thrive only due to the anomaly of cheap oil, will soon be dead, starved by the lack of Cheesy Poofs after Peak Oil, and if that doesn't get them, Al Gore's Big Sweat will. No need for any messy trains, camps, and ovens. And then the smug, if not meek, will inherit the Earth.

There's an even bigger picture here, extending beyond tele-vision, movies and even the fossil fuel culture; consider this interesting observation from Maury Knudson on the "Shifting Other":

Prior to 1920, the Great Other in American culture was the seducer in the big city. The innocent young girl from

---

[13] http://dieoff.org/

the country would be picked up by the man with oily, slicked-back hair and pencil thin moustache. Or, an innocent young man from the country would find himself in the clutches of a painted lady. Oh, the horrors! This began to change in 1920 because the census revealed more people were living in the city than the country.

By the 1970s we had the movie *Deliverance* which showed the dangers that city folks faced in the rural backwoods. There were inbred mutants laying in wait, ever ready to cornhole you and maybe even bite your pecker off. Oh, the horrors![14]

How did we get from Gomer Pyle, played by Jim Nabors in CBS "rural sitcoms," to "Gomer Pyle" played by Vincent D'Onofrio in *Full Metal Jacket*?

It's Connelly's take on Kunstler that give us the clue: the Judaic dominance of both the liberal Left and the neo-conned Right.

It's as if Mayberry were being fought over by two evil real estate interests. One, the Liberals, want to clean out the locals and replace them with students; here we find Kunstlerville and Stars Hollow and perhaps Zucotti Park. The other, the Right, wants to ship the jobs overseas and drive everyone to the trailer parks outside town, perhaps imprison what's left, and have Trump build luxury condos financed by Wall Street.

What unites both is a more or less unspoken view of "those people" not as The People, salt of the earth—remember when political movements were proud to call themselves "populist"?—but as basically ignorant and potentially dangerous rural yahoos, a bunch of anti-Semites who don't matter anyhow.

No wonder that when Charlie Sheen's *bête noire*, Chuck Lorre, was looking for a way to instantly characterize Charlie's character's potential mother-in-law as far worse than his own mother (a manipulative WASP, of course) he made her a Midwesterner who announces her arrival by complaining about

---

[14] http://mauryk2.wordpress.com/2010/09/19/the-shifting-other-american-hysteria/

spending her flight "sitting next to some big Jew."

The Wall Street Occupiers are the Gilmore Girls, *en masse*, hating Big Money but hating "the people" — you know, the "Tea Party morons" — just as much; the problem with having such refined standards is that it's hard to make a revolution with just a handful of smart-mouthed hipsters as your constituency.

The Occupation-haters share their disdain for the People, though they are willing to be paid to pose as the People's Tribunes; they love the Big Money — the 1% — who pay for their hypocrisy, and since Big Money already calls the shots, they don't need no stinking revolution anyway.

In Godforsaken America, the Old Right's dream of a nation of rooted communities of farmers and small business has been abandoned for Star Wars fantasies of high tech and globalization, and only survives now on the Left, in the distorted form of the Liberal's dream of College Forever.

It was the future Senator Blutarsky who gave us the epitaph for Occupy Wall Street many years ago, in a movie — *Animal House* — that oddly enough seems to evoke both the preciosity of Stars Hollow real estate and the funky chaos of an OWS encampment: "Seven years of college down the drain."

POSTSCRIPT

Readers may be aware that since this was written, the town of Stars Hollow has morphed into Portlandia, the eponymous setting of the "indie" comedy series on IFC. Portland is indeed the next turn of the screw, a Stars Hollow where everyone went to Yale, or at least took some courses in Postmodern Anthropology or Deconstructing Native American Cuisine at the community center.

The vibe from the opening credits is what Greg Johnson has identified as the root of "West Coast White Nationalism"; he notes that Seattle and Portland are the Whitest cities in America; the states of Washington and Oregon are among the Whitest as well. Yet they have preserved, from frontier days, a genuine openness to eccentricity that one doesn't find in the usual Whitopias.

A sign, apparently official, exhorts "Keep Portland Weird," but while we see some crusty old-timers, they seldom if ever show up in the skits; even the Mayor, played by weird-icon Kyle McLaughlin, runs off to join a reggae band.

No old-timers, no tradition-minded Mayor like Stars Hollow's Doosie, and above all, no WASPy adults like Lorelei's parents. Lacking that critical, "outsider" perspective (which the Left, and the Jews, supposedly value so highly), the series never rises to "White Nationalism" but only "Implicit Whiteness." The jokes about homicidally aggressive cyclists and restaurants that offer personal introductions to the animal you will be eating show that, left to its own devices, political correctness will spiral into forms so obnoxious as to become fair game for satire even among the cultural Left; but that same lack of any old-timers or stuffy Establishment figures prevents any sense of an alternative — White but non-PC — from presenting itself.

If Lorelei and Rory ran a bookstore instead of an inn, they might eventually resemble the proprietresses of Women and Women First; but without her parents to politely tut-tut, the series would, like *Portlandia*, lack any historical context. That's why *Portlandia* is a very funny sketch comedy series, and *The Gilmore Girls* is the 21st century equivalent of *The Magnificent Ambersons*, just like Welles would have wanted it: in color, and seven years long.

Counter-Currents/*North American New Right*
November 21, 2011

"GOD, I'M WITH A HEATHEN."
THE REBIRTH OF THE *MÄNNERBUND* IN
BRIAN DE PALMA'S *THE UNTOUCHABLES*

Brian De Palma's 1987 film, from a script by David Mamet, is usually seen as a Hero's Quest film, like *Star Wars* (or *The Final Sacrifice*), or at least an Epic of some sort,[1] but I find it more interesting to see it as a film that, probably unconsciously, delineates the re-creation of the ancient Aryan *Männerbund*.[2]

---

[1] For example, "It isn't ancient Sparta (like *300*), or The Trojan War (as in *Troy*). But make no mistake, De Palma brings to *The Untouchables* the same archetypal flourishes we might reasonably expect in any cinematic depiction of those legends. He transforms real historical figures into larger-than-life scoundrels, saints, and angels. As dramatized by De Palma, *The Untouchables* is nothing less than the Timeless Heroic Poem of Avenger Eliot Ness." See *John Kenneth Muir's Reflections on Film/TV*, Friday, July 31, 2009, at http://tinyurl.com/yf2psv7.

[2] I want to emphasize that these reflections are based on the Brian De Palma film, not the 1950s TV show, the autobiography Ness wrote near his death to make money for his family, or "actual" history, whatever that is. For what it's worth, "the real Al Capone and Eliot Ness never met face-to-face; there were eleven 'Untouchables' who all lived after Prohibition; but most notably, the real Frank Nitti lived several years after Capone's conviction, rather than being thrown off a roof by Ness" (tvtropes.org). Incredibly, though, the most absurd scene (other than the train station shoot-out), namely, the switching of the juries, really did happen. As Aristotle said, art was more true than history, as it narrates what ought to be.

The script is by David Mamet, who here, and in *Glengarry Glen Ross*, shows a most un-Judaic, perhaps unconscious, understanding of male group dynamics.

Finally, it needs to be pointed out that it is emblematic of the misunderstanding, at times perhaps deliberate, of Tradition by Westerners and Westernized Hindus like Gandhi, to portray as "untouchables" the supposedly downtrodden lowest castes. Actually, the Untouchable was the highest caste, the Brahmin. See Alain Daniélou, *The Way to the Labyrinth: Memories of East and West*, trans. Marie-Claire Cournand (New York: New Directions, 1987), p. 137, where he adds "One of the most

WHAT IS THE *MÄNNERBUND*?

Although the study of the *Männerbund* dates to the 19th century, it was Hans Blüher who first championed its significance, using it first to analyze the German youth movement, the Wandervogel, and later as the key to a non-Freudian, indeed, anti-Freudian, understanding of civilization, especially that of the Aryans.[3] Later, Julius Evola would incorporate the idea in his post-war writings on the origin and possibilities for the rebirth of the Aryan State.[4]

Today, the foremost exponent of the *Männerbund* is Wulf Grimsson, who has devoted several volumes to it, most recently

typical characteristics of the European mentality is *the ability to present everything backwards.*"

[3] Hans Blüher, *Wandervogel: Geschichte einer Jugendbewegung* (Berlin-Tempelhof, 1912/23); *Die Rolle der Erotik in der männlichen Gesellschaft: Eine Theorie der Menschlichen Staatsbildung* (Jena, 1917/19). Neither has ever appeared in English, other than a few excerpts, but see Alisdair Clarke's "Hans Blüher and the Wandervogel," a talk from sixth New Right meeting in London, February 2006, available at http://tinyurl.com/24cwn5f.

[4] "It was this *Männerbund*, in which the qualification of 'man' had simultaneously an initiatory (i.e., sacred) and a warrior meaning, that wielded the power in the social group or clan. This *Männerbund* was characterized by special tasks and responsibilities; it was different from all other societies to which members of the tribe belonged. In this primordial scheme we find the fundamental 'categories' differentiating the political order from the 'social' order. First among these is a special chrism—namely, that proper to 'man' in the highest sense of the word (*vir* was the term employed in Roman times) and not merely a generic *homo*: this condition is marked by a spiritual breakthrough and by detachment from the naturalistic and vegetative plane. Its integration is power, the principle of command belonging to the *Männerbund*. We could rightfully see in this one of the 'constants' (i.e., basic ideas) that in very different applications, formulations and derivations are uniformly found in theory or, better, in the metaphysics of the State that was professed even by the greatest civilizations of the past." See Julius Evola, *Men Among the Ruins: Post-War Reflections of a Radical Traditionalist*, ed. Michael Moynihan, trans. Guido Stucco (Rochester, Vt.: Inner Traditions, 2002).

Male Mysteries and the Secret of the Männerbund,[5] where he delineates the idea thus:

> The *Männerbund* is a system of social ties found in tradi-
> tional Indo-European societies which is very difficult for
> men living in a modernist (and/or monotheistic) society to
> understand. . . . Among our Germanic ancestors these
> groups were composed of sexually mature male youths
> who under guidance of an elder formed a closed cult or
> society. They were dedicated to Odin, had special rites of
> pedagogical training, initiation and esoteric practise and
> combined the functions of a sorcerer or shaman and a war-
> rior. To appreciate the importance of such a unit is difficult
> until we realize that the role of the blood brother and the
> *Männerbund* was seen as the foundation of Germanic socie-
> ty with the family unit of far less significance. This changes
> the whole structure of how we see archaic society when we
> realize that these societies held a virile warrior ethic based
> in male-male affection superior to family life.[6]

> The *Männerbund* was a unique social and initiatory institu-
> tion, it stood at the centre of the hierarchy of archaic socie-
> ty offering a path to initiation into the esoteric Mysteries
> and providing stability to the tribe below it. In comparison
> to the Third Function of the tribe and family the *Männer-*
> *bund* was certainly an outsider institution yet it was this
> outsidernesss that allowed it to take such a significant role
> within the traditional hierarchy. It was not swayed by
> nepotism or by tribal or familial pressures; it was a sepa-
> rate, distinct and unique structure. It had a warrior ethic
> yet also trained scribes, shamans, rune masters and many
> others; it combined the First and Second Functions in a
> very special and profound way. . . . The bund was Andro-

---

[5] Available at http://lulu.com/spotlight/lokisway. Grimsson, by the
way, agrees with Aristotle when it comes to dealing with history: truth is
"more often than not in myth legends, traditions and symbols; literal
history needs to be decoded by it, not vice versa" (p. 19).

[6] Grimsson, p. 7.

philic in practice and focused on the unique bond created by blood brothers. These bonds continued even if a comrade left the Bund, the blood brother was the most significant bond even above that of a wife, family or the tribe. A brother would help another even at the cost of his life. The bond created with a blood brother would last till death, and it is considered by many, thereafter.[7]

One important point Grimsson raises is the value of the *Männerbund* to a society, like ours, facing seemingly endless crises:

> [I]t is an immense loss to our way of life that this structure has all but vanished and it may be that such a system of social ties will be the key to surviving the many catastrophes which are around the corner.[8]

One such crisis is the decay of everyday legal order, despite an evermore massively intrusive government, a situation Sam Francis called "anarcho-tyranny." Such a situation might be compared, in a limited way, to America, especially cities like Chicago, under Prohibition. As John Kenneth Muir says:

> Importantly, not one of these men (especially Ness) declares any fealty to the government's (wrongheaded) policy of Prohibition. On the contrary, what this foursome defends to the death is the very principle that makes America great: *the rule of law.* This is the meat of Ness's inner crisis: *can the rule of law be re-established by violating the law?*[9]

As Carl Schmitt emphasized, the political is defined by the exception; he is sovereign who can in an emergency declare an exception to the rule of law —*and get away with it.* However much it may offend the delicate sensibilities of the Liberal, not everything is subject to debate and proper procedure. If it is the law itself that no longer works, how can it be restored *legally*? No

---

[7] Grimsson, p. 89.

[8] Grimsson, p. 7.

[9] http://tinyurl.com/yf2psv7

wonder the Tea Party's costumes freak them out.

Indeed, as Evola emphasizes, only the *Männerbund* can do so, because it is not only outside the State, as it is outside the family structure, but also prior to it, being the true origin of the State itself.

BEWARE OF IMITATIONS

Since the *Männerbund* is not a typical subject of "mainstream" discourse, most people are unaware of it, and thus susceptible to fraudulent substitutes. *The Untouchables* begins with the most flagrant one, the Capone mob.

Far from either creating or restoring the State, the mob is responsible for the collapse of Chicago into violence and anarchy. In real life, Chicago had been horrified by the brutality of the St. Valentine's Day Massacre, which is what led to Ness' assignment, but Mamet wisely ignores this overdone episode and starts the film with a little girl, holding a suitcase which explodes, blowing her to bits along with a non-cooperating pub. As Frankie Five Angels sneers in *The Godfather: Part II*, "They do violence in their grandmother's neighborhood."

And speaking of *The Godfather: Part II*, the next shot gives us Robert De Niro, playing a very different character than that man of honor, Don Corleone ("I mean, we're not murderers, in spite of what this undertaker thinks"). Instead, we have a well-fed hypocrite:

> **Capone**: Yes! There is violence in Chicago. But not by me, and not by anybody who works for me, and I'll tell you why—because it's bad for business.

The only truth in that statement is that Capone is a businessman. In Chicago, the castes have regressed, and now the *sudra* rules. Capone's mob (note the word!) is neither a State nor a *Männerbund*, but, in another loaded phrase, a "criminal enterprise," which is to say an enterprise, a business, which no longer operates under society's laws. In contemporary terms, one might cite Wall Street in general, especially the gigantic frauds and outright thefts (MF Global) that have gone entirely uninvestigated, to say nothing of punished. Who indeed is sovereign?

Contrary to the "free market" myth, from Adam Smith to Ayn Rand to Alan Greenspan, business transactions are not a "natural" activity, prior to, and superior to, the State. As seen most recently in the ex-Soviet Union, the collapse of the State does not produce a peaceful society of "capitalist acts between consenting adults" but a gangster's paradise.[10]

Later in the film, we'll get a chance to see Capone discoursing on "teamwork" only to wind-up by bashing in a gang member's skull with a baseball bat. Like Captain Ahab, Capone uses the rhetoric of Traditional honor and leadership, but despite his "charisma" and "romantic aura" he is

> . . . not just some fine old warrior-aristocrat who has somehow fallen into the wrong age. Ahab is just such a man as nineteenth-century America was producing, a man who could and did ruthlessly exploit the land and the people for his own grandiose, self-aggrandizing ends.[11]

We next meet his presumed nemesis, Elliot Ness, with his wife and children. Well, we know that the family unit isn't going to be the source of a *Männerbund*. But when he goes to work, carrying the lunch he wife has made for him, we learn that the Chicago Police aren't either. They've been corrupted, penetrated, as it were, by Capone. His first ridiculously earnest raid — "Let's do

---

[10] One could argue, in another essay, that the particular law, Prohibition, was itself responsible for the breakdown in respect for the Law as such, as well as providing the *entrée* for Capone. In this way, Prohibition is a synecdoche for the Judeo-Christianity which brought about the regression of the castes, or degeneration of the functions, by demonizing the *Männerbund* (Judaism's well-known and unique "homophobia"). See Grimsson, ch. 6. In addition, not only did ordinary citizens learn to fraternize with criminals, they also became accustomed to hobnobbing with Jews, the financier and businessman *par excellence*, and even welcoming them into their homes. Once more, the small town Protestants, in their war against big city immigrants, shot themselves in the foot.

[11] Tony Tanner, "Introduction" to the Oxford World Classics edition of *Moby Dick* (Oxford: Oxford University Press, 1998), p. xix.

some good!"—is an embarrassing "bust out," netting him only a shipment of Japanese parasols, and a nickname in the press: "Poor Butterfly." (Even the press is on Capone's side—during the raid Ness mistakes a reporter for a gangster.)

Ness learns he is not cast as a Hero, this time, but a clown— perhaps Canio in *Pagliacci*, a bit of which we see Capone enjoying later in the movie—or even a forlorn geisha. He started the day as a little boy; he ends it completely emasculated.

As Jack Donovan says in *The Way of Men*, while Ness is a "good man," but he's not so "good at being a man."[12] Despite his empty boast, he doesn't know how to "do some good." To learn how to be good at being a man, Ness will obviously need a teacher; but as we have seen, the primary method of initiation in the West has been not the teacher as such, but the *Männerbund*,[13] which also, conveniently, has been the primary means of establishing, and re-establishing, the State.

Ness won't surrender to, and certainly won't join, Capone; he won't go along with the corrupt cops or politicians, or curry favor with the press. To beat them, he can't join them; he needs to find another group, or create his own.

FROM SACK LUNCH TO BLOOD OATH

"The first and most important feature of groups is the fact that groups are not constituted according to the wish and choice of their members. Groups are constituted by the teacher, who selects types which, from the point of view of his aims, can be useful to one another."

—Gurdjieff[14]

---

[12] Jack Donovan, *The Way of Men* (Portland, Or.: Dissonant Hum, 2012).

[13] ". . . the point is that a 'group' is the beginning of everything. One man can do nothing, can attain nothing. A group with a real leader can do more. A group of people can do what one man can never do." G. I. Gurdjieff, quoted in by P. D. Ouspensky's *In Search of the Miraculous: Fragments of an Unknown Teaching* (New York: Harcourt, 1949), p. 30.

[14] *In Search of the Miraculous*, p. 222.

Enter the last honest cop, Jimmy Malone (Sean Connery) who will become the teacher who selects the men who will become known as *The Untouchables*. Malone is so honest that he's never risen above beat cop. It's not clear why Ness trusts Malone to be the last honest cop in Chicago. Connery's bogus "Irish" accent alone might set bells off.[15]

As we shall see, however, Connery's character will indeed manifest a shamanic ability to shape-shift. One more clue *we* have that Malone is on the up and up is that they meet *on a bridge*.

> The sorcerer and warrior are always liminal, while they may enter into the community their values and allegiances set them apart. Sorcerers, shamans and witches in most traditions are often pictured as living at the edge of the village or in forests or caves.[16]

Malone will eventually agree to teach Ness "the Way," in this case, "the Chicago Way," which is a kind of karma-yoga in which appropriate, or *svadharmic*, action is all:

> **Malone**: You wanna get Capone? Here's how you get him. He pulls a knife, you pull a gun. He sends one of yours to the hospital, you send one of his to the morgue!

Malone starts with the first of many tricks and inversions of society's norms, in this case, both inverting Ness' oath of duty and tricking him into affirming a new one:

> **Malone**: I'm making you a deal. Do you want this deal?

(Unlike Ness' wife, who only *made him a meal*, the characteristic

---

[15] While Connery won his only Oscar for the role, his performance has been voted "Worst Movie Accent of All Time" in several surveys over the years; in 2009, his runner up was co-star Kevin Costner, for *Robin Hood: Prince of Thieves*. See http://tinyurl.com/boy79nv

[16] Grimsson, p. 65.

family activity.)

> **Ness**: I have sworn to put this man away with any and all legal means at my disposal, and I will do so.
> **Malone**: Well, the Lord hates a coward. Do you know what a blood oath is, Mr. Ness?
> **Ness**: Yes.
> **Malone**: Good. 'Cause you just took one.

At the trial, Ness admits he has "foresworn" himself by eventually being led to choose to hunt Capone with Capone's own methods, not the State's.

Now Malone begins to put together the warrior band. But who can they trust in the department?

> **Malone**: If you're afraid of getting a rotten apple, don't go to the barrel. Get it off the tree.

The allusion to the Garden of Eden is clear, although we will see that it is Malone's double, Frank Nitti, who embodies reptilian evil.

> The . . . leader [of] any *Männerbund* must take great care when selecting comrades and develop a preinitiation training program which will weed out those unsuited or unwilling to commit. Such programs should not only be intellectual but include "homework" to prove dedication and "challenges" would-be comrades should overcome. . . . It should be made very clear to any potential comrades the nature of the commitment, that a *Männerbund* is an Androphilic organization and that no outside relationships are permitted.[17]

First, though, Ness makes his own demand: no married men, even though, as Malone quickly points out, Ness is himself married. Ness doesn't seem to have quite figured out what will be

---

[17] Grimsson, p. 79.

required of him. When Nitti threatens them with the ironic "It's nice to have a family," Ness ships them off the countryside.[18]

> Thor curses Starkadr telling him that if undertakes Odin's requests he will have no children, no individual land or property and be despised by the common folk.[19]

Malone rejects with contempt a recruit who recites the police motto, then insults and strikes another, whose violent but controlled response passes the tests.

> **Malone**: Why do you want to join the force?
>
> **George Stone**: "To protect the property and citizenry of . . ."
>
> **Malone**: Ah, don't waste my time with that bullshit. Where you from, Stone?
>
> **George Stone**: I'm from the south side.
>
> **Malone**: Stone. George Stone. That's your name? What's your real name?
>
> **George Stone**: That is my real name.
>
> **Malone**: Nah. What was it before you changed it?
>
> **George Stone**: Giuseppe Petri.
>
> **Malone**: Ah, I knew it. That's all you need, one thieving wop on the team.
>
> **George Stone**: Hey, what's that you say?
>
> **Malone**: I said that you're a lying member of a no good race. [He cuffs Stone across the face. As he draws back his arm again, Stone presses a gun under his chin]
>
> **George Stone**: Much better than you, you stinking Irish pig.

---

[18] Interestingly, the real Capone was married, like the standard Mafia "family man," but in the movie we see no women anywhere around him or his mob, and Capone lives in sybaritic splendor in a swank hotel suite. Malone also lives alone, but in a rundown apartment; also like Capone, he listens to opera, but on a gramophone, not at a meet-and-greet with Caruso. Unlike Capone, or Ness, he cooks for himself, and even serves Ness tea; all somewhat unmanly traits by the social standards of the time, but right at home in the world of the *Männerbund*.

[19] Grimsson, pp. 90–91.

Malone: Oh, I like him.

This is the first racial note in the movie. Obviously there are no Blacks on the force, but the "racial" antagonisms are there nonetheless. Between Ness, Malone (with Connery's confusing Irish-Scot accent), and "Stone" (another blurry shape-shifter) we seem to have an early attempt at what Greg Johnson has suggested:

> What is emerging is a generic white American, with a sense of his interests merely as a white. . . . America may be the place where we recreate the original unity of the white race before it was divided and pitted against itself.[20]

Ironically, these men are joining together to enforce Prohibition, which was largely the attempt of small town WASPs (like Ness, whose family is now hiding out in the countryside) to "control" the "thieving wops" and "stinking Irish pigs" of the big cities.

Finally, Ness has already been assigned Wallace, a meek little accountant from Treasury. Physically and professionally, he seems to be the Designated Jew, but nothing is ever made explicit, and so for our purposes we can treat him as White. Ness is still living in ignorance, and does not yet appreciate the value of Wallace, both as man, and as the key to the capture of Capone.

Wallace epitomizes the role of the geek or nerd, as Jack Donovan describes it:

> Advanced levels of mastery and technics allow men to compete for improved status within the group by bringing more to the camp, hunt or fight than their bodies would otherwise allow. Mastery can be supplementary—a man who can build, hunt and fight, but who can also do something else well, be it telling jokes or setting traps or making blades, is worth more to the group and is likely to have a

---

[20] Greg Johnson, *Confessions of a Reluctant Hater* (San Francisco: Counter-Currents, 2010), pp. 12–13.

higher status within the group than a man who can merely
build, hunt and fight well. Mastery can also be a compen-
satory virtue, in the sense that a weaker or less courageous
man can earn the esteem of his peers by providing something else of great value. It could well have been a runt
who tamed fire or invented the crossbow or played the
first music, and such a man would have earned the respect
and admiration of his peers. Homer was a blind man, but
his words have been valued by men for thousands of
years.[21]

Or put away Capone by decoding his secret account books.

> **Ness**: We need another man.
> **Wallace**: Mr. Ness? This is very interesting. I've found a
> financial disbursement pattern which shows some irre-
> gu . . .
> **Malone**: You carry a badge?
> **Wallace**: Yes.
> **Malone**: Carry a gun.

There are, then, four Untouchables. The number four is:

> [A] code for its related letter in the Elder Futhark which is
> Ansuz. Traditionally Ansuz is related to Odin but reversed
> is related to the trickster Loki so the correlation seems cor-
> rect. The rune also means the Aesir in general and hence
> the use of this rune emphasizes that Loki has left the
> community of the gods and become a true spiritual out-
> law. Ansuz is related . . . to Venus. In the community Ve-
> nus or love holds the family together while in the *Männer-
> bund* Venus is androphile and focused on individual im-
> mortality through sorcery.[22]

---

[21] Donovan, *The Way of Men*, ch. 2.
[22] Grimsson, p. 95.

Initiation I:
"Outsidering" — "Hey. This is the Post Office . . ."

"The first rites of Initiation are those which help the comrade consolidate his rejection of the functions of the society around him."[23]

"As shamans and sorcerers they must move beyond the tribe and become separate from the rules and regulations of the community. Essentially they become spiritual and social outlaws."

—Wulf Grimsson[24]

Malone: There's nothing like vaudeville.
Police Chief: What the hell are you dressed for? Hallowe'en?
Malone: Shut up. I'm working.
Police Chief: Where? The circus?

Malone has shape-shifted into civilian garb, but still uses his beat cop knowledge to strip the mask off another public institution: behind the façade, literally, of the Post Office is one of Capone's warehouses.

This is the turning point in Ness' career, and the movie, with Morricone's soaring theme music underlining it for us. So does the dialog and action, which pound away at the liminal theme: crossing the street, crossing Capone, crossing the doorway.

Malone: Everybody knows where the booze is. The problem isn't finding it. The problem is who wants to cross Capone. Let's go.
Ness: You'd better be damn sure, Malone.
Malone: If you walk through this door, you're walking into a world of trouble. There's no turning back. Do you understand?
Ness: Yes, I do.

---

[23] Grimsson, p. 90.
[24] Grimsson, p. 93.

Malone: Good. Give me that axe.

The axe, of course, is a traditional symbol of male power, as well as the root of the fasces symbol.

After making his violent and uninvited entrance, Malone is confronted by a portly thug, or postal worker — once more, ambiguity — who demands his "rights."

> **Portly Thug**: Hey! This isn't *right!* Hey! This is no *good!* You got a *warrant?*
> **Malone**: Sure! Here's my warrant. [Delivers the stock of his shotgun to the thug's crotch]
> **Malone**: How do you think he feels now? Better . . . or worse?

Malone delivers butt to crotch, the warrior band's deviant inversion of sodomy, making quite clear that they have gone beyond concern for rights, warrants, and the social good.

Here is the scene, seen, as it were, through Grimsson's lens:

> When I look at the tale I see an initiatory rite, a ritual whereby Loki is becoming a sorcerer. He is ceremonially rejecting his role among the Gods and the tribe [the cops] and becoming a spiritual outlaw. *It begins as Loki is refused entry to the feast.* This is unusual as *Loki as a member of the Aesir would have been invited to such an event even if he sometimes behaves erratically* [Malone as a cop would ordinarily be "in on" the crimes, but he is the one honest cop, whose goody-goody ways are joked about].
>
> He then kills Fimafeng, the name Fimafeng means *service* [the Postal Service?] *and he represents the normal activities of a community such as serving, working and feasting.* By Loki killing Fimafeng he is making it clear *he is going beyond his prior role within the Aesir and within the society.*
>
> He enters the hall but Bragi says he is unwelcome. Bragi is the god of poetry and the storyteller of the community [The Post Office?].
>
> *Loki's insults are staged* and meant to symbolise him sep-

arating from each of the Gods and their functions.[25]

INITIATION II:
THE WORLD TREE — "MANY THINGS ARE HALF THE BATTLE"

"As the initiate moved through the bund other rites were used including the *initiation of the world tree* which was a form of *northern vision quest* giving the initiate an experience of *the power of the runes*. I believe that the *Männerbund* was also secretly devoted to Loki as Odin's blood brother and darker rites were used in his honour. These rites included those of *shape changing* and the *techniques of the Berserker*."

— Wulf Grimsson[26]

Ness has sworn a blood oath, joined a *Männerbund*, and crossed the threshold. Now he and the others face further initiations to acquire further powers — shape-shifting, reading the runes, and the fighting skills of the Berserker.

After the successful raid, Ness decides to take the battle to Capone, *heading North* in an airplane — at time when such flights were rare among ordinary folk, though a common achievement for the shaman — to the Canadian *border* where a shipment of whisky (from Joe Seagram to Joe Kennedy, perhaps) is scheduled to be exchanged for cash *on a bridge*.

Not just a bridge but a border; obviously we are meant to understand this is another, more intense, liminal situation.

> **Mountie**: Thus taking them by surprise *from the rear*. And surprise, as you very well know, Mr. Ness, is half the battle.
> **Ness**: Surprise is half the battle. Many things are half the battle. Losing is half the battle. Let's think about what is all the battle.

The Mounties riding in is a film and cultural icon. Here, how-

---

25 Grimsson, p. 94.
26 Grimsson, p. 36.

ever, they seem to have forgotten their motto, "We always get our man" and become symbols of careful, bureaucratic procedure, like Canada itself. They are another false *Männerbund*, mere agents of the State. They're not corrupt, like the Chicago cops, but they're not helpful either. Their pudgy "captain" (as Ness mistakenly calls him, as if he were a cop) hands out safe and complacent orders (attack from the rear, for surprise), settling for a safe second best, which Ness rejects with some quiet contempt, preferring to be instructed by his guru:

> **Malone**: Wait and watch.
> **Ness**: Are you my tutor?
> **Malone**: Yes sir. That I am. [YHVH?]

"Many things" indeed happen in this complex scene, and most of them, I suggest, involve either the acquisition or demonstration of shamanic powers.

> This suffering was part of a birth, death and rebirth motif but without the role of the biological female, the male is reborn through the agency of men alone and hence becomes part of a new "family" structure which is of a single sex.[27]

The bureaucratic Mounties' safe and secret strategy goes awry, creating chaos (from behind, *au rebours* indeed) in which the men are tested.

> Since belonging to Odin means becoming a comrade of the Einherjar (or Odin's Army), this means the comrade can be taken to Valhalla at any time, and he is considered already dead or literally dead among the living, regardless of whether he literally dies in battle or not.[28]

> This condition also creates a unique psychological state for the warrior preparing him for Berserker training, if he is

---

[27] Grimsson, p. 90.
[28] Grimsson, p. 97.

already undead and eternally in Odin's service then pain and death are minor transitionary stages and nothing to be feared.[29]

Stone is the first and as yet only one of the Untouchables to be shot, thus pierced, but quickly jumps back up; he is either invulnerable, a trickster, or already dead and hence fearless.

The candidate is first given a basic education in ethics and the teachings of the lore. He then withdraws from the community and fasts and undertakes ascetic activities including being pierced with a spear.[30]

Stone, however, is down long enough to literally infuriate the meek Wallace, who acquires the spirit of the Berserker; shrieking in rage, he rushes the gangsters like Achilles avenging Patroclus, killing several and, when out of shells, resorts to what is now the signature Untouchables method, using the butt of the shotgun to dispatch the last thug.

Ness escapes being run over by diving under the car, a symbolic death, and then, trailing a gangster back to their cabin, himself kills his first man.

Finally, Malone, the Trickster, will use the dead man to fool the captured bookkeeper into agreeing to decode the account books. Only he and Ness know the man on the porch is the one Ness killed earlier; Malone goes outside, picks him up, holds him against the window, pretends to threaten him, sticks his gun in the corpse's mouth, and blows out the back of his head. The Canadian is horrified by all this violence.

Finding the code has been their ultimate goal, not just stopping a shipment of whiskey. In other words, *interpreting the runes*. The corpse, pushed up against the window and pinned their by Malone's pistol, may suggest Odin's self-hanging to acquire the knowledge of the runes.

---

[29] Grimsson, p. 98.
[30] Grimsson, p. 101.

Malone: *Translate* this ledger for us!
Thug: In hell.
Malone: In hell?! *You will hang high* unless you cooperate.

And we can also go back to a bit of comic relief, when Wallace, after his Berserk outburst, and to solidify his Outlaw status, helps himself to some of the booze leaking from the truck. The use of socially forbidden intoxicants is a well-known Shamanic, and Tantric, technique; one also may recall Siegfried who drinks the blood of the slain dragon and acquires understanding of the language of the birds.[31]

SACRIFICES

As a result of Malone's capture of Capone's books—and trick with the corpse having convinced the bookkeeper to talk—Wallace can now prove Capone's tax evasion. Unfortunately, Nitti manages to kill all three, leaving Ness without his sole witness. Once more, Ness is unmanned.

Capone: And *if you were a man*, you would've done it now!
You don't got a thing, you *punk*!

Since none of the "real" Untouchables was killed, it's hard to see why De Palma kills off half of them. Wallace's death is particularly unmotivated; in the language of Internet movie discussions, they all seem to have the Stupid Ball at this point—ironic, since Wallace is presumably the smart guy. It may be just cinematic: create conflict, pare down the cast to focus on Ness, etc. Or what?

---

[31] Discussing this "Language of the Birds," René Guénon recalls that in the Gospels the "birds of the air" that settle in the branches of the tree that grows from the mustard seed of faith, represent angels in various levels of the spiritual hierarchy, the tree itself being the World Tree which links all the levels, bringing us back to Odin's hanging, the bridge at the border, which like the tree is a means of changing states, and even the airplane flight with which the sequence opens. See *The Sword of Gnosis: Metaphysics, Cosmology, Tradition, Symbolism*, ed. by Jacob Needleman (New York: Penguin, 1988), pp. 299–300.

The Untouchables has been a fairly "PG" film up to this point: no ears cut off, no gangsters being carved up in trunks, no exploding heads, the obsession with which Scorsese seems to be satirizing at the end of *The Departed* (which also involves a main character killed in an elevator by a rogue cop). Starting with Malone's shooting the corpse in Canada, blood starts to flow; in Malone's case, ridiculous amounts, as befitting the importance of his character.[32]

The only sense I can make out of them is that both deaths are sacrifices, part of some kind of ritual. Wallace, having already made his point about Capone's tax liabilities, is expendable. Malone's death seems to be some kind of payback or "boomerang" from the etheric realm for his corpse shooting stunt.[33]

Thus we don't have to rack it up to stupidity. When Nitti fools Malone with the decoy killer (few people who quote it remember that Malone's "Just like a wop, bringing a knife to a gunfight" line is followed by his being cut apart by a machine gun) it's psychic payback for the corpse stunt. Malone, like the corpse, is already dead anyway ("It's a dead man talking to me" said the corrupt cop earlier), and as Grimsson emphasizes, the whole point of being initiated into the warrior band is to be already dead, hence able to fight fearlessly.[34]

---

[32] Malone's literally operatic death has been mocked endlessly; even Connery refused to do more than two takes, saying it epitomized "everything he hates about moviemaking." See
http://www.moviedeaths.com/untouchables,_the/jim_malone/

[33] Baron Evola observed that the Magus, despite his powers, may appear poor, downtrodden, or even in danger of death or injury in this realm, precisely because of his achievements in the higher realms, due to the law of cosmic compensation.

[34] Nitti is the shape-shifting Malone's own double. He's dressed entirely in white, which is a nice flipping of conventions, like Henry Fonda's blue-eyed killer, also named Frank, in Sergio Leone's *Once Upon a Time in America*, also scored by Morricone. It works nicely cinematically, as his stark white figure is seen yet barely registered on the edges of his crimes, but not so well against the blue screen in his fall. As played by B-movie favorite Billy Drago, he takes the womanless Capone gang over the edge into effeminacy, although perhaps he's just European.

If Nitti is Malone's twin, then he seems to play the role of Lo-ki to Malone's Wotan, in accordance with Grimsson's suggestion that the *Männerbünde* were led by Wotan but had more secret rites associated with Loki. Nitti's gender-ambiguity, sudden or subliminal appearances around crimes, and above all his fooling Malone with the decoy assassin (cleverly inverting Malone's gun vs. knife with shotgun vs. tommy gun) suggest Loki's shape-shifting, while his Loki-like boasting about Malone's death will lead to his own demise, and Ness's triumph.

Malone's death, then, is a self-sacrifice, and just as Wotan's sacrifice leads to knowledge of the runes, both of these deaths are related to communication in some way, an appropriate role for the dead.

Nitti has *hung* Wallace's body in the elevator, suggesting one of the odd ways Loki would "assist" Wotan, and used his blood to smear the message "touchable" on the elevator wall, remind-ing Ness of his mortality. Malone, despite losing about 90% of his blood, is still able to gasp out the train information, but more importantly, he inspires Ness; first, when Ness discovers him and Malone asks, "What are you prepared to do?" and later, when Nitti makes the mistake of mocking his ridiculously bloody death, leading us to see just where Ness in fact is pre-pared to go. Like Obi-Wan, Malone is even able to inspire Ness after what we would call "death."

The Train Station sequence, while the final bravura set piece, is really quite dispensable. De Palma added it to Mamet's script,[35] perhaps to show Ness is still capable of defending

---

(Later he'll play the call-boy that ruins Steven Lang's life in that mon-ument to despair, *Last Exit to Brooklyn*.) When a bailiff puts a hand on his shoulder, he shakes it off with the haughty annoyance of a drag queen dismissing an unwanted bar patron. He suggests both the femi-nine and the reptilian, and thus the snake in the Garden, thus forbid-den knowledge, and ultimately his own Fall. He is the Evil Tutor to the Evil *Männerbund*, just as the real Frank Nitti was not a killer but more of a *consigliore*. (While red-haired Tom Hagen was always shown as a family man, in accordance with the Don's views, the balding actor, Robert Duvall, suggests a kind of James Carville snakiness.)

[35] "That cockamamie baby carriage"; see Ben Kenber, "David Mam-

"family values" despite his increasingly outlaw status,[36] or to reinforce our memory of the child's death at the beginning, as well as the threats to Ness' family; or just as an homage to Eisenstein.

THE LAW ON TRIAL: "YOUR HONOR, IS THIS JUSTICE?"

Using the knowledge provided by Wallace and Malone, Ness is able to bring Capone to trial, but perhaps not to justice; the judicial system is as corrupt as the police.

Nitti seems to have the stupid ball now; in other words, some kind of karmic payback for his previous cleverness. First, he stupidly lets Ness spot his gun in the courtroom (even Ness mumbles an incredulous "Unbelievable"), which gives him a perfectly good excuse to have him removed and searched, which yields the list of bribed jurors. Then, Nitti hands over a matchbook that links him to Malone's death. (What? Has he been carrying it around for weeks?) Panicking, Nitti steals a gun, shoots a cop, and makes his escape up the stairs to the roof. (Has this ever worked out in movies?)

After failing to escape from the roof by—stupidly—climbing down the ivy-covered building (another Eden connection), Ness captures Nitti by successfully executing the same trick, using his superior shamanic powers of deathlessness and shape-shifting. He rolls over the edge of the building, and when Nitti—stupidly—ambles over to check out the corpse, Ness, in corpse pose, has the drop on him.

Ness seems willing to let the system take over at this point, but in a final Act of Stupid, Nitti decides have a little Loki-like laugh about Malone's death:

---

et Talks About *The Untouchables* on Tax Day," *Yahoo Voices*: http://voices.yahoo.com/david-mamet-talks-untouchables-5905806.html?cat=2

[36] "Ness collects a small bunch of would-be vigilante cops (vigilante in the sense that since the rest of the force is corruptly suckling on the teat of organized crime payouts, their righteousness could be considered transgressive)"—Eric Henderson on Oct. 4, 2004 http://www.slantmagazine.com/dvd/review/the-untouchables/463

Nitti: I said that your friend died screaming like a stuck Irish pig. Now you think about that while I beat the rap. [Nitti is now doubling Stone, who called Malone "a stinking Irish pig."]

Which causes Ness to revert to full Berserker mode, frog-marching Nitti right off the roof, and shape-shifting him into Malone:

Nitti: [Screaming as he falls to his death]
Ness: Did he sound like that?

As he falls, Nitti not only shrieks like a little girl, he flaps his arms wildly, as if trying to transform into a white bird against the bright blue sky (or blue screen), but his shamanic powers to fly or shape-shift have been misplaced along with his wisdom.

It's conceivable that Malone's death was an elaborate scheme to not only lead Ness to Nitti but insure he would be enraged enough to kill him outright. As Grimsson has pointed out, the member of Odin's band, the initiate, is already dead, and so does not fear death.

From the alchemical thriller, *Red Dragon*:

Dr. Frederick Chilton: You caught him. What was your trick?
Will Graham: I let him kill me.

Now Ness has to finish with Capone. Knowing about the bribed jurors, Ness the Trickster bluffs the judge into thinking Ness knows his name is in Capone's coded ledger, and the judge responds by executing the largest shape-shifting yet:

Judge: Bailiff, I want you to go next door to Judge Hawton's court, where they've just begun hearing a divorce action. I want you to bring that jury in here, and take this jury to his court. Bailiff, are those instructions clear?
Bailiff: [*puzzled*] Yes, sir, they're . . . clear . . .
Capone: [*to his attorney*] What's he talking about? What is it?

Judge: Bailiff, *I want you to switch the juries.*
Bailiff: Yes sir.
Defense Attorney: Your honor, I object!
Judge: Overruled!

Remember, Capone is in a civil court, for tax evasion, not murder, but now he will face a family court jury, since in the film's terms he is guilty of the child's death at the beginning, whose mother asked Ness for justice.

Capone's attorney reacts by *switching his plea* to guilty (unlike the jury switching, not really a possible defense motion at this point, but whatever; this is a philosophical fiction), and, as the cliché has it, the courtroom "explodes."

Ness has achieved his shamanic purpose: he and his androphilic band has inverted reality, ripping the façade off society, and even turned back time. We are back at the beginning of the movie. The elite courtroom of false justice explodes, not the bar full of honest working people. Frank Nitti has exploded into a pile of bloody flesh in the back of a car, not the little girl who found his bomb in the bar. Capone, who we first met telling us that there was no violence in Chicago, at least "not by me," is now swinging punches wildly, like a common juvenile delinquent.

Capone: I'm askin', your honor, is this justice?

Better he should ask the child's mother, or Ness' family in hiding.

"HERE ENDETH THE LESSON."

In the aftermath, Ness is cleaning out his office and finds Malone's call box key, with its religious medal, St. Jude, patron saint of police and lost causes ("God, I'm with a heathen" Malone had said when having to explain it to Ness). Ness gives it to Stone: "He'd wanted a cop to have it." Apparently, while Ness is moving on, back with his family (choosing The Path of the Ancestors), Stone will remain.

Here we uncover a final *Männerbund*: the Twelve Disciples (there were eleven Untouchables in reality, the twelve minus Judas). Stone, born Giuseppe Petri, has received the key(s), and upon this rock a new, uncorrupt police force and cleansed society will be built, safe for Ness and his family to return.[37]

We've learned that the *Männerbund* is not an archaic, literally primitive feature of Aryan culture in a dead past, as the Christians and secular "Progressives" would have us believe (conveniently for them) but an eternal principle, which can always and anywhere be re-accessed and re-created when needed. As Krishna said, in a verse frequently quoted by Savitri Devi:

> *yada yada hi dharmasya*
> *glanir bhavati bharata*
> *abhyutthanam adharmasya*
> *tadatmanam srjamy aham*

Whenever there is decline of righteousness
and rise of unrighteousness;
To protect the virtuous, to destroy the wicked and
to re-establish Dharma,
I manifest myself, through the ages.[38]

Counter-Currents/*North American New Right*
April 11, 2012

---

[37] If assimilating the Apostles to the warrior band seems forced, it is, like the switched juries, absurdly real. Christianity was presented to the Germanic tribes in the form of a revamped gospel story, the *Heliand*, in which Jesus leads his warriors on raids between Fort Rome and Fort Jerusalem. See G. Ronald Murphy, S.J., *The Saxon Savior: The Germanic Transformation of the Gospel in the Ninth-Century Heliand* (New York: Oxford University Press, 1995) and James C. Russell, *The Germanization of Early Medieval Christianity: A Sociohistorical Approach to Religious Transformation* (New York: Oxford University Press, 1996).

[38] *Bhagavad-Gita*, Chapter 4, Verse 7.

Of Costner, Corpses, & Conception:
Mother's Day Meditations on
The Untouchables & The Big Chill

Okay, I missed Mother's Day, but hey, every day's a holiday for the unemployed! So, in the holiday spirit, I offer some Second Thoughts on a couple of films recently discussed here.

Malone's Death

Readers of my essay on *The Untouchables* as an initiatic work will recall that I was somewhat puzzled by the reasons for Malone's death. I speculated that he had sacrificed himself, rather like Odin, to further Ness's initiatory journey.

I was recently re-reading an essay by "Abraxas" (Ercole Quadrelli) collected by Baron Evola in the first volume of his *Introduction to Magic*, viz. "Three Ways."

> You must generate—first by imagining and then by realizing it—a superior principle confronting everything you usually are (e.g., an instinctive life, thoughts, feelings). This principle must be able to control, contemplate, and measure what you are, in a clear knowledge, moment by moment. *There will be two of you: yourself standing before "the other."* Then you will know the meaning of "inner dialogues," the inward commanding and obeying, the inward asking for and obtaining of advice, as in the case of many Christian and Muslim mystics, and similarly reflected in many Hindu texts that were compiled in dialogue form; the characters depicted in them are not real persons, but are seen by a skilled disciple as two parts of his own soul.
>
> All in all, *the work consists of a "reversal": you have to turn the "other" into "me" and the "me" into the "other."*[1]

---

[1] Abraxas, "Three Ways," in Julius Evola and the Ur Group, *Intro-*

Then, in contrast to the mystical, or Christian, path, where the Other remains Other, and the Self remains in the feminine position of need and desire:

> In the magical, dry, or solar way, you will create a duality in your being not in an unconscious and passive manner (as the mystic does), but consciously and willingly; you will shift directly on the higher part and *identify yourself with that superior and subsistent principle*, whereas the mystic tends to identify with his lower part, in a relationship of need and of abandonment. Slowly but gradually, you will strengthen *this "other" (which is yourself)* and create for it a supremacy, until it knows how to dominate all the powers of the natural part and master them totally.[2]

Then, "the entire being, ready and compliant, *reaffirms itself, digests and lets itself be digested, leaving nothing behind.*"[3]

In short, as the New Agers like to say, if you meet the Buddha on the road, kill him.

If Malone is a projection of Ness, embodying what Ness knows about being a man, but manifested as an external being able to function as a teacher and then dismissed (like Tyler Durden in *Fight Club*), this would not only be consistent with the shape-shifting and other shamanic attributes of Malone, but also explain most of the oddities I called attention to. How do they just happen to meet on a bridge at Ness's point of greatest need? If, as Malone himself says, the whole police force is corrupt, why does Ness trust Malone himself?

And above all, why does Malone, an Irish cop, speak in a

---

duction to Magic: Rituals and Practical Techniques for the Magus, ed. Michael Moynihan, trans. Guido Stucco (Rochester, Vt.: Inner Traditions, 2001), p. 48. The process of "cultivating" the Other as part of the process of initiation is referenced in *The Silence of the Lambs*, where Buffalo Bill cultivates a rare species of moth: "Somebody grew this guy, fed him honey and nightshade, kept him warm. Somebody loved him."

[2] Abraxas, pp. 50–51.
[3] Abraxas, p. 51.

quasi-Scottish brogue? Because Ness, the *ur*-Norwegian Midwesterner, has probably never heard a real Irishman; Ness has just arrived in Chicago; talkies were only recently invented; even Cagney's *The Public Enemy* won't be released until after he leaves in 1931.

SHE'S HAVING MY BABY

Speaking of Kevin Costner playing dead, I also failed to point out that Costner made his big screen debut playing a corpse. This was in *The Big Chill*, where the opening credits play over a body being dressed for viewing. According to the commentary track by the writer-director, Lawrence Kasdan,[4] Costner was to portray Alex, the erstwhile leader of the gang back at the U. of M. whose suicide brings them back together for the funeral. These flashbacks were the first scenes shot — the whole film was made in chronological order for effect — but Kasdan decided to scrap them and only deal with present time. As a sop, Costner was given the unaccredited role of Alex's corpse.

Kasdan' commentary goes on to state that audiences were supposed to be fooled, thinking that a woman was dressing a man for a formal event, perhaps Glenn Close and Kevin Kline, as just seen in the previous sequence, and then the last shot was a "reveal" of the sutured wrist of the corpse. Perhaps I had seen a review beforehand, but I don't recall ever being fooled that way, always taking it to be Alex's corpse. On Kasdan's interpretation, though, we have another layer: not only is (real) Costner playing a (fake) corpse, but the (fake) corpse is playing a (fake) Costner.

Readers will also recall that I previously discussed, briefly,

---

[4] Kasdan was one of the most bankable men in Hollywood, and thus able to make this more personal project, due to his work on *Raiders of the Lost Ark*, which connects him to Sean Connery, who plays Indiana's father in the later sequel, *The Last Crusade*, which is based on the figure of Otto Rahn, author of *Crusade Against the Grail* and Himmler's pet grailologist; suspected of disloyalty and homosexuality, he wound up a corpse as well, committing a Cathar-style suicide in the frozen Alps, like Alex before the Big Chill starts in.

The Big Chill in "The Gilmore Girls Occupy Wall Street" but only in the context of what might be called Liberal Psycho-Geography, their strange preference for living in small towns, even rural communities, once they have been cleansed of those dirty White Others who actually created the towns and communities.

In the case of the sad sacks gathered at Alex's funeral, they were only happy living together back in Ann Arbor, under the charismatic leadership of Alex, some kind of sophomore Tim Leary or Mark Rudd (these would have been the deleted Costner scenes). Now, his suicide has brought them back together in a similar locus, the conveniently large house of the most adult couple among them, now living in conveniently rural but Yuppie-friendly South Carolina.[5]

The gang is clearly some kind of *Männerbund*, now bereft of their spiritual leader. But it's an unusual one: multi-sexual and multi-ethnic,[6] and above all, characterized by fakery and failure.

---

[5] Kline and Close are adults because, not only are they married homeowners with children, all this is possible because he has set up a company, "ironically" called Running Dog, which seems to be on the ground floor of the running shoe phenomenon. The Big House, subservient locals—even the infamous "Southern Sheriff" is a friend and "some kinda guy"—and no doubt slave labor abroad for products sold to inner city youth strongly suggests some kind of Southern antebellum fantasy. But we know he's a "good guy" because Procul Harum and Motown are "the only kind of music here." Kline angrily announces "I'm dug in here" while, unlike the "12 Southerners" who defended agrarian rootedness in *I'll Take My Stand*, wearing a "Michigan" sweatshirt. As I mentioned before, this shot is perhaps the iconic Modern Liberal, and I like to imagine his shirt has a Made in Thailand tag.

[6] Jeff Goldblum plays what can only be called "a Real New York Jew" (*Annie Hall*) and is consequently intensely unlikable, unlike his later roles as gawky but sympathetic and even heroic (*The Fly, Jurassic Park, Independence Day*), or indeed any Jew's movie portrayal since about 1945.

Michael: Everyone does everything just to get laid.
Karen: Who said that? Freud?

The complete failure of their lives, most dramatically Alex himself, might lead one to question his *bona fides* as a guru, but like most Liberals, what they've learned is mostly an intense self-regard, which makes it impossible to "check their premises," as Ayn Rand used to say.[7]

> **Michael**: No, I did.
>
> **Michael**: That's the great thing about the outdoors, it's one giant toilet.
>
> **Harold**: (preparing to order shoes for everyone) Feet grow as you get older.
> **Michael**: I wish everything did.

Despite his smarmy approaches to every woman around, he is the only character to not manage to get laid that weekend.

[7] Jo Beth Williams' square, stodgy husband, played by Don Galloway —I remember thinking, hey, it's that guy from *Ironside*!— delivers the only words of wisdom in the film: no one ever said it was supposed to be easy.

> **Richard**: [Richard is having a late-night snack while talking to Sam and Nick] There's some asshole at work you have to kowtow to, and you find yourself doing things you thought you'd never do. But you try and minimize that stuff; be the best person you can be. But you set your priorities. And that's the way life is. I wonder if your friend Alex knew that. One thing's for sure, he couldn't live with it. I know I shouldn't talk; you guys knew him. But the thing is . . . no one ever said it would be fun. At least . . . no one ever said it to me.

That's because he didn't have the misfortune of falling under Alex's spell, with Alex's fake-Zen "ironic" *non sequiturs*:

> **Nick**: I know what Alex would say.
> **Harold**: What?
> **Nick**: What's for dessert?

His insomnia may be supposed to indicate one of those "sublimat-

Nick: Wise up, folks. We're all alone out there and tomorrow we're going out there again.

Rather than the more obviously *Männerbund*-ish features, I'd like to focus on something at first glance entirely different: Sarah has the bright idea to solve Meg's worries about never finding a man to have a child with, by loaning her husband, Harold.

In my previous essay, I passed this off as an ostentatious, Bloomsbury-like nose-thumbing of "bourgeois morality." Oddly enough, Hans Blüher, the theorist of the *Männerbund*, provides a more interesting perspective.

Through Wulf Grimsson, whose work we drew on for our *Untouchables* essay, I've obtained one of the few English translations of one of Blüher's public lectures, in which he lays out his theory of sexuality, the family, and the *Männerbund*.

In "Family and Male Fraternity," he discusses at one point the role of creativity in responding to the demands of new situations. Traditions, to be vital, must respond to new conditions, and in the process, what once were sins may become moral, as they facilitate the creation of a new tradition. (One thinks perhaps of Carl Schmitt's doctrine of the Exception.) In considering the modern problems besetting the tradition of monogamy, Blüher spurns the advocates of "free love" as not having thought out and found a creative solution to the practical problems, such as jealousy. Here he writes:

Jealousy is the will to have an exclusive right on the

---

ed" conditions Frankfurt Schooled Leftists like to postulate to explain why their opponents happily ignore them, but I would suggest it hints at a natural talent for vigils and contacting the Jungian active imagination, source of wisdom. No one pays attention to him, of course. William Hurt's insufferable character just walks away when first introduced to him, and he is shipped home to Detroit to take care of the kids so that Williams can finally sleep with, and be disappointed with, her old flame. But before he goes he both predicts her disillusionment with Sam and hints at the essential fakeness of this group: "I can't believe these are the same people you've been talking about all these years."

sexual partner and illustrates all over again the myth of the human being cut in two and deprived of his other half. Because after all there can only be *one* other half! Jealousy is really the destructive element within a polygamous marriage. Jealousy can never be eliminated by affectionate persuasions, by calming appeasements or any kind of rational arrangement, but only by a great creative act of the Eros itself. Let me give a comparison from German philosophy. Arthur Schopenhauer speaks at several points in his work of so-called "conversions." A criminal, who is just going to the scaffold and who until recently has had no remorse for his crime, is suddenly enlightened. . . .

A man is not purified through a gradual diminution of sin—to believe this would just be muddled ignorance and rationalism—but through a sudden change of his whole nature. The bigger his sin was, the more he is purified. The same thing can happen with jealousy.

Jealousy is the real sin against the creative Eros. *In the case of exceptional women, there are rare moments where this usually destructive passion can turn around, can place itself into the service of the former rival and can increase the love of two women for the man whom they both love.* On such a basis the will of the man is creating the sacrament of polygamy. Without this sacrament, which the Greeks called *mysterion,* all polygamous relationships are doomed to end in the most distressful disaster. Something permanent can only come about where a sacrament (a mystery in the Greek sense) stands between people, where devotion, sacrifice and service are involved. Polygamy needs a state of grace and cannot be "made."

Are Meg and Sarah such *exceptional* women? (Note Blüher's use of the Schmittian term.) Sarah, despite her marriage, children, and homemaking, and her general "earth mother" portrayal,[8] and Meg, despite her distinctly non-hip obsession with

---

[8] Close in the film bears a strong resemblance to '60s female icon Carole King—who wrote the theme to, and appears occasionally in,

finding a man to have a child with (which would be mocked as '60s stupidity on *Mad Men* today), are both played by decidedly "mannish" actresses. Glenn Close, who received her first Oscar nomination for this role, received her most recent this year for a role in which she portrays a woman living as a man, while Mary Kay Place eventually "came out" as a lesbian.

When she first arrives, Meg wears neither the '80s shoulder-padded woman's "power suit" nor the later Hilary-style "pants suit" but what looks like a boy's suit, complete with white shirt, striped tie, and attache case—in the contemporaneous *Official Preppy Handbook*, women were advised to check out the boy's department at Brooks Brothers for appropriate attire.

She and Richard are the only ones dressed like real grown up men, and both have thought a lot about what a man should be. Like Richard's late night speech, she provides a surprisingly contemporary meditation on modern manhood:

> **Meg**: They're either married or gay. And if they're not gay, they've just broken up with the most wonderful woman in the world, or they've just broken up with a bitch who looks exactly like me. They're in transition from a monogamous relationship, and they need more space. Or they're tired of space, but they just can't commit. Or they want to commit, but they're afraid to get close. They want to get close, you don't want to get near them.

Finding no acceptable men, Meg has had to become a man, or a facsimile thereof, just as Costner's Ness had to learn how to become a man by creating his own double, the wise and honest Malone.

> **Meg**: It's a cold world out there. Sometimes I feel like I'm

---

The Gilmore Girls! Cringingly but all too appropriately, King's "You Make Me Feel Like a Natural Woman" accompanies Sarah's decision, although, also in keeping with the proto-SWPL atmosphere, it's Aretha Franklin's version—so much more earthy!

getting a little frosty myself.

As Capone says, "If you were a man, you'd have done it." And we know what "doing it" means. As Blüher says, "Where is the important man who would be content with just one woman?"[9]

Meg accepts Sarah's offer of Harold only as last resort, having considered and dismissed all the inadequate man-children available that weekend (including a "return engagement" with the Jew, Michael). Her choice, adultery if not quite a *ménage à trois*, is made to further a higher tradition, motherhood.

It's even possible, though it passes as a joke, that Meg's wisdom was what killed Alex:

Meg: The last time I spoke with Alex, we had a fight. I yelled at him.
Nick: That's probably why he killed himself. . . . What was the argument about?
Meg: I told him he was wasting his life.

In *The Untouchables*, Costner's Ness conjures up an authentic teacher of manhood and then kills him off when no longer needed for the task of re-establishing the ideal of justice. In *The Big Chill*, Costner plays a fake guru—or perhaps, a Guru of Fakeness—who is killed off by Meg, in order for her to set up the funeral weekend where she will finally conceive a child. Meg is the authentic Shaman, who can shape-shift across gender lines and break traditional vows—monogamy—in order to pursue a higher calling: motherhood.

Counter-Currents/*North American New Right*
May 22, 2012

---

[9] A similar triangle occurs in the WWII German film *Opfergang*; see Derek Hawthorne's "*Opfergang*: Masterpiece of National Socialist Cinema," http://www.counter-currents.com/2011/ 12/opfergang-masterpiece-of-national-socialist-cinema/

THE BAKER STREET *MÄNNERBUND*:
SOME THOUGHTS ON HOLMES, WATSON, BOND, & BONDING

"These," he pointed around, "are my other guns. The parallel is exact!"
          —Sherlock Holmes, "The Empty House."[1]

Having devoted considerable time and attention to the genres of weird fiction and science fiction,[2] it is perhaps long overdue that I should spend some time considering the remaining one of the Three Disreputable Genres,[3] detective fiction.

The transition is made easier by the fact that the inventor of the detective tale, by most accounts, is that master of the weird tale, Edgar A. Poe, who in turn Lovecraft considered his own master.[4]

I suspect that, as with weird fiction and science fiction, the persistent popularity of this looked-down-upon genre—one

---

[1] "I wonder that my very simple stratagem could deceive so old a SHIKARI," said Holmes. "It must be very familiar to you. Have you not tethered a young kid under a tree, lain above it with your rifle, and waited for the bait to bring up your tiger? This empty house is my tree, and you are my tiger. You have possibly had other guns in reserve in case there should be several tigers, or in the unlikely supposition of your own aim failing you. These," he pointed around, "are my other guns. The parallel is exact."

[2] See the essays mostly collected in *The Eldritch Evola … & Others* and *Green Nazis in Space!*

[3] The ascension of first, Chandler and Hammett, and then Lovecraft and Philip K. Dick, to the Library of America indicates a bit of a sea change, though accompanied by the usual grumbling from contemporary Edmund Wilsons who value *bourgeois status quo* rather than Tradition.

[4] *The Eldritch Evola* contains "Mike Hammer, Occult Dick: *Kiss Me Deadly* as a Lovecraftian Tale," which considers the parallels between the overly-inquisitive protagonists of detective fiction and Lovecraft's weird fiction.

often considered no more than a mere personal quirk or obsession—lies in its ability to present Traditional metaphysical
themes no longer countenanced by mainstream fiction, or culture in general. Let's see!

In dealing with detective fiction, one must, of course, deal
with the epoch-making figure of Sherlock Holmes.

The first thing writers on Sherlock Holmes feel the need to
tackle is the question of the overwhelming cultural impact of
these tales of a late Victorian/early Edwardian private (or
"consulting") detective. The only rival, though still subject to
far less fan obsession, is that other British chap, James Bond,
secret agent, of whom more anon.

As usual, Colin Wilson has an interesting and useful theory
about this.[5] He attributes the overwhelming and continued fas-
cination with Holmes to Doyle having, quite inadvertently,
solved an important problem in spiritual evolution:

> Holmes was more than a fictional character: he was a re-
> sponse to a deep-rooted psychological need of the late
> Victorians, a need for reassurance, for belief in the effica-
> cy of reason and for man's power to overcome the chaos
> produced by this new disease of alienation.[6]

The rise of literacy among the populace led to an obsession
with the realistic novel (itself an innovation of Cervantes, Rich-
ardson, Defoe and others).

You would have to imagine that Sir Walter Raleigh brought
back marijuana from the New World, and all Europe became
pot smokers. This taste for escaping into worlds of fantasy
swept across Europe, and literature gained an important that it
had never possessed in any previous age.[7]

---

[5] *The Books in My Life* (Charlottesville, Vir.: Hampton Roads, 1998);
see Chapter 5, "Sherlock Holmes, the Flawed Superman."

[6] Symptomatic of which illness is the other new character type, the
anti-Holmes, the master criminal such as Prof. Moriarty, or fiend,
such as Jack the Ripper.

[7] I don't really agree with Wilson that this was some kind of evolutionary leap, "the most decisive steps in the evolution of man since

A point often missed, especially by literary critics of the Realist camp,[8] is that this involves more than the accumulation of precise detail, important though that is.[9] Among realists, Dumas would always be more popular than Balzac, and even within Dickens, *Pickwick Papers* would be more popular than "better" novels like *Hard Times*. "They are too 'real,'" says Wilson, "and they lack the element of the wish-fulfillment fantasy."

The point is, to get the two together, in the right proportion: the wish-fulfillment fantasy, with enough realistic detail to assure us that this, unlike a child's fairy-tale, is *real*.

Consider *Manhunter,* Michael Mann's 1986 film based on Thomas Harris' *Red Dragon*. In pursuing the Tooth Fairy, FBI "manhunter" Will Graham knows that he can't be caught unless Graham can figure out what his fantasy is: to find his motive, he must find out what he kills "to fuel his fantasy." By the end,

> The psychological paths of Graham and Dollarhyde finally converge. Graham tells Crawford how he understands the Tooth Fairy. "He dreams about being wanted and desired. So he changes people into beings who will want and desire him . . . Killing and arranging the people to imitate it . . . *You put it together*, you get, *if our boy imitates being wanted and desired enough times, he believes he will be-*

---

the invention of the wheel"; but certainly, after centuries of Christian cretinizing, it was a distinct improvement.

[8] As well as ideologues like Tom Wolfe; see his polemical articles on the New Journalists as *The New Realists* reprinted as the introduction to *The New Journalism* (New York: Harper & Row, 1973). "Believe me, there is no new journalism. It is a gimmick to say there is . . . Story telling is older than the alphabet and that is what it is all about." — Jimmy Breslin, quoted in Philip M. Howard, Jr., "The New Journalism: A Nonfiction Concept of Writing," unpublished master's thesis, University of Utah, August, 1971; quoted on *Wikipedia, op. cit.*

[9] I discuss the maniacal accumulation of detail as a key method in writers as different as Lovecraft, Henry James, and Baron Evola in "The Eldritch Evola" and elsewhere in *The Eldritch Evola, op. cit.*

come one who is wanted and desired and accepted. It will all come true."

There is an uneasy parallel and confluence in the modern mode of genre fiction, one of fantasy/reality, child/adult:

"Are you sympathizing with this guy, Will?" Crawford asks offscreen. Mann keeps the camera on Graham's face. "Absolutely," he answers. "My heart bleeds for him as a child. . . . As an adult, someone should blow the sick fuck out of his socks. Do you think that's a contradiction, Jack? Does this kind of understanding make you uncomfortable?"[10]

---

[10] See the remarkable analysis of *Taxi Driver* and *Manhunter*, "God's Lonely Men: Cinema Psychopaths" at *The Niles Files*, http://nilesfilmfiles.blogspot.com/2011/04/gods-lonely-men-cinema-psychopaths.html. Here's a sample:

More interestingly, they both have the same cinematographer, Dante Spinotti. But whereas *Red Dragon* briskly moves along with its plot and suspense thriller tropes in terms of how it uses lighting, music, editing, and sound, *every element in Manhunter is able to be savored again and again*: the compositions, the colors of window blinds behind a character, Mel Bourne's amazing production design, the moody synthesizer music, the highly experimental editing and sound. All this could at first be perceived as a flaw of over-stylization; indeed, whereas *The Silence of the Lambs, Hannibal,* and *Red Dragon* come off as gothic horror, *Manhunter* feels like a cousin to the New German Cinema of the 1970s. But this criticism is off-set by two things: Mann is totally invested in his characters and his meticulous research reveals itself in the slightest nuances of his performers; (even the fantastic Fiennes feels trivial and shallow when compared to Noonan's Dollarhyde; and Ed Norton's Graham seems to have no struggle whatsoever); and secondly, the aestheticism of the film is integral to the substance, being that Francis Dollarhyde, one of cinema's great creepy *gazers*, looks and then elevates or perverts everything that he sees. Like Mark Lewis, he is a filmic cyborg and what we see in *Manhunt-*

But then, around the turn of the 19th century, a problem developed; people began to live too much, perhaps entirely, in their imaginations. Enter the literary figure of the aesthete—Axel, Dorian Gray, and most notably Des Esseintes, the protagonist of Huysmans' *À rebours* (*Against the Grain*)—all living apart from, and hostile to, the outside world, constructing their own, superior counter-world at home.[11] Unfortunately, as Wilson points out, the world always wins; Des Esseintes ultimately sickens and must return to the hated Paris for treatment.[12]

Holmes was at first a similar figure, holed up in his rooms at 221b Baker Street, taking cocaine and Turkish coffee, gesturing "languidly." As Wilson notes, Doyle was commissioned to write the second Holmes novel, *The Sign of the Four*, by the same publisher, at the same dinner party, that produced *The Picture of Dorian Gray*, just two years after *À rebours*.

But unlike either character, Holmes evolves a solution to the problem: crime; or rather, the solution of crimes, the pursuit of justice: "He has not turned his back on the world; on the contrary, he regards himself as a last court of appeal."

> Quite unconsciously, certainly unaware of what he was doing, Conan Doyle had solved the problem that had tormented and frustrated the novelist since Richardson. He had created a romantic hero, a man whose life is entirely the life of the mind ("I cannot live without brain-work), yet succeeded in steering him out of the *cul-de-sac* of despair and defeat that destroyed so many of the best

---

er is filtered through a lens of complete aestheticism.

For more on the intense re-view-ability of *Manhunter*, see my "Essential Films … & Others," https://www.counter-currents.com/2015/02/essential-films-and-others/.

[11] Here again, Poe was first; his detective, Dupin, already lives shut away from the Paris noise, preferring to live by night. Other than the aesthetic veneer, on might compare such creatures to today's basement-dwelling video-gamers.

[12] Wilson later devotes a chapter to "Huysmans: The Ultimate Decadent."

minds of the *fin-de-siècle* period.

This has a sound basis in Tradition. From Plato (The Myth of the Cave) to Emericus Durden,[13] the path of the Realized Man involves not only rising to the heights but also a return to live among us. [14]

As Krishna explains his role as avatar:

Whenever there is a decline of righteousness,
and the rise of unrighteousness,
then I re-incarnate myself
to teach dharma.[15]

Indeed, soon an even more fascinating development occurred. Fired by his interests in detection, Holmes acquires more and more knowledge and skill, until, no longer a languid aesthete who claimed to not know, or have an interest in, whether the Earth revolved around the Sun or vice versa, to a polymath, a universal genius—a superman, or, as Wilson add,

---

[13] See my review of his *Aiming Higher Than Mere Civilization: How Skeptical Nihilism Will Remind Humanity of Its Long-Forgotten Purpose* (Emericus Durden Philosophy Series Book 1), https://www.counter-currents.com/2015/05/aiming-higher-than-mere-civilization/.

[14] In *The Hermetic Tradition*, Evola discusses how the Realized Man rebuilds for himself a new, glorified body (the Body of Light in various traditions); see Chapter 32, "The Red Work: Return to Earth." In his autobiography, *The Path of Cinnabar*, Evola explains his interest in Guénon and Tradition as arising from the idea that the Absolute Ego that he had arrived at in his studies in philosophical Idealism needed to be "grounded" in history, and this he identified with the historical founders of the various Traditions, such as Manu, Solon, or the Yellow Emperor.

[15] *Bhagavad Gita*, 4.7. I discuss this avataric role in "The Babysitting Bachelor as Aryan Avatar: Clifton Webb in *Sitting Pretty*, Part 2," https://www.counter-currents.com/2013/02/the-babysitting-bachelor-as-aryan-avatarclifton-webb-in-sitting-pretty-part-2/, as well as its relevance to the *Männerbund* theme in "'God, I'm with a heathen': The Rebirth of the *Männerbund* in Brian De Palma's *The Untouchables*," herein.

"a true magician." He becomes that figure we have frequently cited, the *Chakravartin*, the Unmoved Mover turning things from the Center of the World; as Wilson quotes Watson on Holmes: "He loved *to lie in the very center of five millions of people, with his filaments stretching out and running through them*, responsive to every little rumor or suspicion of unsolved crime."[16]

Wilson thinks Doyle's writer's instinct was right to try to kill off Holmes, because he was unable to find a way to develop the character further.[17] He sounds a bit like a Liberal Goodthinker when he suggests that "a man like Holmes" should have naturally become interested in the socio-economic causes of crimes, not just solving them, but this was too mundane to interest Doyle.

What interested Doyle was spiritualism, séances, and such like, and "it's hard to imagine Holmes at a séance." True, but I find it hard to imagine Holmes campaigning for slum clearance, hot school lunches, or midnight basketball, either.

The real problem is that Doyle's interests were not in real Tradition but in the modern, deviant areas of "spiritualism" or what Guénon disparaged as "Spiritism,"[18] an interest Wilson shares [19] and to which we will be returning.

---

[16] "The Adventure of the Cardboard Box," in the last collection, *His Last Bow*.

[17] As I have frequently emphasized, unlike "moral" fiction, in genre fiction the death of a character—especially a Big Bad who, as Trevor Lynch notes, is usually the only spokesman allowed for Traditional, or non-PC, views—results only superficially from "just retribution" (the cover story) but simply because there is nothing else to be done with him. "When you get the message, you hang up the phone," as Alan Watts liked to say. Tura Satana's character in *Faster Pussycat, Kill, Kill* is herself killed at the end not because the wimpy girlfriend triumphs but because the film has to end at some point.

[18] See *The Spiritist Fallacy* (Ghent, NY: Sophia Perennis, 2003) and *Theosophy: History of a Pseudo-Religion* (Ghent, NY: Sophia Perennis, 2001).

[19] A somewhat hostile critic calls Wilson "somewhat innocent and over-trusting, like Sir Arthur Conan Doyle. Both Conan Doyle and

Wilson gives us a compelling portrait of Holmes and the reasons for the Holmes phenomenon. Still, it might be useful to see what the "professional" literary critics have to say about it.

There are, of course, gazillions of editions of the Holmes novels and tales, ranging from expensive "limited edition" volumes to pricy, vastly annotated slipcovered editions[20] to free Kindle versions from Amazon sellers.

The Oxford volume I will employ, whose second edition recently appeared, collects most of the famous tales as well as the short, early novel *The Sign of the Four*, all gently annotated, and with a useful introduction by Barry McCrea.[21] Prof. McCrea

---

Wilson gave credence to the Cottingley fairies, for example" (https://philosophynow.org/issues/85/Colin_Wilson_As_Hydra). For his part, Wilson said:

> Like Joe Cooper, I am willing to believe the girls were telling the truth. Both had had many psychic experiences, which Joe records (and which anyone who wants to explore further can find summarised in my son Damon's article on fairies in our joint book *Unsolved Mysteries Past and Present*). Joe's book *The Case of the Cottingley Fairies* received little publicity and is still not widely known. This has given me the opportunity to speak of my own attitude to these things, and to explain why, like Joyce [Collin Smith], I accept the reality of these 'elementals', as did the poet W. B. Yeats and his friend Lady Gregory, and as did the writer and researcher Evans Wentz in his classic book on the subject, *The Fairy Faith in Celtic Countries*. (http://www.joycecollinsmith.co.uk/an-introduction-by-colin-wilson)

[20] Before publishing the more modest *New Annotated Lovecraft* we reviewed https://www.counter-currents.com/2014/10/notes-on-the-new-annotated-h-p-lovecraft/, Leslie S. Klinger prepared *The New Annotated Sherlock Holmes*, described by Wikipedia as "a series of three annotated books edited by Leslie S. Klinger, collecting all of Arthur Conan Doyle's short stories and novels about Sherlock Holmes. The books were originally published by W. W. Norton in oversized slip-cased hardcover editions. . . . This publication of the Sherlock Holmes canon has been called 'definitive.'"

[21] *Sherlock Holmes: Selected Stories*, 2nd ed. (Oxford: Oxford Univer-

reminds me of what my mentor, Plotinus scholar Dr. John N. Deck, once said about Walter Kaufmann and his attempts to popularize Nietzsche and Hegel: He's seldom wrong but never profound. As such, he provides a useful framework which we can, as Dr. Deck would also say, *aprofondise* with our own expansions of his comments.

McCrea and Wilson agree, and it is good that they agree, that "There is simply no other fictional character who comes close to having the cultural influence of Holmes," and that he is "clearly a product of his times." However, since Doyle fails to give Holmes any PC speeches about racism, sexism, etc., Prof. McCrea has to exercise a bit of academic legerdemain to get his quota of goodthinking in: "The mechanism of the stories is to focus our attention entirely on the mystery while imperceptibly exposing us to social, economic, psychological and historical realities."

Ah yes, love that "imperceptibly"; it's there, but you can't see it until the critic comes along. Double points!

McCrea's still got something on the ball, though; in his own PC way, he does manage to notice many of the points we and Wilson have been hammering away on. Holmes' stories manage to insinuate the plight of women under patriarchy, the toiling of the oppressed workers, the ruthless exploitation of the colored masses, etc., because Holmes exercises the superhuman powers of the *Chakravartin*:

> Holmes sees almost everything and he understands everything he sees, often immediately. Holmes' work . . . reveal[s] the connections that remain otherwise hidden, or unspeakable. Holmes is an appealing figure in an overcrowded world and a bewildering global economic system because reveals unseen or disavowed connections. Holmes reveals new, unexpected connections and conjunctions generated from the new circumstances of metropolitan living.

---

sity Press, 2014).

McCrea, of course, does not attribute this to any mystical, superhuman achievements. Rather, he brings it back to another of our themes; Holmes' method of deduction depends on the same patient, exhaustive, perhaps neurotic and suffocating, *accumulation of details* that we have identified as the literary method of weird fiction. In "The Red-Headed League,"

> Holmes sees something invisible to the police, to the characters who are victims of the scam, and, of course to the eternally astonished Watson:—namely, that "the line of fine shops and stately business premises . . . really abutted on the other side upon the faded and stagnant square." The fact that the two neighborhoods are physically next to each other is invisible to Watson because socially and imaginatively they are so far apart.[22]

Like Poe, Lovecraft, and other writers of weird fiction (as well as such Traditionalists as Guénon and Evola),

> Strangeness is hidden somewhere within ordinary life. For the mystery to be solved or the criminal identified, commonplace doings and commonplace people, not usually worthy of enquiry, *must be scrutinized.*[23] Holmes is able to see or make these connections *due to his social isolation.* He is *not of the world* he investigates. The only ones who see the world the way Holmes does are the criminals and *family outsiders.*

---

[22] Of course, this also reminds us of Jim Garrison's method of "guilt by geography," where, for example, a "connection" is established between Lee Oswald and Guy Bannister by noting they had offices in the same building; see Patricia Lambert's *False Witness: The Real Story of Jim Garrison's Investigation and Oliver Stone's Film* JFK (New York: Evans & Co., 2000).

[23] Whether McCrea intends it or not, that word always recalls to my mind F. R. Leavis' journal, *Scrutiny*, as well as the certainly unintended "Central Scrutinizer" of Frank Zappa.

McCrea also agrees with Wilson in seeing Holmes as a *fin de siècle* figure, a withdrawn dandy, but fails to notice any development of the sort Wilson descries. Instead, he takes the idea in a different and equally intriguing direction: "Holmes is a bohemian bachelor who abhors family life."

> Yet Holmes himself is a confirmed bachelor who lives, on and off, with a male companion. Watson, just as he intermediates between Holmes and the reader, is never fully part of either realm, the bohemian bachelor life he shares with Holmes or the heterosexual family world which he ostensibly joins when he marries. . . . Watson shuttles anxiously back and forth between them, supposedly living at home with Mary, but moving back to Baker Street whenever there is a crime to solve. . . . From the point of view of the reader, he is married to Holmes. What seems to engrave itself more than anything else on our reading memories is *the domestic life of 221b Baker Street*. Holmes and Watson sitting in their rooms, reading the newspapers, discussing Mrs. Hudson's cooking, or waiting for the door bell to ring and a stranger to arrive with a new mystery to solve.

Refreshingly, McCrea dismisses any concern over the question "Is Holmes gay?" one way or another. Instead, he picks a different thread to unravel:

> What we can say for sure is that Holmes stands emblematically *outside of the economy of marriage and reproduction*.

> Holmes is most often called in to help *where the family is failing or under threat*.

Here we see Holmes and Watson taking on the role we've called attention to before: the *Männerbund*, the "band apart," outside of but not hostile to the family unit; indeed, by its very isolation, able to come to its defense in desperate times.[24]

---

[24] The *Ur*-text is "'God, I'm with a heathen': The Rebirth of the

This cultural role parallels the (paradoxical, to some) biological role of homosexuality in enabling large groups of mammals to survive, by allowing some members to be always available for defense, food gathering, etc.[25]

221b Baker Street is inhabited by a "couple" whose partnership cannot bear biological fruit, a household which will not leave a genetic legacy. By the same token, Holmes's professional eye is resolutely turned away from thoughts of the future. . . . Where we find clarity and solace is not in the comfort of family life, the marriage and fertility that offers comfort in so many other kinds of narrative, but in the unconventional homestead of 221b Baker Street, *a queer source of order* from which the strangeness of the world, and *how it came to be as it is*, is *visible with a unique kind of clarity*.[26]

This raises another, subtle point (though I doubt McCrean

Männerbund in Brian De Palma's *The Untouchables*," herein. As the future M, Judi Dench, intones at the beginning of *The Chronicles of Riddick*: "In normal times, evil would be fought with good. But in times like these, well, it should be fought by another kind of evil."

[25] See James Neill, *The Origins and Role of Same-Sex Relations in Human Societies* and my review-essay thereon, available as an Amazon Kindle. Needless to say, this is all subverted by the "gay" identity manufactured by the Left, in which marriage and family are "redefined" so as to merge the happy homosexual in the mix: he's just like us! As Ann Sterzinger puts it in her review of our *Green Nazis*, "can you imagine William Burroughs writing about the Wild Boys with an adopted baby strapped to his chest and a yuppie husband yapping in his ear about *Glee*?" (https://www.counter-currents.com/2016/05/fashy-homos-and-green-nazis-in-space/).

[26] The ethnic outsider tears down and "develops" — like *Caddyshack*'s Al Czervik — while the homosexual of one's own ethnic group reclaims and gentrifies the old; see our "This Old Gay House," herein. Is it not the Jew, with his "family values," that gifted us with capitalism and its obsessive concern with the new and the future? A concern shared by the Marxist, with his "New Soviet Man" and the total destruction of the old order.

notices). The homosexual is often the homophobic Right's favorite straw man for "those with no concern for future generations."[27] And yet isn't the Right—the non-libertarian, at least—concerned above all with the past, and the preservation thereof? In a word, archeofuturism?

> The gaze of the stories is *fixed firmly on the past, on how things turned out as they did, not on what they will or might become*. The mysteries, even when solved, leave us with a sense that *underneath ordinary daily life there might always lie something old and dark and violent that will return in an unpredictable form*.

McCrea also make an important point about the use of Watson, which returns us to our them of wish-fulfillment:

> There is something in the stories' form as opposed to content, that has nothing to do with historical context but which draws us in wholly and inexplicably. . . . *Watson is our way into the stories*. . . . because his blindness and puzzlement in the face of these facts mirror our own experience of reading the story. The sense that Watson incarnates of missing the big picture, of not "getting" how everything really fits together, is part of our experience of life itself.
>
> It is one of the sources of *fellowship between ourselves and Watson* that we never master Holmes' skill, and it is part of the stories' compulsive hold on our attention that *we keep feeling we might*.

This is an essential component to the wish-fulfilment aspect that Wilson emphasized. Kingsley Amis made the same point in his invaluable study of the Bond phenomenon: Bond, like all wish-fulfilment figures, must be enough like us to plausibly suggest that, "I could do that if given half the chance."[28] He's a

---

[27] Keynes is often "explained" this way: "Well, he said 'in the long run we are all dead' because he was queer, you know?"

[28] Kingsley Amis, *The James Bond Dossier* (London: Jonathan Cape,

good shot, not the best in the Service; he needs to train, to read up on card tricks, etc. He's Batman, not Superman.

Unlike Batman, of course, he's not a vigilante (except, notably, when pursuing Blofeld), but, as Amis emphasizes, a loyal, old-fashioned King and Empire Brit, a mere "civil servant," and certainly not a grubby little spy. This makes him even more like Green Lantern, as opposed to both Bats and Supe, as I noted in the title essay of *Green Nazis*.[29]

In tune with the times, Bond, unlike Holmes, is presented as a relentless womanizer, and even (in the books) make occasional homophobic observations, usually in the context of bemoaning feminism and other aspects of modernity.

Thus, in the novel *Goldfinger*, Bond muses that Tilly Masterson is:

> One of those girls whose hormones had got mixed up. He knew the type well and thought they and their male counterparts were a direct consequence of giving votes to women and "sex equality." As a result of fifty years of emancipation, feminine qualities were dying out or being

---

1965), which I've frequently called the very model of genre criticism.

[29] *Op. cit.* Trevor Lynch has noted the same essential opposition when reviewing the new *Batman vs. Superman* movie:

> In any matchup between Batman and Superman, I side with Batman. I've never liked the character of Superman, because he is not a man at all. He's basically a god. He's not a human being who has raised himself to the pinnacles of human excellence. He's an alien who is simply endowed with superior abilities. There is nothing heroic about Superman, because he is almost invulnerable. He faces no risks. There's nothing he must struggle to overcome. Batman, however, is a true Nietzschean superman, a man who has made himself more than a man, a man who faces injury, death, and imprisonment night after night in order to fight evil. I don't want to live in a godless universe, but frankly I would prefer that we make ourselves into gods rather than find them readymade.
> (https://www.counter-currents.com/2016/05/batman-v-superman-dawn-of-justice/)

transferred to males. Pansies of both sexes were everywhere, not yet completely homosexual, but confused, not
knowing what they were. . . . He was sorry for them, but
he had no time for them."

Sounds like something right out of today's man-o-sphere. [30]
Bond is really rather a crusty old reactionary—part of his
"Queen and country" mentality that explains his perverse
championing of the British, who haven't mattered since the
days of Bulldog Drummond.[31]
    Amis, however, is at pains to point out, in that carefully cat-

-----

[30] Right-wing types who might cheer Bond/Fleming's homophobia should note that Fleming associates sexual deviance with "furriners" *including* the US. For the film version, Tilly was ret-conned as
straight, and Pussy Galore became a fantasy lipstick Lesbian who
would succumb to Bond's charms. In the book, however, Pussy's
backstory is: "I come from the South. You know the definition of a
virgin down there? Well, it's a girl who can run faster than her brother. In my case, I couldn't run as fast as my uncle. I was twelve. That's
not so good James. You ought to be able to guess that." As Tricia Jen-
kins points out, "Here, Fleming specifically implies that Pussy's *lesbi-
anism emerges from the familial and cultural dysfunction of the American
South*, and given the Bond formula, *this deviancy can only reflect the
degeneracy of the United States.*" See her invaluable essay "James
Bond's 'Pussy' and Anglo-American Cold War Sexuality,"
http://www.the007dossier.com/007dossier/post/2014/06/04/Jame
s-Bonds-Pussy. While American "conservatives" laud down-home
Southern family values and sneer about the British queers, Fleming
sees "degeneracy" right there in the Flannery O'Connor heartland,
not from "cultural Marxism" but from the primitive conditions of the
family-obsessed conservatives of the colonial world; real men are the
bachelor products of public schools, like Bond.
    [31] The American Bond phenom' really ran on the coat-tails (a two
button, soft shouldered, single-vented suit, of course) of the Camelot
mystique, when JFK, supposed champion of "youth," averred to having a Fleming novel at his bedside. One wonders who was fooling
whom; after all, how much time did JFK really spend in the White
House bedroom *per se*? "My bedroom! Where my wife sleeps! Where
my children play with their toys!" —Michael Corleone, *The Godfather
Part II*.

aloging way of his, that Bond seldom beds more than one or two ladies per book, a rather modest count, well within the "I could do that" mode of successful wish fulfilment.[32]

More importantly, Don Juanism is easily seen as a cover for latent homosexuality; Bond's marriage is quickly erased by Blofeld,[33] who then replaces Tracy as the object of Bond's obsessions. Once Blofeld too is dispatched, the energy of the series—perhaps also due to Fleming's physical decline—drops off dramatically, and it really just peters out.

Amis is correct to suggest that both M and the various super-villains function as surrogate fathers for Bond, who is intimidated by their worldly sophistication and punished for his transgressions and inadequacies; M and the villains both do so with snide comments and other displays of superiority, the villains ultimately inflicting corporal punishment as well.

All this is echoed in the recent (supposed) Internet surge to have Gillian Anderson take over the role of Bond. Although popular with a certain generation of post-humanist nerds,[34] a

---

[32] By contrast, Bond rip-offs and spoofs like the Derek Flint or Matt Helm series have their heroes surrounded by veritable harems, the typical exaggeration of satire. I suspect any adult woman would be immune to, and able to easy handle, or break free from, Helm's boozy "charm." Austin Powers' comically frustrated satyriasis is fully in line with Fleming's creation. On Matt Helm and other pseudo-Bonds see Jef Costello's "'The Flash in the Pan': Fascism *&* Fascist Insignia in the Spy Spoofs of the 1960s" in his collection *The Importance of James Bond* (San Francisco: Counter-Currents, 2017).

[33] Bond kills Blofeld in the book *You Only Live Twice* using only his own hands, an intensely up-close, personal, one might almost say sadistically homosexual way; typically, movie Bond, having become Roger Moore, picks up the wheelchair bound Blofeld with a helicopter and dumps him into a factory smokestack (sexual inversion?) as he pleads "I'll buy you a delicatessen—in stainless steel!" Perhaps that curious line is meant as a taunt about Bond's Judaic, middle-class mindset?

[34] "Dear Agent Scully; Did not appreciate your lawyer's tone . . ." *Mystery Science Theater*, Episode 1010, *The Final Sacrifice*. "Look, he's filed all his letters to Gillian Anderson." Episode 1005, *Blood Waters of Dr. Z.*

number of problems seem obvious.

First, the whole "Jane Bond" idea has already been exploited by the porn industry.[35]

More importantly, a female Bond completely ruins the ratio of detailed realism vs. wish fulfillment; as New Rightists frequently point out, real world women just can't do that stuff, and it's even dangerous — to them — to pretend otherwise.[36]

As Tim Stanley insists:

> Here's what I'm not saying: that women can't play men's parts. They can, they have and it can be illuminating. The problem is that the switch is almost always highly self-conscious — it's done to make an artistic point.
>
> When a woman plays Hamlet, the audience is in on the conceit and feminising the role adds new depths to it. When Cate Blanchett played Bob Dylan in Todd Haynes' *I'm Not There* it was to make the point that Dylan's constant search for meaning, and his ready identity with outlaws, meant that he could just as easily be played a woman as by Marcus Carl Franklin, a black adolescent, or Richard Gere, an ageing Billy the Kid.
>
> By contrast, the desire to see a woman play Bond is purely so that a woman can play Bond — and *with the absurd proviso that we'd all have to act like we hadn't noticed.*

---

[35] *Jane Bond Meets Thunderballs* (Jack Remy, 1986), and various sequels. Or so I've heard.

[36] Unless, of course, we go full video-game, or virtual reality. And indeed, this isn't the first time Anderson has been to this rodeo. Season 7 of *The X-Files* brought us "First Person Shooter" by none other than William Gibson himself, where Scully ultimately needs to enter the virtual world of a video game to save Mulder from a rogue female warrior. Interestingly, critics regard this episode as "legendarily bad," while it "became one of Gillian Anderson's favorite episodes, despite 'its reliance on big guns and raging testosterone.' Anderson explained that she enjoyed the opportunity 'to show Scully wearing heavy metal and firing oversized weapons'" (https://en.wikipedia.org/wiki/First_Person_Shooter_(The_X-Files)#Broadcast_and_reception). This doesn't bode well for an Anderson Bond.

The idea is both dumb and dishonest.

Sure, make a film about an ass-kicking female spy who beds everyone she meets and drives a Lotus underwater. But don't call her Bond.[37]

The Bond world as a whole, then, is a *Männerbund*,[38] or rather, a sort of world-wide public school in which Bond is trained for membership. The dynamic is all two-way, Bond/M or Bond/Villain, with the villain trying to win Bond over to "the dark side" like Emperor Palpatine.[39] The famous "Bond Girl" can at most take the place of Watson, with generally unsatisfactory results.[40]

---

[37] "The name's not Jane Bond: why 007 can never be a woman," *The Telegraph*, 25 May 2016, http://www.telegraph.co.uk/films/ 2016/05/25/the-names-not-jane-bond-why-007-can-never-be-a- woman/. Jef Costello made similar points about the ultimate unsuitability of a female M in his review of *Skyfall, op. cit.*

[38] The titular Skyfall is the *Bond manor*, I suppose.

[39] As the film series was "modernized" M of course became a mother figure (the last season of TV's *The Avengers* had already given us the wheelchair confined Mother), and Bond ultimately the Judaic Daniel Craig. Book Bond is almost embarrassingly enthused about Sir Hugo Drax at the start of *Moonraker*; Dr. No hosts Bond to dinner because he thinks he's smart enough to appreciate his status, but dismisses him as "only a stupid policeman." Goldfinger absurdly carries Bond to Kentucky (New York in the book) to witness Operation Grand Slam. As always, the question is: why don't you just kill him? Because, of course, Bond is the potential apprentice; "there are always two."

[40] In the *Goldfinger* book, Bond is not captured so much as shanghaied, along with Tilly Masterton, as Goldfinger's "secretary," which emphasizes their equivalence as protégés of the master. Male secretaries were still common in Britain, a point leading to some comic interaction on *Mad Men* between the ladies of Sterling Cooper and Lane Pryce's male secretary when London agency PPL takes over. In *Dr. No*, the book makes much of Honeychile's muscles and "boyish behind," leading Cyril Connelly to ask "What on Earth was he thinking?" *The Spy Who Loved Me* is the only book narrated by the Bond Girl, with results universally regarded as dire (she even gets his title

I suspect that the lack of a Watson figure accounts for the relatively lower level of personal obsession with Bond, whatever his world-wide fame;[41] for all his solitude and singularity, Holmes needs a Watson, not a Bond Girl, for the reader's interest to crystalize around. But as always, your mileage may differ:

> I've learned a whole lot about life from James Bond, and I will continue to defend Bond and continue seeing these films from now till my dying breath . . . unless they make Bond black.[42]

Counter-Currents/*North American New Right*
June 6, 2016

---

wrong; as noted above, he's a secret agent, not a "spy").

[41] Felix Leiter hardly counts; although he might be thought of as an attempt to give Bond an American partner for the bigger US market, he is, in accord with his CIA background, a cipher; his numerous beatings and dismemberments suggest not so much a stand-in for Bond as a sadistic figure of fun, a Judy to the villain's Punch; the movies have fun with him being played by a different actor each time, in line with his nonentity.

[42] Jef Costello, "The Importance of James Bond," *op. cit.*

HUMPHREY BOGART:
MAN AMONG THE COCKROACHES

"Bogart was a medium-sized man," said John Huston. "Not particularly impressive off-screen." Put him on camera, however, and "those lights and shadows organized themselves into another nobler personality, heroic."

Recently Andrew Hamilton wrote about "The Courage of Jodi Foster" at Counter-Currents/*North American New Right*,[1] the courage in question being her outspoken standing by, if not exactly "supporting," the always controversial Mel Gibson.

Looking at Ms. Foster, as many of us like to do anyway, and meditating on her life and work, one word comes to mind: Aryan.

What also comes to mind is Stefan Kanfer's new book, *Tough Without a Gun: The Life and Extraordinary Afterlife of Humphrey Bogart*,[2] where the subject's "outstanding characteristics—integrity, stoicism, a sexual charisma accompanied by a cool indifference to [the opposite sex]" are not only "never out of style when he's on-screen" but applicable to Ms. Foster as well.

I don't mean to sound like I'm pushing Ms. Foster as the new Bogart—although she probably wouldn't mind—but the task Mr. Kanfer sets himself is to not merely provide another Bogart bio. You could say he wants to explain why adding another bio is unnecessary; for Bogart, even over fifty years after his death (from cigarette-induced esophageal cancer, which today would be the ironic death of a *Mad Men* character) is as well-known, as popular with movie-goers, as quoted, as imitated (a point we will return to), and as influential on filmmakers and actors as he was at the height of his Hollywood career.

How, then, did this not particularly handsome or multi-

---

[1] http://www.counter-currents.com/2011/05/the-courage-of-jodie-foster/

[2] Stefan Kanfer, *Tough Without a Gun: The Life and Extraordinary Afterlife of Humphrey Bogart* (New York: Knopf, 2011).

talented guy, born in 1899 (!) manage to make such a mark that the American Film Academy named him the Greatest Hollywood Legend?

Hamilton has already suggested the answer:

> Foster is a member of that curious set of Hollywood figures who come from privileged backgrounds: John Lodge, Katherine Hepburn, Humphrey Bogart, Otto Kruger, director Robert Aldrich. She attended a French-language prep school, the Lycée Français de Los Angeles, and since her teens has frequently lived and worked in France.

For "privileged" read: upper class WASP; in Foster's case, descendants of *Mayflower* passengers; for Bogart, a society doctor and a famed illustrator. He attended, but was expelled from, Phillips Andover; and while he may never have dubbed his own films like Foster, I heard he's really big in France anyway.

Kanfer says he needs to examine not only the social context Bogart emerged from, but also "the changing image of masculinity in the movies"—at which point I, and perhaps you, usually cringe. But fear not, there's no "queer theorizing" or anything particularly feminist here. What emerges, perhaps unconsciously, is a portrait of the actor as the embodiment of Aryan Virtue.

> For all his rebellions against [his parents], for all his drunken sprees and surly postures, Humphrey could not escape the central fact of his life. He was the son of straitlaced parents whose roots were in another time. Their customs and attitudes may have become outmoded, but they were deeply ingrained in their son. . . . They showed in his upright carriage and in his careful manner of speaking, in his courtesy to women and frank dealing with men. He came to recognize that he gave "the impression of being a Nineteenth Century guy," no matter how hard he tried to be *au courant*. But it worked in his favor. (p. 20)

It helped first of all because the theatrical fashion at the time was for indolent playboys, but although looking the part, Bogart was actually not very good playing it; as we shall see, it was miscasting that made his career. (Near the end of his career he made another, failed stab at playing a Long Island playboy-industrialist in *Sabrina*.) It played a more important role behind the scenes; Bogart learned early that "there were only two kinds of actors, professionals and bums" (pp. 19–20), and he had resolved never to be a bum.

Directors liked how dependable Bogart was, always showing up on time and knowing his lines, and saving the drinking, though heavy, for after hours. (His frustration on *Sabrina* showed when he insisted on leaving the set each day at the contractual 6 p.m., no matter what, after an assistant handed him his highball.) Actresses liked to work with him because there was no funny business, and actors trusted him not to upstage them. Once he got a leg up in the movie business, he remembered his friends, and lent a helping hand to Peter Lorre, Fatty Arbuckle, Gene Tierney, and Joan Bennett.

During the run of *Petrified Forest* Bogart "made a special point of being courtly offstage, in direct contrast to [his character's] snarling persona."

> It was now apparent to all . . . that he was truly old school. He never believed in totally immersing himself in a character; there was no fusing of the performer and the part that was to mark film and stage acting in the decades to come. (p. 39)

One recalls Noël Coward's similar dismissal of "The Method School," describing his method as finding the emotion in oneself, learning how to imitate it on stage, and then dismissing it.

Once he got to Hollywood, Bogart's career got many unexpected boosts from his "old school" professionalism. His very debut, reprising the Broadway role of Duke Mantee for the film, came about when Edward G. Robinson got a swell head after *Little Caesar* and began demanding more money and deference. Though he was the obvious choice, Jack Warner decided to teach him a lesson and gave Bogart a call. Robinson would get his revenge by killing him in numerous films, until Bogart finally got the drop on him in *Key Largo*.

Later, George Raft made the same mistake, began believing his own press, and Warner again turned to the unassuming professional, Bogart, for *High Sierra*, one of the last great *noirs*.

Meanwhile, Bogart was driving a battered Chevy, wearing old suits, and telling reporters he wouldn't make the rookie mistake of "blow[ing] themselves on Cadillacs and big houses." Bogart put every cent in his FU fund (p. 45).

His genetic endowment didn't just shape his attitudes; even his appearance was a plus:

> Bogart was something new onscreen. . . . The appeal of [Robinson, Muni, and Cagney] was ethnic [each was half or wholly Judaic]. . . . In contrast to those stars, Humphrey was a WASP. . . . He represented the notorious malefactors from the heart of the heart of the country . . . all of whom had been dramatically and savagely hunted down and killed in 1934. . . . Duke Mantee seemed a guarded and intense man who lived outside the law, yet had a speck of nobility buried deep within. (p. 43)

Although the country was well over 90% white, apparently Hollywood was so Judaificated by 1934 that a real WASP was a hot new commodity; and just the thing to portray the new White Rage rising in the heartland. Today, Bogart might be playing Timothy McVeigh, or debuting in *Natural Born Killers*.

Tom Shone's review has nicely summarized the interplay of Bogart's heritage, career, and legend:

> His entire film career was to rest on a single, judiciously prolonged piece of miscasting: his stiff, slightly old-fashioned patrician bearing was slightly redundant when deployed in the service of patricians, but transplanted into the bodies of toughs, condemned men, and private eyes — the closest the modern world has to the knights of

the round table—and the result was a brand of hard-bitten, rueful integrity that fit the times like a glove.[3]

The whole premise of Kanfer's book—Bogart as the greatest film legend—makes it unnecessary to go through the classic films to come; except perhaps to note that Bogart was no ingénue; he was well into his 40s, and had made over 30 films before becoming a "star." Kanfer does an excellent job explaining the old studio system, the backstage business, and general cultural background, in order to provide us the context in which Bogart created some of the most iconic film roles.

And Kanfer also documents what he calls Bogart's greatest role, a man dying relatively young from cancer, hiding his pain to spare his family and fans. The doctor treating him said: "When a man is sick, you get to know him. You find out whether he's made of soft wood or hard wood. I began to get fonder of Bogie with each visit. He was made of very hard wood indeed" (p. 220).

Earlier, he had given a more public display of manhood when dealing with the tangled loyalties of the Hollywood blacklist.

Kanfer seems to be a pretty standard liberal guy, but he's refreshingly independent of what he calls "the romantic wish dream" (p. 131) of the Hollywood Left: the blacklisted as brave men and women, just ordinary citizens, standing up to ignorant, corrupt, badly-shaved politicos, as epitomized (of course) by Woody Allen's *The Front*.

In fact, as Kanfer says:

> More than half of the hostile witnesses had lied to their own lawyers about their Communist past or present, and presented themselves to the Committee for the First Amendment [the support group Bogart had joined] as innocent victims framed by the government.
>
> After witnessing their performance at the hearings,

---

[3] http://tomshone.blogspot.com/2011/02/his-toughness-was-inside-job.html

and making a few inquiries of his own, "Bogart was furious" one blacklistee recalled, "shouting at Danny Kaye, 'You fuckers sold me out.'" (p. 127)

Though he remained liberal in private life, he felt a justifiable anger about the way his name and reputation had been used. (p. 132)

Alistair Cooke later recalled: "Bogart was aghast" to discover how many of the protestors "were down-the-line Communists coolly exploiting the protection of the First and Fifth Amendments. . . . He had thought they were just freewheeling anarchists, like himself" (p. 127).

If Bogart was an anarchist, he was a Conservative Anarchist, in the tradition of Céline or Jünger, whose "Anarch" sounds like the typical Bogart character:

[A]n extreme aloofness, which nourishes itself and risks itself in the borderline situations, but only stands in an observational relationship to the world, as all instances of true order are dissolving and an "organic construction" is not yet, or no longer, possible.[4]

Or even a "Bohemian Tory" like Noël Coward, men for whom personal integrity, professionalism and loyalty to friends—like Foster with Gibson, Bogart stood behind those he could personally vouch for, using his star power to keep them working—were more important that politics or ideological purity. And to that extent Kanfer is justified in finding Bogart to have created a "new" masculinity, not the "post-feminist" sort but more like one of Evola's "men among the ruins."

[To name names or not] was a matter of great importance to those affected, but it was not the only way to take the measure of a man, and many refused to be defined in such narrow terms. Humphrey Bogart was one of them.

---

[4] http://www.counter-currents.com/2010/08/right-wing-anarchism/

As the decade wound down, he continued to present his own brand of masculinity, which had nothing to do with polemics [such as the contrasting but self-exculpating works of Miller or Kazan]. (p. 132)

In his recent book *Dupes: How America's Adversaries Have Manipulated Progressives for a Century*, Paul Kengor presents some intriguing bits of evidence to suggest a "Bogart" enrolled in a New York City indoctrination program in the 1930s could have been Bogart.[5]

Speaking of communism, Aryan masculinity, and Noël Coward, consider their interplay in *Beat the Devil*, based on the novel by Communist Claud Cockburn (whose son, Alex, has just published a new edition),[6] with a screenplay by Truman Capote. We know how Bogie hated commies, what about queers?

Bogart's attitude to homosexuals seems to have been amusement or puzzlement, but capable of changing to good will when they showed the same professionalism he embodied. The famously flamboyant Capote earned Bogart's respect for his ability to crank out countless rewrites, sometimes daily, even from a hospital bed. Capote returned the compliment after Bogie's death, recalling the way he divided the world into professionals and bums, and "God knows he was [a professional]."

Moreover, he even beat Bogart at arm wrestling, and hustled $50 out of him doing it; an incident oddly reminiscent of an episode of *All in the Family* where Archie's old pal comes out while they arm wrestle.

It's also reminiscent of the way Sam Spade deals with Joel Cairo in *The Maltese Falcon*, the first time Bogart, Huston, and Lorre teamed up. And yes, I know Bogart isn't Sam Spade and

---

[5] Paul Kengor, *Dupes: How America's Adversaries Have Manipulated Progressives for a Century* (Wilmington, Del.: ISI Books, 2010). See Kevin Mooney, "Was Staunch Anti-Communist Humphrey Bogart Once a Young Communist Dupe?," http://netrightdaily.com/2010/10/was-staunch-anti-communist-humphrey-bogart-once-a-young-commie-dupe/

[6] Claud Cockburn, *Beat the Devil* (Oakland, Cal.: AK Press, 2012).

that Spade is in fact an entirely fictional character. But what made Bogart's Spade unforgettable, when studios had already flopped twice with other actors, was Bogart himself, and Spade's character does give us a chance to see the range of Bogart's response to sexual deviation.

Cairo, played by Peter Lorre, with his lisp, piss-elegant clothes, and scented handkerchief, even resembles Capote. He is easily knocked out and disarmed, almost playfully (Spade allows himself a puzzled sniff of the handkerchief); but at the end of the scene Cairo gets the drop on Spade and insists on carrying out a search of his office. Spade, impressed by Cairo's persistence and competence, lifts up his arms and says "Go ahead, go ahead" while Bogart gives a rather forced giggle. Fade to black; is there a sexual undercurrent here?

Spade deals otherwise with the *gunsel*, Wilmer (seemingly pronounced "Wilma" by everyone). Played by Elisha Cook, Jr., he's an obviously overcompensating fruit, swathing his scrawny frame in a thick overcoat, carrying two guns in his pockets, and talking in "tough guy" lingo. ("The cheaper the hood, the gaudier the patter," Spade sneers, articulating the Aryan's contempt for theatricality.) "What is it?" says the hotel dick, and Spade answers, "I don't know, I've been watching it." His conclusion is that Wilmer is weak and incompetent; Spade enjoys disarming him and then displays Aryan modesty: "A crippled newsie took them away, I made him give them back."

Spade is right in his evaluation. Wilmer is incompetent and a coward, who literally kicks Spade when he's down and out; Spade repays him by offering him up as the fall guy, and the gang eagerly agrees. The actor will redeem himself in Bogart's next detective film, *The Big Sleep*, where his wimpy character is killed protecting his girlfriend; "Your little man died to keep you out of trouble," Marlowe points out to the ungrateful shrew.

Finally, Kasper Gutman, Oxford scholar gone bad; Wodehousian accent, possibly Jewish, searching the world for the Maltese Falcon, like his contemporary, Otto Rahn, another homosexual academic Grail hunter (and possible inspiration for Indiana Jones); and a classic, even Classical, pederast. Here,

Spade's Aryan virtues play him false; his respect for Gutman's age and erudition allows Gutman to mesmerize him, first with words and then with a mickey. A parable for the history of Aryan-Jewish interaction?

And yes, Bogart even teamed up, after a fashion, with Coward himself. Here's how Lauren Bacall tells it:

> He and Bogie were guests of Clifton Webb one weekend. Bogie and Noël were assigned to the same room, and Noël was gay, as everybody on Earth knew, but nobody cared, because he was so great. Just to be in his presence was quite enough. And at the end of the evening one night, they were changing into their PJs to hit the sack. Bogie was sitting on the edge of the bed, and at one point put his hand on Noël's knee. Bogie said: "Noël, I have to tell you that if I had my druthers and I liked guys you would be the one I'd want to be with. But, unfortunately, I like girls." And from that moment on Noël never mentioned it, and Bogie never mentioned it. Class behavior! And they became fast, fast friends.[7]

In his final chapter Kanfer addresses his broader theme: the unprecedented dominance of the Bogie icon. He gave us the answer already on his very first page, when he corrects Norma Desmond: the pictures did become bigger, and the actors smaller. The 20 highest-grossing films of all time are all "blockbusters" made for teen audiences, and their actors have the same dewy innocence and immaturity. Since it's experience that produces character, today's actors, however highly trained, are indistinguishable and interchangeable; no one, Kanfer points out, impersonates Tobey Maguire, Leonardo DiCaprio, or Christian Bale, the way men like Bogart or Cagney or even wispy Jimmy Stewart were a staple part of a comedian's repertoire.

One could quibble a bit here; Christian Bale, certainly, has given comics from South Park to Riff Trax a comedic foothold

---

[7] http://www.advocate.com/news/daily-news/2011/02/07/bacall-capote-didnt-have-sex-bogie

with his raspy Batman voice. And Bale's *The Dark Knight*, despite showing up as Number 8 on Kanfer's list, is arguably at least an attempt to create a more mature, more conflicted, Batman, perhaps not unlike one of Bogart's bad guys with principles, making hard choices in a world morally adrift (See Trevor Lynch's meditations on *The Dark Knight*.)[8]

On the other hand, I confess that even after watching it about eight times, I still don't understand the narrative of *The Departed*, since the three principals, Mark Wahlberg, Matt Damon, and, yes, DiCaprio, seem exactly the same person to these old eyes. (Or was that deliberate?) Needless to say, no problem recognizing old school Jack Nicholson. Of course, Bogart's scars, lisp, and cigarette-rasp were only the external signs, useful for an actor, of his inner maturity. In his review of Kanfer cited above, Shone also says: "These days, we measure toughness by the damage dished out to others—by body counts and kill ratios. Bogart's toughness was an inside job."

In *Men Among the Ruins*, Baron Evola summarized The Roman, and generally The Aryan, style as:

The sober, austere, active style, free from exhibitionism, measured, endowed with a calm awareness of one's dignity. To have the sense of what one is and of one's value independently of any external reference, loving distance as well as actions and expressions reduced to the essential, devoid of any exhibition and cheap showmanship— all these are fundamental elements for the eventual formation of a superior type.[9]

That was Bogart: tough without a gun.

Counter-Currents/ *North American New Right*
May 30, 2011

---

[8] http://www.counter-currents.com/2010/09/the-dark-knight/
[9] Julius Evola, *Men Among the Ruins: Post-War Reflections of a Radical Traditionalist*, ed. Michael Moynihan, trans. Guido Stucco (Rochester, Vt.: Inner Traditions, 2002), p. 261.

HE WRITES! YOU READ!
THEY LIVE

Constant readers will know that I not infrequently make use of images or lines from John Carpenter's schlock-cult classic *They Live*. But it was only the other day, my financial situation being but a few steps away from Roddy Piper's in the film, that I had to luck to find a $1.99 proof copy of Jonathan Lethem's excellent book,[1] part of the "Deep Focus" series, from which I also recommend the one on *Death Wish*.[2]

Both are written from the Default Liberal Position (otherwise they wouldn't be published), but both are relatively free of ideological cant and more than a little willing to contemplate, for example, whether Bronson's vigilante might have a point or two to make, so they make easy enough reading for those who might actually have a Bronson poster on the wall.

It's only 200 pages, and moreover it's a small-sized book, so you can probably read it in one relatively short sitting. In fact, a movie time code appears throughout, so you can probably read it along with your Netflix stream. So in the spirit of such brevity, let's do so, and I'll just make a few notes along the way.

1. Carpenter's screenplay pseudonym, "Frank Armitage," alludes to Lovecraft's "Dunwich Horror," while the originating short story is by an obscure author best known as one of the few to collaborate with Philip K. Dick, thus linking "two now esteemed artists situated in disreputable genres." I would myself add, as noted here before, that these are the two greatest American writers of the 20th century, one in each half. Lethem does note, however, the irony that Lovecraft's trans-dimensional Elder Gods have now become yuppies shopping for blue corn tortillas.

2. He also notes that in the summer between the film's pro-

---

[1] Jonathan Lethem, *They Live* (Berkeley: Soft Skull Press, 2010).
[2] Christopher Sorrentino, *Death Wish* (Berkeley: Soft Skull Press, 2010).

duction and release saw the riots in NYC's Tompkins Square Park, which calls to mind the homeless encampment at the start of the film. However, not so much; these are "sheepish, demoralized, obedient" and seem to want to do nothing but watch television all day, which is convenient for the plot points, of course. More on these losers later.

3. The use of '50s sci-fi clips on the TVs leads him to speculate if, to Carpenter, the '50s "seem a whole lot deeper than the '80s," which is a nice way to put what a lot of us here have been thinking. As Lethem later says, the glasses reveal that "color is lies, black and white the truth" or, as one revolutionary shouts, "They colorized it!"

4. Lethem is all upset about the ways that the phrase "Hoffman Lenses" has been mutated in pop culture; Albert Hofmann? Abbie Hoffman? He likes pop culture re-appropriation, but like most good-thinkers, thinks some standards—his—should apply. Some people have dared to associate them with "holocaust denier" Michael A. Hoffman II, which he take as a warning to those who would set their memes loose on the world: "Free your mind, and an ass may follow." Har-de-har-har. However, just to blow Lethem's mind, here's another: entheogenic drug researcher and cultural historian (and Heavy Metal theorist) Michael [no relation to Hoffman II] Hoffman. Take that!

5. Now back to those hapless homeless. Lethem notes at various points one of the most interesting memes in the movie, quoting at length (as we will here) no less than NPR poster-boy Slavoj Žižek:

> [I]t totally turns around the usual new age idea of critique of ideology, which would be: "in everyday life we have ideological glasses, learn to put down, take off, the glasses, and see with your own eyes reality the way it is." No, unfortunately, it doesn't work like this. Liberation hurts. You have to be forced to put your glasses on. (Slavoj Žižek, "They Live! Hollywood as an Ideological Machine")

6. This is in reference to the (in)famous "longest fight scene in movie history" but it also crops up throughout the film. Lethem notes that Frank is not a "Magic Negro" (even using the term!) but more of a Danny Glover sidekick, then goes on to point out that while the White hero, Nada (which makes me recall *Showgirls'* "Nomi") is naïve, the Black guy is too-knowing in his cynicism: "a nice twist is in the works: Nada will eventually have to bludgeon his Black friend into seeing the truth Frank seemingly already possesses." The "twist" being on the now-audience-expected theme, White guy learns grudging respect for the street wisdom of Black partner forced on him. In general, "knowledge in *They Live* is associated with head pain, grogginess and eyestrain. . . . It's more comfortable not to see." Moral? Even the most obvious victims of the system are more likely to just "tune in for more" as they used to say during station breaks, than rise up and throw off their mental chains.

7. If the good ol' American family won't rise up (I think that's why, along with budget restraints, Carpenter makes use of suspiciously normal looking families among his homeless group), then what to do? Who you gonna call? The *Männerbund*!

EXCURSUS ON THE *MÄNNERBUND*

Lethem starts off by calling to our attention that once we get away from the homeless camp, the LA scenes, especially Holly's apartment, look like porn sets. True, but I'd just say that all of Southern California looks like a porn set to these New York eyes and leave it at that; *Curb Your Enthusiasm*, for example, looks like a porn shoot to me; but Lethem wants to use this to set up his notion that there's some kinda homoeroticism going on between Frank and Nada. Noting their obvious racial polarity, he trots out the tired Huck and Jim thesis of Judaic critic Leslie Fiedler, who tried to reduce all American literature to variations on boys on the raft.

(The *ne plus ultra* of this was probably the Penguin Classics edition of *Moby Dick*, where critic Harry Beaver [!] created a 300 page text with 200 pages of endnotes detailing line by line Melville's "phallic imagination"—Harpoons! Coffins! Peg-legs! Oysters! Dogs and cats living together!)

I take Frank's invitation to introduce Nada to the homeless encampment (hot food and showers!) as recruitment not into a sexual liaison but into a proto-*Männerbund* of working class types banding together in the economic chaos (though, as we have seen, not a very lively one, but serving to get him across the street to the fake church were he meets the real revolutionaries). Nada will return the favor when he later beats the truth into Frank, *Fight Club* style.

Lethem would have saved himself some idle speculations, and real puzzlements, such as why Nada later takes a younger version of himself under his wing, if he had understood better that, as he says: "If it's not that kind of hookup scene, it's still a hookup scene." As he says later, when Nada spews stupid, supposedly clever one-liners about ugly female ghouls, "this man of the people is more of the male than the female people." And later, during the shoot-em-up at the Cable 54 offices, "He really shouldn't be looking for Holly; he's got no knack with women."

The *Männerbund* theme continues even when Nada "hooks up" with Holly, played by the "eerie" and ineffable Meg Foster.

Lethem is correct to point out she is indeed strikingly "mannish" for a nevertheless attractive woman (originally cast in TV's *Cagney and Lacey*, she was dropped because she made Tyne Daly look too feminine!), which may have something to do with Nada's oddly unmotivated rage against how ugly the female ghouls appear to him; he has firm though offbeat ideas about beauty.

And though dark haired she has eyes that "are such a pale shade of blue they're nearly a special effect" by themselves. He alludes to her roles in *The Scarlet Letter* (19th century American lit again!) and *The Osterman Weekend*, but I find it more interesting to compare her role just the year before in the otherwise atrocious *Masters of the Universe*, where her hard face and unearthly eyes work well for the straightforwardly and extradimensionally evil character called Evil-lyn (it's that kind of movie), playing against another muscular blonde hero, Dolph Lundgren as He-Man.

Mannish though she is, Holly will, of course, turn out to be the *femme fatale* to infiltrate the group and betray everyone, even killing Frank. Lethem nicely points out that this unexpected turn makes it seem like genre conventions are attacking our poor heroes; like *Full Metal Jacket* or *The Shining*, halfway through the film, the sci-fi metaphysics stop, and suddenly it's an action flick, then a *film noir*.

Throughout the book, Lethem comments on the oddly pedestrian, that is, walk-around, *flâneur*-like LA in the film, so unlike the freeway-LA we think we know, and comes up with various explanations, including budget restraints. To me, the answer is simple; Carpenter sets the whole film in some kind of post-Reagan hyper-recession; jobs have disappeared, workers are migratory (Frank from Detroit, Nada from Denver), riding the rails, working under the counter, etc. Who can afford to drive, except the "Well Dressed Man" at the newsstand, who's a ghoul, or Holly, who's a mole for the ghouls? The supposed "real face" of Reagan's Morning in America.

8. Making the film as early as 1988 gives it the look of Leftist hysteria, but in fact the process was underway, it just took 30 years and two busted bubbles to make everyone realize that while we were putting everything on the card, the real jobs were shipped out, and the real money was siphoned off, not so much by yuppies (who are as mortgage-strapped as the rest of us, just with bigger houses) but the really big guys, the bankers. Frank and Nada's car-less wanderings, and the packed streets, give the film a contemporary, not a dated, look.

9. Another theme dear to the New Right: the ghouls are outright colonizers and parasites, not even illegal aliens (like *District Nine*) you might work up some Ellis Island sympathy for, like the sociopathic Sicilians we now welcome as "Italian American patriots," and they're coruscating ugly, and even worse, they want to wear our best clothes (like "Well Dressed Man") and make it with our smooth, pink bodies.

There's no chance for the "traditional science-fiction platitude, with its overtones of Franz Boas cultural relativism." When a ghoul cop tries the Good Cop routine and suggests "You look just as ugly to us" Nada responds with Randian certitude and contempt: "Impossible." It reminds me of the scene where Toohey tries to confront Roark, but Roark just walks away. Lethem refers to Carpenter's '50s film outlook again, and he's right. Not for nothing does Carpenter idolize John Ford and admire the Ford-influenced *The Thing* enough to remake it. The comparable exchange in the '50s *Thing*: "What do you do with a carrot? You cook it."

10. Lethem contrasts this with another late '80s sci-fi film, *Blade Runner*, where the replicants are more sympathetic than the humans, and the controversies over whether Deckard himself is a replicant. I would again match him with Lovecraft. Lovecraft certainly loathed furriners, especially immigrants. The Old Ones certainly seem to covet warm human flesh, and several characters are half-breeds of such couplings, who, in accordance with Lovecraft's strict morality (or bigotry) must be evil and come to bad ends, like Wilbur in "The Dunwich Horror" that Carpenter's pseudonym alludes to. His brother, "who looked more like the father," is a monster killed by the scientists at the end; the narrator of *The Shadow Over Innsmouth* gradually realizes he is one of the fish-people himself and presumably will shoot himself at the end; the eponymous Arthur Jermyn discovers he is the offspring of an ape mother, and burns himself alive (although this might be one of the Darwinian Lovecraft's little jokes). Poor Akeley, beset by Plutonian immigrant miners in "The Whisperer in Darkness" is fooled into joining the Plutonian race, having his brain boxed up with the promise of being shipped off to see the sights of the galaxy, perhaps the ones Roy recalls at the end of *Blade Runner*. Most notably, Professor Peaslee in *The Shadow Out of Time* has his mind "kidnapped" and transferred into the "rugose cone" body of a Cyclopean prehistoric race—brain rape!—when he finally works up the courage to look in a mirror at his new body, he shrieks and faints, as does "The Outsider" when a mirror reveals that he is a rotting corpse. Nada, Lethem points out, never turns the glasses on himself in a mirror.

But there is another vein in Lovecraft, part of his "cosmic awe." Peaslee learns to appreciate and admire the super-intelligent cones, rugose or not; the narrator in *At the Mountains of Madness* sympathizes with the specimens of the ancient race dug out of the ice only to be attacked by dogs. As the Templars came to admire the Moslem warriors they fought, anyone who peers deeply into a religion or culture of his own may be able to recognize the value of an alien's, but at such a deep, shared level that talk of conversion or "relativism" is inane. But still, not with these guys. They're space yuppies, practicing plane-tary gentrification, and ugly as cheese dip from 1957. Nada kills the cop and steals his weapons.

11. As a boomer myself, I find it mind-boggling that Lethem attributes the line "ten thousand holes in Blackburn, Lanca-shire" to "Yellow Submarine"; in fact, since "A Day in the Life" is usually held up as some kind of "classic work of timeless ge-nius," to misattribute an image, and to such a dopey song, seems unforgivable in general; or is he deliberately thumbing his nose at the middle-brows?

12. But, just a page or two later, he redeems himself with this: "it's hard to imagine that at the ghouls' first job fair the position of Fatuous Cocktail-swilling Jackass didn't have will-ing applicants lined up around the block." I can't wait to use that line myself, maybe even on myself.

13. Holy cow, now Lethem's calling the same character "the cockroach of the human spirit." He's using my meme!

14. Lethem's giving us some freeze-dried lecture on how "post-Freudian, post-Virginia Woolf" readers demand charac-ters that are flawed, even treacherous; he thinks this is an index of how seriously a work is intended, or even, he adds ominous-ly, "how seriously it is likely to be received" —by the literary gatekeepers, like him, of course. If you don't know where this is going, he tells us "If Shakespeare had written *The Lord of the Rings*, its title would be *Gollum*." (And I guess if Shakespeare had written *Hamlet*, its title would have been *Rosencrantz and Guildenstern*.)

And there, in admittedly a neat little phrase, is a perfect ex-ample of the Judaic Plan for Culture Distortion; how even already existing classic literature can be "taught" in ways that inculcate the cockroach mentality. And after all, is not the plea that "we" prefer such "complex" and twisted characters simple egotism? Does the Jew not recognize himself in such figures (just as Freud's so-called science was an impudent projection of the Judaic domestic scene onto all mankind)? Surely Gollum is the Jew of the *Ring* films; did people not complain of the role's "anti-Semitism"? It is the Jew who finds such characters "intriguing," not the Aryan public, which is why normal stories keep getting written and filmed, since they are demanded by the public (adjusted for inflation, the all-time box office hit: *Gone with the Wind*), and the Judaic gatekeepers keep having to push them back underwater and "demand" "more serious" ones.

Lethem keeps trying to insinuate, in that Judaic way, that we really like the bum-turned-traitorous big-shot, Drifter, that we'd really like to be him, in fact, far more than that dumb, boring blond hero. It surfaces again when he discusses the poor Pregnant Woman with Coffee Pot who gets in Nada's way during the shoot-out, specifically connecting her with Frances Dormand's character in *Fargo*, the Coen Brothers' festival of Judaic paranoia, dividing the *goyim* into two groups, murderous blond beasts and simple-minded law enforcers (who, implicitly, will protect the Jews from the first group). You want to play that game, Jonathan? OK, Nada embodies both; while we know he's a simple guy just trying to save us, to the office workers he's just a murderous workplace psycho. Oh, and your precious Coen Bros. stole Lebowski from . . . *Drifter*!

Maybe it was a mistake to try and read this all in one sitting. I'm starting to feel a little woozy, more than a little cranky. If you took my suggestion at the beginning to do this, go back, you fools! Only a few pages of the book, less than two minutes of the film, are left, and Lethem is really working my nerves. First, he quotes G. K. Chesterton—when's the last time you saw that, outside the *New Oxford Review* or maybe that Catholic cable channel? But then, he follows it up some "film curator" guy who says that "we who live in the urban centers" both fear and loathe the denizens of the heartland, whom "we" perceive as "Bible-thumping, gun-toting" nut jobs "like the Unabomber."

Uh, the Unabomber? Harvard, brilliant mathematician, Mani-festo published in the *New York Times*, oh yeah, that cracker dumbass. Alright buddy, Mr. "Milan Film Festival" jag-off, you've asked for it. I've run out of bubble gun . . . I mean, gum.

15. But wait, as I move down the hallway for my stolen police rifle, I pass a mirror . . . look in . . . My God! The blue skin, the robotic eyes! You others, drop the book, before it's too late . . . save yourselves! As for me . . . I have fallen into the cheese dip . . .

Counter-Currents/*North American New Right*
September 5, 2011

I'll Have a White Rock, Please:
Implicit Whiteness, Aryan Futurism,
& the Godlike Genius of Scott Walker

"Was listening to this during a rocket attack at DaNang Vietnam in '71 . . . what a rush . . . after smoking 3 bowls of Thai Stick. Still get a rush to this day at age 64 . . . there was teeth, hair, and eyeballs all around my barracks, but we survived."

—YouTube comment on "Jim Dandy to the Rescue"
by Black Oak Arkansas

Over the last year or two, the value or usefulness of popular music, and rock in particular, to the struggle to renew White Consciousness has been subject to debate. These discussions have made important points, but too often they suffer from a lack of historical, and perhaps metaphysical, data. In this essay I will examine some of the most interesting of these recent online discussions, and suggest how they might profit from a little re-orientation in the light of such White musical pioneers Varg Vikernes and Scott Walker, as well as the writings of Julius Evola and Alain Daniélou on music from the Traditionalist point of view.

The Woman Question in White Rock

In "How About Some Good Old Love Songs From Alleged 'Right Wing' Groups?"[1] Andrea O. Letania—proprietress of the "Neo-Fascist" pop culture blog *Once Upon a Time in America*,[2] whose title alone makes me want to call her a comrade—calls

---

[1] Andrea O. Letania, "How About Some Good Old Love Songs From Alleged 'Right Wing' Groups?" http://www.wvwnews.net/story.php?id=9536

[2] http://ostrovletania.blogspot.com/

attention to an important issue—"Given that the main point of popular music is to appeal to the opposite sex, how can right-wing rock appeal to most ladies out there?"—and raises some interesting questions, but too many questionable assumptions prevent her from making any real headway toward a solution.

First, she seems to think that the "right wing" milieu is characterized by a love of Metal. This may be broadly true, especially among groups that either themselves or by their music cause the mainstream media to have convulsions, and hence get lots of press, but arguably the most characteristic, and interesting, current is composed of the small but deeply loyal tributaries making up what's been called alt-folk, or apocalyptic folk, etc.,[3] which are hardly male-only when it comes to performers, audience, or even distributors (hello, Jane Elizabeth!). For more on this "scene traditionalism," see the articles on Mark Sedgwick's blog[4] as well as Josh Buckley's comments on the same blog:

> One would expect that a music-based subculture would consist of music groups with an identifiably similar sound. This is certainly the criterion for defining music genres like bluegrass, rhythm & blues, or country/western. Yet the vast majority of (alt.folk groups) play wildly divergent styles of music.[5]

But let's look at Metal itself. Letania finds it either impossibly "hard" or else given to "kitschy mythic airs." As for the latter, I thought girls liked stories of castles and unicorns. And anyway, it's hardly any more "monotonous" than rap (and considerably less vulgar and misogynistic, quite a trick for music that supposedly appeals to adolescent boys) or the olde-tyme moon-June-

[3] See Christopher Pankhurst's "Music of the Future," where David Tibet is compared to Schubert, http:// www.counter-currents.com/2011/11/music-of-the-future/

[4] Mark Sedgwick, "Apoliteic Music," http:// traditional-istblog.blogspot.com/search?q=neo-folk

[5] Joshua Buckley, "Euro-Paganism: One or Many?," http://traditionalistblog.blogspot.com/2008/01/euro-paganism-one-or-many.html

spoon songs our great-grandmothers sang around the parlor piano (while the men, I guess, danced to John Philip Sousa marches).

However, Letania is exactly correct that "a rock band is supposed to do both, which is why even the toughest rock bands have songs ranging from hard to soft." But this hardly sets aside Metal. Indeed, Metal was arguably created, as a genre, by Led Zeppelin, and Zep is arguably still the greatest Metal band, not so much for any specific musical or lyrical accomplishment, as for its ability, as Michael Hoffman[6] emphasized, to rock both hard and soft equally well. In this quote, he states Letania's whole thesis quite well:

> Classic Rock inherently has more potential for acid allusions, because it includes the entire range from Heavy to Soothing, whereas Pop is limited to Soothing, and Metal is limited to Heavy. This is why Led Zeppelin ranks at the top of Rock history: a broad command of the full range of modes. That's why Pop and Metal have a harder time becoming Classic. Pop has the advantage of being acceptable in public.[7]

Hoffman even seems to grant Letania's dichotomy, but this is because he, like most general culture critics, can't be bothered to consider "popular" bands that are popular precisely for their willingness to include the infamous "power ballads" to keep the chicks happy.

In fact, when it comes to the ladies, Metal, despite its media image, has historically had more than a little appeal. Though "hair metal" is universally disparaged today, its continued existence reminds us that heavy music, as well as such "gay" attributes as long hair and spandex attire, can be chick magnets, as they were in the dreaded '80s.

---

[6] The entheogenic researcher, not the holocaust revisionist, although the coincidence is . . . intriguing.

[7] Michael Hoffman, "Mystic Allusions in Heavy Rock Lyrics," http://www.egodeath.com/MysticAllusions.htm

Or, since Letania speaks highly of Southern Rock, consider Black Oak Arkansas. White skin, long blonde hair, and white spandex jeans, but it's not Ann Coulter! The chicks love Jim Dandy! And forget about "don't ask don't tell." Jim Dandy's qualifications are on display for all to fall down before in lust or despair.

What happened? Rather than disparaging Metal as such, we would be better off looking for the cause exactly where "alleged 'right wing' groups" would suggest: the Judaic-Negro conspiracy that, in defiance of market demand, took White rock off MTV and force fed rap and its no-hair, no-ass "aesthetic."

While the boys stayed loyal and metal flourished under the radar (who sold more records, the Stones in 40 years or Metallica in 20? Metallica, of course), the girls seem to have swallowed the whole Britney-and-rap cocktail. One might speculate that the girls' preferences reflect a greater conformism, or susceptibility to media brainwashing, but I suppose that would be sexism.

From her description of what's wrong with metal, I can imagine Varg Vikernes would pretty well sum up her image of the Worst Alleged Right Wing music. Yet, Varg may have the answer she seeks. While Letania wants soft but "rockin'" music with romantic lyrics, Varg has questioned the appropriateness of "guitar based" music entirely, when it come to White people. The music he's been releasing from his prison cell—how romantic is that?—sounds like nothing other than what might just be called Aryan New Age, and what could be more female-friendly than that?

THE RHYTHM QUESTION AND THE NEW WHITE AGE

Letania wants softer music, Varg to get rid of guitars altogether. But what if we got rid of shredding guitars and pounding drums—how would we rock? This leads to another question: does White music have, or need, rhythm? And what does it matter?

Discussions of "implicit Whiteness" in popular music—such as this from Kevin MacDonald[8]—tend to gravitate toward

---

[8] Kevin MacDonald, "Psychology and White Ethnocentrism,"

Heavy Metal and country rather than "New Age" music, for obvious reasons; while all three are reviled, only "New Age" is associated with hippies, yuppies, boomers, and other Left-of-center types.

Yet consider this discussion of "New Directions for 'New Age'":

> But even though Woods sees new-age music as a universal force for change, the fact is that the audience is limited by age (mostly baby boomers), race (mostly White), and class (mostly middle and up). Consider, for example, this definition of new-age music offered by composer-producer Steve Halpern in Patti Jean Birosik's book *The New Age Music Guide*: "Perhaps the most striking aspect of new-age music is its use of rhythm — or, more accurately, its lack of it." This characteristic alienates vast numbers of listeners for whom rhythm is the thing — not just African-Americans and Latinos but people of all origins.[9]

I ran across this while trying to save my lazy White ass by finding whether someone had already typed up for me that quote from Halpern's fine Introduction to said book (an ancient tome from 1989, which, like other culturally scorned material, is easily found for a buck or two).

Although intending exactly the opposite, the writer correctly ascertains the obsession with rhythm characteristic of the primitive Negro mentality. And of course, by "people of all origins" he means "formerly White people who have been brainwashed by MSM and modern society in general into a grotesque overvaluation of one, small, dispensable aspect of music, the better to reject their entire culture in favor of an alien simulacrum." As the White college student famously said, "We don't have any culture."

Contrariwise, the author is unable to appreciate Halpern's intriguing and bracing embrace of the idea of "no rhythm" (and

http://www.kevinmacdonald.net/WhiteEthnocentrism. pdf
[9] www.csmonitor.com/1990/0212/lage.html

he, for his part, would be horrified by my identification of it as "implicitly White"; note his name).

Although I'm sure Halpern is as PC as the rest of the New Age audience, his discussion explicitly denigrates rhythm as a primitive and backward element ("Cro-Magnon man pounding on skins and bones"), and explicitly welcomes the modern technologies that have enabled new instruments, and new uses of old instruments, without the "slave[ry]" of "the time machine."

The surely accidental association of rhythm and slavery is both accurate and, in this context, rather piquant. It's like the railroad foreman in *Blazing Saddles* demanding that his workers sing "a good ol' nigger work song" and reminding them that "when you was slaves, you sang like birds."

Need one point out that, here again, the science and instruments are White creations? Halpern's techno-positivism would fit very comfortably in the late, great Alisdair Clarke's notion of Aryan Futurism.

Of course, it's really just a question of emphasis; New Age music doesn't *lack* rhythm—an Amazon reviewer of the Windham Hill 20 year anniversary sampler complains that it "has some rythmic [*sic*] and percussion pieces that are actually gnarly and you want to hit the skip key on your CD player if you are looking for relaxing and meditative music"[10]—it just isn't *interested* in it, and prefers to emphasize more important elements.[11]

As well, if it weren't part of the PC catechism to praise Negroid rhythm (while the author of the quote above would tear out his own tongue before uttering the phrase "natural rhythm,") we might point out that the much-vaunted "jazz" music of the Negro is largely in basic 4/4 (as the [possibly] Judaic hipster Dave Brubeck observed long ago, thus creating a profitable niche for himself), while "(c)Rap" or "Rap(e)" music is

_____

[10] http://www.amazon.com/Sanctuary-20-Years-Windham-Hill/dp/B000000NLB/ref=sr_1_1?ie=UTF8&s=music&qid=12745617 36&sr=8-1

[11] For a pro-White discussion of those elements, in the vocal context, see Julian Lee's "The White Voice in Rock & Pop," http://www.counter-currents.com/2011/11/the-white-singing-voice-in-rock-and-pop/

even more primitive, merely amplifying said 4/4 "beat" to ear-splitting and gut-punching levels—again, thanks to the White man's technology—while also eliminating melody, which is usually "sampled"—viz., looted—from White rock or pop (a technique already used by jazz, where the compositional resources of oh-so-advanced "be-bop" rarely got beyond stealing the chords of a Gershwin song and then wailing away).

What's at issue here is not rhythm (seriously, did Mozart *lack rhythm*?) but that amorphous thing (without which "it don't mean a thing") called "swing." Self-hating White critic Robert Palmer observed in his notes to the Ornette Coleman box set that European imitators of "free jazz" were boring, because they lacked what American Negroes had learned as entertainers: how to swing.[12] As we have pointed out, this "swing" is by no means any kind of "natural rhythm," but a particular entertainment device, which Louis Armstrong had to teach to Fletcher Henderson's orchestra, despite their being "the finest musicians in Harlem."[13]

In short, a mere bit of early 20th-century show business mumbo-jumbo, easily discarded by anyone interested in serious composition.

The pioneers of hip-hop, perhaps because not writing self-hating essays but actually working with White technologies such as turntables, had more appreciation of the "non-swinging" Europeans than Palmer. Afrika Bambaata famously said of Kraftwerk that they "were so stiff, they swung." He paid tribute to them in the style of the Negro, by imitating—or again, looting—their work.

Still, a lesson for all those pitiable "whiggers" who are, in fact, just a more literal-minded component of the general demoralized White society: the Negro will never respect an imitator; he

---

[12] http://www.amazon.com/Beauty-Rare-Thing-Complete-Recordings/dp/B00000332J/ref=sr_1_1?ie=UTF8&s=music&qid=1274568308&sr=1-1

[13] James J. O'Meara, "Happy Fourth of July! Venerable Jazz Scholar Admits: Negro Musicians Had No Sense of Swing, Had To Be Taught By Louis Armstrong," http://jamesjomeara.blogspot.com/2009/07/happy-fourth-of-july-venerable-jazz.html

will, however, be compelled to admire the sheer audacity of those who either ignore him, or, like Jimmy Page, loot with the alacrity and joy of Viking raiders.

VARG VIKERNES ON THE MUSIC OF THE FUTURE

Speaking of Vikings and other Berserkers: this evolution in the direction of Aryan Futurism is not beyond Heavy Metal itself. No less an icon than Varg Vikernes, the imprisoned, church-burning Godfather of Death Metal, has explicitly rejected all "guitar-based" music as "implicitly Negroid" and thus inappropriate for a White movement:

> The guitar is an European invention, just like the synthesizer. However, the music played on guitar is mostly nigger music—and that goes definitely for all metal music.[14] I have nothing against guitars, as you might know a lot of classical music is played on guitar. If I would make any more guitar music it would be classical music. So, it has nothing (or better; little) to do with the instrument in itself.
>
> I guess I have been a bit unclear when talking about this, until now. Anyway, what I explain above should clear things up for you. I categorize music like this; Aryan music (European classical and folk music, as well as some other more electronic music); Alien music with Aryan lyrics (like all these Viking-metal bands, Oi-rock and the like) and; Alien music with alien lyrics. As simple as that.[15]

His most recent work embraces keyboard, synthesizers, and other electronic methods—perhaps due to their availability in prison, since even Norwegian prisons have their drawbacks—producing what might well be called "Death New Age" (alt-

---

[14] An echo of Spengler, who said in 1932—when you could say this in a book published by Knopf and favorably reviewed in *Time*— "Jazz music and Negro dancing perform the Dead March for a great Culture."

[15] http://www.burzum.com/burzum/library/interviews/varg/

hough "Black New Age" might be more accurate, it might have paradoxical implications in the light of our discussion here).

THE GENIUS OF SCOTT WALKER

The conceptual movement away from rhythm—or at least "blue-eyed soul"—to more purely Aryan modes of music making can be found in exemplary fashion in Scott Walker's curious trajectory from Pop Idol to reclusive "genius."[16] Born in Ohio, Walker had achieved a "big in Europe" kind of superstardom as part of a Righteous Brothers knock-off act called The Walker Brothers (they weren't named Walker or even related). He then, well, walked away from it, living in seclusion for decades, releasing a handful of albums, musically *avant-garde* and alienating, lyrically obscure and tortured, that might be works of genius, either as serious music or else an elaborate post-modern "fuck you" to his fans, sort of Lou Reed via Andy Kaufman.

Walker's reticence—in typical fashion, his "comeback" included contributing a song for a Bond film which was so depressing it wound up over the end credits—could be seen as an exaggerated form of the noble Aryan's traditional self-composure, as Baron Evola has outlined it, in contrast to the hysterical, show-off Mediterranean type so typical of "show bizness."[17]

Anyhow, I was led to link the two by a couple of odd lines from Scott in the recent film biography, *Scott Walker: 30 Century Man*.[18] I mean, odd from the rhythm-worshipping, bongo-

---

[16] The definite biography is still Jeremy Reed's stalker classic, *Scott Walker: Another Tear Falls* (London: Creation Books, 1998). Although outdated by Scott's recent "rediscovery" by the hipsters, and by no means even aware of the Aryan motifs outlined here, it nicely conveys Scott's ability to captivate and obsess his fans, even a man some have called England's greatest living poet; which is probably why the fans hate it.

[17] See Julius Evola. *Men Among the Ruins: Post-War Reflections of a Radical Traditionalist*, ed. Michael Moynihan, trans. Guido Stucco (Rochester, Vt.: Inner Traditions, 2002), ch. 14.

[18] A 2006 film by Stephen Kijak, featuring interviews with such il-

beating perspective of today's critics: When hiring a session sax man Scott points out: "It's not going to be a funk session." Scott explains that he never lets the studio musicians he hires see the whole arrangement, only their own parts, because, "I don't want them getting together and 'grooving.'"

Reticence, loathing of "show business," use of high-technology to make music on his own terms, and an abhorrence of "grooving" and "funk" mark Scott as a true Aryan Artist, his uncompromising self-exile and technological experimentation not dissimilar to Varg Vikernes' prison life and music.

And as already pointed out, this disdain for the easy appeal of "funk" in combination with a penchant for technological so-phistication has nothing to do with a lack of rhythm or physicali-ty when appropriate; in the film, we see Scott installing and painstakingly testing out—with his fists—a slab of beef in order to produce just the right beat; the scenes where Scott somewhat impatiently instructs the "percussionist" how to get the rhythm he wants by punching the slab just right are priceless.

How perfect that the track being recorded—"Clara"—was in-spired by a childhood viewing of newsreel footage of the bloody fate of Mussolini and his mistress: one piece of post-war "let's all hate the Nazis" propaganda—and a rebellion, as Baron Evola pointed out in the same discussion of "Mediterranean Soul," of the Italian slave mentality seeking vengeance on the man who attempted to lift them to a greatness they were no longer capable of in spirit—that doesn't seem to have had the intended effect on this Aryan spirit.

ALEX KURTAGIĆ ON BLACK METAL

My suggestions that White audiences should embrace and ex-tend something that might be called White New Age should not be confused with similar but reactionary and retrograde views

---

lustrious fans as David Bowie (who might be called Scott Lite, having chosen a series of rabidly shifting stage personae rather than seclu-sion), Brian Eno who helps connect us with our New Age/Ambient theme), Marc Almond, Ute Lemper, and Jarvis Cocker.

promoting some kind of "neo-classicism" based on certain tendencies among the neo-folk and even Black Metal genres.

Prominent Alternative Right cultural critic Alex Kurtagić's essay "White Noise" at TakiMag[19] is excellent, though mainly for representing another neo-pagan incursion into the online "conservative" media. On its own merits though, it's useful mainly for identifying what's wrong with the Right's take on "White music."

Kurtagić starts off with this accurate view of the current situation:

> Most of mainstream Pop nowadays is African-American in either origin or derivation, even if the musicians playing it are not. Indeed, one is hard pressed to find even a nano-second of music in the charts that is quintessentially European in its sensibility. The fact that music derived from African-American creativity has come to enjoy maximum visibility in contemporary mainstream culture, however, says more about the policies of corporate record labels and the mass media of news and entertainment than it does about the quality of music originating in the European soul on either side of the Atlantic. This music is alive and well, I am happy to report, thriving purer and truer than ever, aloof from—and completely ignored by—the brainless and banal MTV sausage factory.

Then he asks, "what does this music sound like?" and there the fissures begin to appear.

Lumping together "several genres worthy of examination: neo-folk, Martial Industrial, and various forms of extreme Metal, including Black Metal, Folk Metal, and Viking Metal," Kurtagić describes them as lyrically reflecting "a decidedly pagan and neo-Romantic sensibility, emphasizing—always to a harrowing degree—dark emotion and obscure mysticism" and musically as "quite complex, drawing extensively from Classical and traditional Folk music, with varied and layered instrumentation, ex-

---

[19] http://takimag.com/article/white_noise#axzz1f3LxqV77

pressionistic riffing, elaborate orchestration, an epic sense of melody, and scintillating musicianship."

He sums things up thusly:

> Black Metal artists may be called "conservative revolutionary" in so much as they advocate putting an end to the liberal order, by revolutionary means if necessary, and instituting a new dispensation founded on conservative principles. (Of course, the term "conservative" must not be understood here as having anything to do with the Republicans.)

Indeed. Then why does it all sound so much like a Chamber of Commerce-sponsored concert of Judaic-manned and directed orchestras?

The problem with these genres of Metal, in fact, is exactly this combination of truly "traditional folk" with the sounds, ideals and "musicianship" of what Kurtagić and others take to be some kind of essentially Aryan High Musical Culture—*Kultur*, if you will—which is actually a long- dead post-Renaissance bourgeois taste, although it still apparently controls pop culture, zombie-like.

Rather than "putting an end to the liberal order," these *soi-disant* "pagans" fall to their knees (as Nietzsche described Wagner in composing *Parsifal*) before a Romantic image of "inspired" conductors, overblown and overstaffed orchestras, garish "temples of music," and female-faint inducing "virtuosos" (usually Judaic), shared by both Left and Right but in fact largely a creation of the Judaic-owned gramophone business and the German-Jewish "refugees" from the same *Kultur*-stratum that produced Adorno and the Frankfurt School.

Baron Evola noted in *Ride the Tiger* that all this bourgeois rubbish had deserved to be scooped up and chucked out long ago, and that the only danger had been that the younger generation, seeking—rightly—more authentic musical experiences, had been steered not to their own indigenous music (as Bartók, for example, tried to do) but rather to the sub-rational world of primitive Negroid music which produced jazz and its descendants: the "beat" music Evola discusses and eventually Kurtagić's Metal.[20]

Another Traditionalist, Alain Daniélou, himself an accomplished musician trained by authentic Hindu teachers, established the inferiority of Western "classical" or "art" or "serious" music, based as it was on the Greek misunderstandings of tonality, in comparison to integral musical systems such as the Indian and Chinese, in his *Music and the Power of Sound: The Influence of Tuning and Interval on Consciousness.*[21]

The whole development of Western music, its increasing "complexity" and instrumentation, which the Metallers seem to ape, is really not "progress" but just a desperate attempt to *compensate* for the meager, and increasingly inadequate, expressive possibilities of this misbegotten system, while a Mediaeval Indian musician, as Daniélou notes, could make rain appear by sounding the correct notes!

Paradoxical as it may sound, it is precisely the lack of expressiveness in this "scientific" and "evolving" system that has led, on the one hand, to the constant development of bigger forces and wilder "effects" from Bach to Brahms (Kurtagić's "elaborate orchestrations" and "varied and layered instrumentation"), with more and more "Romantic" virtuosi and "genius" conductors (his "scintillating musicianship" to provide "expressionistic riffing"), finally burning itself out with Strauss (who needed a wind machine!) and settling down with the dour, unpopular—and Judaic—serialists (whose musical language, Colin Wilson pointed out, was good for expressing only confusion and dread); and, on the other hand, to the attraction, among both audience and composers, to "primitive" music that seems, correctly, to be far more expressive and meaningful.[22]

---

[20] Julius Evola, *Ride the Tiger: A Survival Manual for Aristocrats of the Soul*, trans. Joscelyn Godwin and Constance Fontana (Rochester, Vt.: Inner Traditions, 2003).

[21] Alain Daniélou, *Music and the Power of Sound: The Influence of Tuning and Interval on Consciousness* (Rochester, Vt.: Inner Traditions, 1995; first published 1943).

[22] See the discussion of "bent" and "blue" notes in Julian Lee's essay, although he fails to see their significance as Daniélou does: "The

Daniélou tells the story of an Indian during the early Raj, who tried to imitate "Western" music; he got together as many instruments as possible, and had them play as loudly as possible, all different lines at the same time! An "emperor's new clothes" moment for the much vaunted Western "harmonic development" as well as a nightmare recently reproduced, to much fanfare among White "sophisticates," by the Negro jazz cacophony called "Free Jazz." And is it not indeed the experience of the performance of one of these Metal bands?

By promoting the combination of Negro-derived "beat" music and putrescent Klassical Kultur, Kurtagić and Metal are short-circuiting again the legitimate hunger of the White population for its own traditional expressive folk music, as well as delegitimizing new Aryan technical and musical explorations, such as those of Vikernes and even New Age. He is in fact embodying, in one simultaneous stance, Adorno's successive Frankfurt School plans for fomenting Communism by first promoting Schoenberg, then when that failed, concocting a new, "sophisticated" form of jazz.[23]

Of course, it's all a question of tactics. No one is unsullied; "to live is to collaborate" (Burroughs, *Nova Express*). If Vikernes is right, that all guitar-based rock music is Negroid in inspiration, and Daniélou, that Western "serious" music is a dead end, one still can, and must, distinguish that which is entirely harmful to Whites (most pop music) and that which, perhaps due to its lyrical content, is relatively positive (Metal).

---

success of African American music, with its 'blue' notes so alien to equal temperament and therefore so expressive, is not due merely to fashion. It shows the need for an understandable musical system, for logical and true intervals that can remove the veil of inexpressive insipidity which temperament spreads over even the most impassioned movements of the greatest symphonies" (*Music and the Power of Sound*, p. 16).

[23] Elizabeth Whitcombe, "The Mysterious German Professor," http://www.theoccidentalobserver.net/authors/Whitcombe-AdornoII.html; and Elizabeth Whitcombe, "Adorno as Critic: Celebrating the Socially Destructive Force of Music," http://www.theoccidentalobserver.net/2009/08/adorno-as-critic/

Since the beginning of the last century, the White race has been trying to dig its way out from under the Wrong Turn of the Renaissance. Some of those paths, such as the embrace, by both "serious" composers and teenagers, of "more soulful" music in the form of Negroid rhythm, have been further detours or even dead ends. At this point, we need neither more soft ballads nor more neo-classical flourishes. An authentic White music should proudly embody our race's unique characteristics—a Futurist focus not on the telluric mire of primitive "rhythm" but the transcendence of time through technological innovation.

Counter-Currents/*North American New Right*
November 30, 2011

THE COUNTER-CURRENTS
INTERVIEW

NOTE BY GREG JOHNSON

Before beginning this interview, I knew very little about James J. O'Meara. Based simply on his writings, I would describe him as a New Right/Radical Traditionalist-oriented literary and cultural critic residing somewhere Back East. He is a highly valued contributor to Counter-Currents/*North American New Right*. He has also published in journals ranging from *Alexandria* to *Fringe-Ware Review* to *Judaic Book News*.

His own blog is entitled *Where the Wild Boys Are*, http://jamesjomeara.blogspot.com/which has the arresting subtitle "Aryan Futurism, Heavy Metal Entheogenic Mysticism, and pitiless hordes of adolescent warriors in rainbow thongs." At the very least, I hope to get an explanation of that!

James, give us some basic biographical background: When were you born? Where are you from? Who are your people?

I have come to think that everything boils down to being born and raised in Detroit, a late Boomer during the period when Detroit was the true workers' paradise, the High Tide of the American Dream, up to about 1972, when the city, and the country, and the West, entered its swift decline. Workers like my father had good jobs with high pay and amazing benefits; in his case, not in the auto industry, but the New York Central Railroad, itself soon to enter bankruptcy.

These were the last times that one man could support a family, buy a house and car with cash, no loans or mortgages, and men were expected to actually be doers rather than "consumers"; if shelves were needed, he made them, rather than go to some Home Depot. This is the background against which I try to analyze, and immunize myself from, all the post-1980 ideological nonsense of the Identity Left and Free Market Right. Yes, even Richard Nixon, in the light of today, was a wise and decent leader, and his world was the White Utopia.

More particularly, I witnessed in Detroit the utopia of White Youth—which I have identified with the concept of Wild Boys that Burroughs was just publishing at that time, as well as, later, with the Aryan *Männerbund*—that this relative prosperity provided, epitomized by the revolutionary political and musical groups of that time and place, unimaginable today; and also the destruction of all that through the encroachment of the Negro. Let's say that having been exposed to "black educators," I was already long familiar with candidate Obama's idea that there are "really" more than 50 states.

This is not to say that my upbringing was ideal; it was, in fact, quite eccentric, to say the least. I was the only product of the late second marriage of a nearly uneducated, nearly elderly, second generation Irishman to an even less educated middle-aged woman he met in Nassau.

Even aside from this, both parents would likely be diagnosed today as autistic.

My father spent nearly every waking hour at work, by choice; having made a mint and retired to the suburbs when I entered high school, he promptly dropped dead.

My mother spent the entire time I knew her on a sofa, watching soap operas; I believe that she wanted to come to America to see the programs she only knew by radio broadcasts in the islands. It was only later, near her own death, that I discovered, after finding her watching the Joseph Campbell PBS show (her!?) that she had actually been spending her time living in an extensive dream world in which she was continuing to live with her family and friends in the Bahamas. I suspect I inherited not merely their antisocial ways but also a precocious grasp of Jungian active fantasy, and even Corbin's Sufi-inspired "imaginal realm."

You can imagine the sort of dreamy, unpopular good-for-nothing this produced. I was the sort of kid that would attend the premiere of *2001* by myself and too young for drugs, and acquire an interest in Richard Strauss and Nietzsche. The sort of kid that would pick up Hesse's *Steppenwolf* because I knew that was where the band had gotten its name, and then intensely identify with Harry Haller; later, at 50, I realized that I had indeed seen my future and become a 50-year-old misanthrope in a room full of books and cigar ash.

Tell us about your religious upbringing and present beliefs.

My parents were nominally Catholic; my mother had been the daughter of a Welsh Methodist minister and missionary to the Bahamas, whom I think I take after in appearance and interests, but presumably disinterested enough to become apostate. They had no particular interest in my religious upbringing any more than my social or educational, other than a formal interest in making me go to church, until I rebelled against it, and a fixed idea that Catholic schools would be the best, which of course was true.

Once in the best Catholic high school, my parents took no further interest, leaving things like course selection (the age of the "option" was upon us) to me. Hence my eccentric choices of German as a foreign language, the better to read Nietzsche and Hesse, as well as the abandonment of mathematics, a true loss, I believe.

My mother, bless her shop girl's soul, had a fixed idea that I should "take shorthand and typing and you'll always have a job," which I must say did prove helpful in the days of typewriters, but shows the rather low career bar that was set for me.

Your writing shows the signs of a wide and not entirely informal education. Where did you go to school?

Of course, while I can't account for my uniquely odd birth and parenting (although Evola was fond of the idea that we choose our life's course prenatally), I also cannot explain how I arrived at the idea of attending an obscure university in Canada; I can only assume that, growing up in Detroit, Canada, though universally despised by its own natives, had seemed like a colorful bit of the British Empire when visited as a child.

The school I chose had been quite a force in its little world back in the '40s, when Wyndham Lewis and Marshall McLuhan spent some unhappy years of exile there (you can read about it in Lewis's *Self Condemned*, a title which should give you some idea of how backward it was even then).

And for a little-known place, my classmates have had some effect on the world, from the actor Colm Feore, award-winning poet Phil Hall, the presidents of Chrysler and Fiat, to the Dean of the NYU Business School. I studied religion alongside Thomas Moore, whose popularization of archetypal psychology in *The Care of the Soul* was typical of the place, and very much in my own dreamy style; while my colleagues in philosophy included one who went on to become a billionaire as one of the architects of the California subprime mortgage disaster.

Going to an intellectual backwater, however, was I think the best thing for me. "Deconstruction" and other "critical theory" was only a dim rumor, and could be grasped only as some foolish modern misunderstanding of Hegel. We were taught—I'm speaking of philosophy, not physics or chemistry—in the grand French Thomist tradition of Gilson and Maritain. One read original texts, and lectures were devoted to *"explication de texte,"* like the English "close reading," not fashionable PC claptrap.

And even the younger professors who chafed at the old school trappings were themselves useful, as they were pioneering what they called "informal logic," which gave me an additional training in disassembling political arguments. Though short on "real world" facts, much better training, almost scholastic if not Platonic, than some sociology or arts graduate today.

Intellectually, the real influence was John N. Deck, an old school Platonist, a real "old time" Catholic, and an American who had fled to Canada during World War II to avoid fighting what he liked to call "National, I mean, Christian Socialism." His combination of Neoplatonic idealism and personal eccentricity— he wore the same cheap Sears work clothes the rest of the faculty had given up after grad school, and shaved his head once a year, letting it grow out until he resembled Schopenhauer; a similar figure appears, eerily enough, in Mann's *Doctor Faustus*, another book I read obsessively at the time—made a deep appeal to me, and I became one of many disciples of this guru who taught the most popular class on campus: a "kiddie" version of Plato called "Dream Worlds and Real Worlds," a two semester long harangue worthy of a more sober Ignatius P. Reilly. Years later, I learned that an upstate New York guru was using his one slender book as a holy text, and the group still keeps it in print to this day.

What is your occupation when you are not writing?

Reading, of course. As for paid work, well, with such a background, I was no more prepared for work than Reilly as well. I left graduate school and chose a profession simply because the training was easy and inexpensive, and some friends had gone the same route and actually got jobs. Eventually, in an equally somnambulist sequence of events, I came to New York, where I plied my trade at several major firms, until the recent economic downturn.

What is "entheogenic mysticism"?

Perhaps one could consider as my first venture in online writing to be my involvement with Michael Hoffman (not the anti-Judaic crusader, Michael A. Hoffman II, though the coincidence is interesting) and his decades-long personal research project on the roots, literally, of religious experience in psychoactive drugs. He believes that drugs are a more effective means than prayer, meditation, etc. for producing the core religious experience, which he defines as a breakdown of personal control, a "cybernetic crisis" relieved only by a relinquishing of control to a Higher Power. His work is archived at egodeath.com, where some of my own postings can be found, as well as a "main article," "The Entheogen Theory of Religion,"[1] which I partially ghost-wrote for a journal that ultimately never came out. So much for "real" publishing.

I differ from Michael mainly in taking a more Evola-inspired

[1] http://www.egodeath.com/EntheogenTheoryOfReligion.htm

approach, preferring a more active, Aryan, heroic model based on Mithra rather than Christ; consequently, he takes hippie psychedelia as his model for "modern mystery ritual for the youth," while I prefer implicitly White Heavy Metal for that role.

Who are your literary and philosophical idols and influences?

Again, it all comes back to Detroit in the late '60s, early '70s. In those days, the FCC required radio stations to broadcast some kind of religious content, so the local "underground" station played lectures by Alan Watts early Sunday morning. Other than my immature reading of Nietzsche, this was my first exposure to philosophy and mysticism, and something like his "spiritual materialism" has remained my touchstone ever since. His autobiography, *In My Own Way*, is a model for a well-lived, interesting life. By the way, Michael Hoffman thinks his essay "Zen and the Problem of Control" in the book *This Is It*, is the greatest philosophical work of the 20th century.

Watts of course was something of a Traditionalist, but he broke away for reasons I think more of personal style than principle. Later, after absorbing a certain amount of Thomism and Hegelianism, I found a Penguin paperback of Guénon's *The Reign of Quantity* in the college bookstore, and having seen the name in Watts's books tried to read it, but found it impossible to assimilate; a combination of puzzlement over his radically different perspective on the "metaphysics" I had been taught, and, frankly, a sense of dread and terror at his matter-of-fact presentation of the unstoppable pulverizing and disintegration of the universe. I can only compare it to the sense of "cosmic indifference" present in the long, late works of Lovecraft; though less intense than in Guénon, it arises from similar reasons, as I explore in my essays on James and Lovecraft.[2]

Eventually, I was able to assimilate some of his more purely "principial" works, such as *The Symbolism of the Cross*, and actually found his perspective, or "personal equation," as Evola would say of himself, to be *muy simpatico*. A purely intellectual

---

[2] http://www.counter-currents.com/author/jjomeara/

perspective on a world unworthy of notice anyway, was just what my dreamy, withdrawn nature craved. Around middle age, however, sometime after arriving in New York, I experienced something of a personal crisis, feeling a great need for more involvement with the "real world."

My old schoolmate Thomas Moore provided a clue, with his attempt to translate or adapt Ficino's Renaissance Platonism first to archetypal psychology, then to everyday life, which I leaned to find value in as an intermediate level, between Matter and Spirit, Dream and Real, called "Soul." Archetypal psychology brought me in touch with Peter Lamborn Wilson, a popularizing Sufi scholar who made Watts seem like a Presbyterian elder, and who also, like Watts, had his own radio show, this time on WBAI. A chance mention by Wilson of a "happening" on the Lower East Side led me to make contact with the most degenerate levels of the New York arts scene, perhaps the most currently well-known and respectable survivor being the torch-singer Antony.

Archetypes, Soul, angels, the "imaginal realm" of the Sufis (and thus, through Schuon, of the Traditionalists); reading around about these, I stumbled on the work of Jeremy Reed, who shared my obsessions with Bowie and Brian Jones, but also introduced me to J. G. Ballard, and above all, to the ultimate angelic White soul, Scott Walker.

Just at the point where I might have entirely drowned in pop ephemera, I finally made the acquaintance of the man of iron, Baron Julius Evola. His name had never been mentioned by Watts or any Traditionalist I had read in English up at that time, despite his long and close collaboration with Guénon. And why should they, since he presented an entirely different perspective from theirs, and on them? Evola was the first person I knew who neither ignored the Traditionalists nor ridiculed them nor slavishly adhered to them, but came with a fully-formed worldview of his own, and was more than a match for them intellectually. Like Marx with Hegel, Evola turned Guénon upside down, as it were, and made use of their much vaunted "principles" as a way to give form to his nebulous ideas of the ideal civilization for Aryan man, how it had been, how it degenerated, how it could be revived today. Evola was all about doing something in the world, and provided an excellent antidote to Guénonian inertia.

So much for what might be called intellectual influences.

In literary terms, *Rolling Stone* was the biggest influence, hard as it may be to believe today. In those days, Hunter Thompson, along with Lester Bangs from Detroit's rival music rag, *Creem*, were early and I think bad influences on my writing and lifestyle, especially when it came to producing existential nonsense in all-night binges in lieu of term papers. More importantly, the *Stone* introduced me to David Bowie, and, through Bowie, William Burroughs, since he contrived to be "interviewed" by Burroughs and gushed on about their "mutual" influences. *The Wild Boys* had just been published (Bowie later turned it into his *Diamond Dogs* epic), and I acquired the symbol for what eventually became my blog musings.

So we have now, what—rock music, etheogens, and, courtesy of Burroughs's British publisher, the blurb about "pitiless hordes of adolescents in rainbow thongs." All clear?

Jeremy Reed revealed that the obsessive attention a fan pays to pop trivia can be the equivalent of a poet's heightened perception, and I try to do something similar in looking at pop culture from a Traditionalist perspective.

But the most important influence was provided by Danny Drennan, who published, in the early days of the Internet, a "weekly wrap-up" of *Beverly Hills 90210*. Drennan was the anti-Reed; having started as an obsessed fan, he grew to hate and despise the show as only a former lover could, and was creating pages and pages of weekly commentary, minutely chronicling the show's idiocies, lazy habits of writing ("So here comes the Obligatory Moment of Donna Praise"), aging and inept actors, etc. But what was liberating was the breathless, *faux* Valley Girl style, with its Homeric epithets and easy transitions from one part of speech to another, all facilitated by the paperless, non-quantitative medium of the Internet ("So Noah Look Away, Smirk, and Reply Hunter looks away, smirks and replies . . .").

This was Thompson's mania, Burroughs' cut-ups, Reed's pop idolatry, taken to a new digital synthesis, and delivered weekly with a knowing smirk. This was how I wanted to write.

But of what?

Wasting time at work Googling various "Evola and . . ." searches, I stumbled upon Alisdair Clarke's blog, Aryan Futurism. Here was someone putting Evola's ideas to work in the modern political and social context, and in particular attacking that great contradiction at the heart of The Right, the Judaic antipathy to homoeroticism. The circle was completed, and I had a comprehensive worldview, from wild boys to drugs to pop and Heavy Metal to imaginal realms to Traditionalist metaphysics to the Aryan *Männerbund* to the New Right.

I also had a medium—the blog—where my Drennanesque rants could be easily "published" and even endlessly rewritten, thus finally conforming to my way of having a bright idea suddenly pop up, feverishly writing it down lest it pass into oblivion, and then consigning it to oblivion by losing interest in developing it into something publishable months later; what I liked to call my "Nietzschean aphorisms" or "McLuhanesque probes" but really more like ADD.

If I consider my work in what Guénon liked to call "principial" terms, I would say that I took from F. R. Leavis the importance of criticism as the application and policing of standards; from Nietzsche the vow to only attack people as when they serve as the vehicles of ideas significant or dangerous enough to be worth consideration; and never the less, from both A. E. Housman and Paul Feyerabend (a modern, yet outré enough to find his way into my school's odd curriculum) the taking of a gleeful interest in ripping apart those who have publicly failed to uphold those standards yet sit back and smugly expect acclaim.

And on that note, perhaps my biggest critical "influence" is a fictional character, Chaim Breisacher, also from Mann's *Doctor Faustus*. This Judaic "private scholar" in 1920s Munich delights in discombobulating his stuffy, Prussian "conservative" hosts by constantly pulling the rug out from under their *haute bourgeois* ideals, such as Goethe and Bach, by diagnosing their "cultural degeneration" and finding "true" conservatism in ever more primitive, "barbaric" forms, such as Christianity and Prophetic Judaism in favor of the blood sacrifices of the Temple.

Some have lately speculated that he was based on a Judaic scholar known to Evola, and, perhaps, Evola himself! I find myself in a similar position, using the historical facts of Traditionalism to prove to "conservatives," and even *soi-disant* Traditionalists themselves, that they are hardly as "conservative" or "anti-Liberal" as they may think; for example, using Evola to show that "family values" is a Judaic attack on the homoerotic and entheogen-based male groups that created Aryan civilization, or Alain Daniélou to prove that jazz is more valid, with its "blue" notes and microtones, than "equal tempered" Western Classical music.

Who are your favorite literary and cultural critics?

Seriously, it may sound like a commercial, or shamelessly self-indulgent, but my go-to cultural critics are the folks at Counter-Currents: yourself, Michael O'Meara (no relation, by the way), and Collin Cleary; for film, Derek Hawthorne and Trevor Lynch. Reading your blog is the first thing I do online each day. Also, anything by Troy Southgate or Keith Preston.

Jim Goad is always a good read, iconoclastic in the true sense, and hilarious as well. The aforementioned Michael A. Hoffman II is essential for keeping abreast of the Judaic and Zionist machinations of the our time; of course, being a Christian Fundamentalist, he's actually extremely pro-Hebrew, he just thinks the current rabbinic sort aren't the real Jews. As Robert Anton Wilson said of his book on the Kennedy assassination as a Masonic mind-control ritual, "he has the strangest reality tunnel I've ever encountered."

Although technically deceased, the late Alisdair Clarke's blog is recent enough to continue serve as a relevant and incisive commentary on contemporary happenings. I like to think of my blog, and now this book, as a continuation of, and tribute to, his work.

Thank you, James.

INDEX

ABOUT THE AUTHOR

James J. O'Meara was born in Detroit, educated in Canada, and now lives in an abandoned glove factory in America's Rust Belt. From atop this crumbling remnant of America's industrial might, he broods with morose delectation over the inevitable reappearance of the hordes of White youth known to history as the *Männerbünde*, or Wild Boys.

He is the author of *The Eldritch Evola . . . & Others: Traditionalist Meditations on Literature, Art, & Culture* (San Francisco: Counter-Currents, 2014); *The End of an Era: Mad Men & the Ordeal of Civility* (San Francisco: Counter-Currents, 2015); *Green Nazis in Space! New Essays on Literature, Art, & Culture* (San Francisco: Counter-Currents, 2015); *A Review of James Neill's "The Origins & Role of Same-Sex Relations in Human Societies"* (Amazon Kindle, 2013); *Trump: The Art of the Meme* (Amazon Kindle, 2016); *Coffee? I Like Coffee!: The Metaphysical Cinema of Coleman Francis* (Amazon Kindle, 2017); and *Aryan Imperium: The Worldview & Geopolitics of the Alt-Right* (Amazon Kindle, 2017). His articles and reviews have been published by Counter-Currents/*North American New Right*, *Alexandria*, *FringeWare Review*, *Aristokratia*, and *Judaic Book News*, and on his blog, *Where the Wild Boys Are*.

www.ingramcontent.com/pod-product-compliance
Lightning Source LLC
Chambersburg PA
CBHW031427270326
41930CB00007B/605